CLEAN FOOD

TERRY WALTERS
CLEAN FOOD

A SEASONAL GUIDE TO EATING CLOSE TO THE SOURCE

Photography by Gentl & Hyers

STERLING EPICURE

New York

STERLING EPICURE
New York

An Imprint of Sterling Publishing
387 Park Avenue South
New York, NY 10016

STERLING EPICURE is a trademark of Sterling Publishing Co., Inc.
The distinctive Sterling logo is a registered trademark of Sterling Publishing Co., Inc..

Originally published in 2007 by Terry Walters

First Sterling Publishing edition published in 2009

Designed by MacKenzie Brown Design
Chicago, Illinois
www.mackenziebrown.com

Photography by Gentl & Hyers
New York, New York

Cover photo by Julie Bidwell
West Hartford, Connecticut

ISBN 978-1-4549-0010-8

Library of Congress Cataloging-in-Publication Data

Walters, Terry
   Clean food: a seasonal guide to eating close to the source with more than 200 recipes
for a healthy and sustainable you / Terry Walters.
       p. cm.
   Includes bibliographical references and index.
   ISBN 978-1-4027-6814-9 (hc-trade cloth : alk. paper)
   1. Vegan cookery. 2. Natural foods. I. Title.
   TX837.W2755 2009
   641.5'636--dc22
                        2009010149

Distributed in Canada by Sterling Publishing
c/o Canadian Manda Group, 165 Dufferin Street
Toronto, Ontario, Canada M6K 3H6
Distributed in the United Kingdom by GMC Distribution Services
Castle Place, 166 High Street, Lewes, East Sussex, England BN7 1XU
Distributed in Australia by Capricorn Link (Australia) Pty. Ltd.
P.O. Box 704, Windsor, NSW 2756, Australia

For information about custom editions, special sales, and premium and corporate purchases,
please contact Sterling Special Sales at 800-805-5489 or specialsales@sterlingpublishing.com.

Manufactured in Canada

10 9 8 7 6 5 4 3 2 1

www.sterlingpublishing.com

Dedicated with love
to Chip, Sarah and Sydney,
for bringing sunshine to my life
every day of every season.

With thanks...

to all with whom I have shared this CLEAN FOOD journey – your energy nourishes and inspires me. Thank you for gracing my life with your passion and your search for knowledge, community, support, delicious locally grown produce, and sustainable good health. Eat clean and live well!

to the friends who are my family and the family who are my friends: Pam Powell, Gary Jacobs, David and Fernanda Jacobs, Barbara Gadd, Jerilyn Brownstein, Susan Case, Sue Davies, Nancy Frodermann, Maria and Peter Uzzi, Beth Zapatka and Michael Zudonyi.

to my agent, Tony Gardner – my friend, mentor and tour guide on this adventure of a lifetime.

to my Sterling Publishing family for its support creating a cleaner future. With special thanks to Marcus Leaver, Carlo Devito, Jason Prince, Leigh Ann Ambrosi, Diane Abrams, Blanca Oliviery and Jeff Batzli.

to the photographic genius of Andrea Gentl and Marty Hyers, digital technician Meredith Munn, prop stylist Alpha Smoot and food stylist Susan Spungen. Thank you for blessing this book with your incredible talent.

to friend and photographer, Julie Bidwell, for making it so easy to be in front of the camera.

to Mario Batali, for his enthusiastic support.

to Mike Kandefer and Urban Oaks Organic Farm for your friendship and incredible organic produce, and in memory of Tony Norris, a pioneer in urban sustainable farming.

to Carol Leggett PR for spreading the good clean word far and wide.

to Steve Riggio, for his online book order that meant the world to me.

to MacKenzie Brown Design, for its vision, unwavering commitment and for designing books that express what's in my heart. To Pete Kowalski, for his artistic contributions. To Kurt MacKenzie, my deepest gratitude. And to Andrew Brown, always by my side, the greatest partner and friend one could ask for.

Finally, to the people who not only make my life, but are my life:

to my mother and father, my greatest role models, friends, fans, editors, cheerleaders and teachers.

to my husband Chip, for supporting and believing in me from the start, and for his honor, respect, pride and love.

and to my daughters Sarah and Sydney, who give meaning and purpose to every day, who honor me with their friendship, and who fill my heart and soul with their love.

You are the greatest gift of all.

Contents

INTRODUCTION

Note from Terry
My Mother's Kitchen 1
A Universal Approach to Diet 2

GETTING STARTED

A Cleaner and Healthier Way 4
Clean Food 6
Eating for Balance 7
Ways to Improve Health and Well-being 8

THE BASICS

Tools 11
Basic Cooking Methods 12
Grains 13
Vegetables 15
Legumes/Beans 16
Soy 17
Nuts and Seeds 18
Oils 19
Fruit 20
Notes About Oxalic and Phytic Acids 21
Organic, Conventional or Locally Grown? 22
Guide to Using Recipes 24
Commonly Used Ingredients 25
What's That? 27

RECIPES

Spring 38
Summer 94
Fall 158
Winter 234
Snacks 302

Index 335

Note from Terry

When I first published CLEAN FOOD in 2007, people questioned the word clean. "Are you telling me my food is dirty?" they would ask. Today, clean is widely understood, and the ideals of eating minimally processed foods, close to the source, for maximum nutrition and wellbeing have been widely embraced. I am thrilled to be able to update CLEAN FOOD to reflect new insights about food and health, to support our ever-changing lifestyles and nutritional needs, and to inspire even greater awareness, positive change and a sustainable future.

As a cookbook author and clean food advocate, I'm constantly immersed in new recipes, new ingredients, new resources and new knowledge. While my next cookbook is in the works, I simply couldn't wait to share with you some of my favorite new creations, so I added them here. With more than twenty new recipes and an all-new snack section for between meal energy, there's a clean recipe to satisfy you and your family's every need and most stubborn cravings. CLEAN FOOD is now even cleaner with refined foods such as Canola oil and agave nectar removed, and superfoods such as virgin coconut oil added. I've made sure there are options for making every recipe gluten-free. And most noticeably, this revised edition has been brought to life by the beautiful photography of Andrea Gentl and Marty Hyers, whose work was featured in my second book, CLEAN START.

Eating clean is not a diet, but rather a comprehensive guide to creating delicious and nutritious meals made from the foods we all need more of no matter what else is on our plate. And now more than ever, CLEAN FOOD delivers inspiration, seasonal recipes and the tools and knowledge you'll need to enjoy good health — one healthy choice at a time, without judgment, without rigidity and without deprivation. This book is your complete go-to resource for clean food so that you have everything you need not only to embrace change, but to create it.

It continues to be an honor to share this journey with you. May you savor every bite, and may you be nourished by a healthy serving of love each and every day.

When my mother put dinner on the table, it was a well-orchestrated affair. She insisted on clean food – rich in protein, fiber, vitamins and minerals – a virtual symphony of colors and tastes all of which occurred naturally. Our food was not altered with additives, growth hormones or pesticides, and our meals were made from scratch with natural ingredients, with intention and with love. Every evening the family sat around the table and infused our meals with laughter, mischief, conversation, and most importantly, connection. We did not eat perfect diets, nor were we a model family, but we were nourished and nurtured by wholesome foods, the energy and love that was cooked into them and by the ritual of mealtime.

My Mother's Kitchen

Over the years, my mother's meals have changed. Natural meats and dairy products have been replaced with organic black beans and kale, chicken and eggs with miso and wild Alaskan salmon, bread and butter with quinoa and extra virgin olive oil. I nourish myself with a balanced diet of locally grown, organic, unprocessed foods prepared fresh daily. Yet, when I am in my mother's home, there is a force that pulls me to explore her refrigerator and cupboards.

If hunger and nutrition are not what drive me to scavenge through my mother's kitchen, what is it that I'm searching for? Could it be the same thing I search for after the children are in bed and I am drawn to my own kitchen to find that elusive little something that's going to make me feel complete?

In this country, the topic of food is charged with emotion and controversy. The whole meals of my past are now an illusion. Nothing is as it appears on the surface. Our produce departments and grocery shelves are lined with unknowns – pesticides, herbicides, growth hormones, chemical additives and process upon process, stripping our food of its inherent nutritional value. Behind each glass of milk or piece of meat is an agenda, a lobbyist, a Fortune 500 company, a distribution chain, a processing plant. . . you need to squint to see the farmer and you need binoculars to find the cow!

The further we remove ourselves from the source of our food, the less we are able to maintain physical and emotional balance. Our processed food diets are so lacking in nutrition that we require coffee to wake up, sugar to get through the day, television to calm down, alcohol to let go of our inhibitions, chocolate and ice cream to feel satisfied, pills to sleep through the night and drugs to provide us with the illusion of health. The vitamins and nutrients that were so rich in my mother's whole meals are hard to come by, and the nourishment from that mealtime is even more rare. Have we become a society that is artificially sustained?

Perhaps what I am searching for in my mother's kitchen is not in the food at all. Perhaps the craving that never seems satisfied is actually a desire for connection, for mealtime.

The more we eliminate processed foods from our diets, the more aware we become of our physical and emotional being. And yet, a perfect diet alone will not fully nourish us. What we need is connection – to our bodies, hearts and spirits, to our families, to community, the environment, the land, the season and to a purpose. That is what my mother created around our kitchen table, what I strive to create around mine and what I hope to help you create around yours.

There are no nutritional supplements that will replace the love and good intention infused in a home-cooked meal. The cleaner we eat, the clearer we think, and the better we can embrace good health and nutrition. I hope that this book inspires and empowers you to nourish yourself with delicious, healthy, balanced meals. I wish for you the fulfillment of a greater connection with your environment, your community and, most importantly, yourself.

Eat clean. Live well.

Terry

A Universal Approach to Diet

Bestseller books on diet, nutrition and wellness flood the shelves of bookstores offering a variety of approaches and much to consider. While many of these authors have discovered the diet that works perfectly for *them*, that does not mean their approach will work perfectly for *you*. However, the more knowledge we gain, the more empowered we become to tap in to the nutritionist within and to serve our own unique needs.

What we need is a master formula that takes everything into consideration – season, environment, metabolism, activity level, stress, hormonal activity, alkalinity, age, sex. There are so many factors that come into play, and just when we think we've got the answers, our bodies go and change! Ultimately, the best way to serve our unique nutritional needs is to empower ourselves with knowledge, listen to our bodies and respond with healthy, nourishing choices.

To do this, we need to realize that we have choices in the first place. A little knowledge goes a long way. Without it, we are vulnerable to deceptive marketing and labeling, and easily influenced by time-saving cooking techniques and appliances that diminish the nutritional value of our food and that can introduce harmful elements.

Consider not only the source of your food but the consequences to your health. Shiny red tomatoes in winter lure us in with their novelty, but where do they come from? The source of those tomatoes is a warm, sunny, faraway place. To withstand the long journey from farm to shelf and continue to look fresh and perfect, even I would need to be artificially enhanced! And what if I eat that "modified" tomato? It won't help me stay warm in winter, nor will it provide the nutrients that I got from the fresh local tomatoes just months earlier. **For maximum nutrition, we're better off eating closer to the source and relying on Mother Nature for seasonal produce to keep us in balance.**

Intention is equally difficult to cultivate and just as important when it comes to improving health. Before you walk into a grocery store, a restaurant or even your own kitchen, pause, take a deep breath and connect with the intention to select only foods that serve you. The goal is to say no to the junk and fill the pantry and your body with healthy foods. If you make the healthier choice at the store, you won't be faced with making it every time you open your pantry.

The final step is to suspend our judgments about food and nutrition. Perhaps you believe that fat is a four-letter word or that certain foods are more appealing for one meal over another. These notions can be handed down to us or passed on through marketing and industry. Cereal and toast may be an easy grab in the morning, but do they really provide the complete nutrition we need to get through the day? You may never eat meat again or you may never stop, but would your more nutritionally balanced dinner fuel you better if you ate it for breakfast?

For many, health improvements can be accomplished by improving habits, reducing stress on our bodies and increasing efficiency. All in all, the more you know about your food and your body, the more easily you can distinguish the foods and habits that harm from those that heal, and the more successful you can be at maintaining health and balance.

The seasons are what a symphony ought to be:
four perfect movements in harmony with each other.

ARTHUR RUBENSTEIN

A Cleaner and Healthier Way

It's time to erase the line between nutrition and nourishment. Clean food is minimally processed, so our bodies get the maximum nutritional value needed to fuel metabolism. The more clean food we bring in, the cleaner and more efficiently our bodies function. But, maintaining good health encompasses much more than clean food. True nourishment must feed our unique constitutions, and fulfill our emotional and spiritual needs. In our fast-paced culture this holistic approach is frequently overlooked and undervalued. It's time to look within for the answers.

Eating clean is a great way to make healthy dietary choices, but significant health benefits can also be achieved simply by slowing down. The results are less mental and physical stress, more oxygen circulating through the body, more toxins eliminated, more strength and more efficiency of nearly every system. Imagine how tired your organs must be from keeping up with your fast pace, not to mention your fast food!

Here's an easy exercise to incorporate into each day:

DAILY MEDITATION

Take five minutes and sit in a quiet place. Close your eyes and focus on your breath. Let your shoulders drop. Relax your facial muscles. Breathe into your belly. Turn off the conversations in your head. Notice how your breath starts to slow down and deepen. Slowly increase the duration of your session until you are comfortably meditating for 30 minutes a day. From this place of stillness, you are more in tune with your whole being, and improved balance and health are possible.

To truly nourish ourselves, we need this healing stillness, as well as an understanding of how we fuel our activity and how we are affected by the foods we eat. Does a bagel for breakfast make you feel sluggish? Can a bowl of oatmeal keep you running strong for hours? Maybe you opt for coffee instead of breakfast or a snack instead of lunch. Are you dragging by the end of the day?

You can't drive your car all day with no gas in the tank and then stop to fill up on the way home. Yet we expect our bodies to operate exactly this way.

One way to achieve greater understanding of your body is to keep a journal. Record what you eat, when you eat it and how you feel throughout the day. Check in with yourself for one day, two days or a week. I find the change of season to be the perfect time for this kind of introspection. Include everything from mood, sleep patterns, energy levels and digestive issues to menstrual symptoms, headaches, exercise regimen and more.

The more thoroughly you journal, the more insight you will gain into your physical and emotional being. Patterns will reveal themselves, and the foods and habits that nourish you (and those that don't) will become apparent. This awareness is essential for becoming empowered to make positive changes in your health and in your life.

By slowing down, experimenting with different foods and food combinations and paying greater attention to your body's responses, YOU can become your own "in-house nutritionist."

SAMPLE FOOD JOURNAL		
DAILY ACTIVITY AND DIET	TIME OF DAY	EMOTIONAL AND PHYSICAL OUTCOMES
WAKE UP 8 oz. water Walk the dog – 25 mins. Black coffee, bagel with cream cheese	6:30 AM	Didn't sleep well. Several trips to the bathroom. Difficulty getting started.
	7:30 AM	
	8:30 AM	Feeling better
WORK 8 oz. water Coffee, cream and sugar	9:30 AM	Focused
	10:30 AM	
	11:30 AM	Hungry; feeling worn out
GET LUNCH Green salad and grilled chicken	12:30 PM	
	1:30 PM	Not productive, bad mood
Can of cola and a nutrition bar	2:30 PM	Much more energy
	3:30 PM	Tired, dragging, hard time focusing, slight headache
GO TO GYM Workout – 1 hr	4:30 PM	Feel a bit more energy and better mood
	5:30 PM	
HOME Late dinner – pasta with vegetables, salad and bread. Snack on cheese while making dinner.	6:30 PM	Insatiable appetite
	7:30 PM	Bloated after dinner
	8:30 PM	Tired, low energy
Chocolate	9:30 PM	Unsatisfied
8 oz. water	10:30 PM	Hard time staying awake to watch TV
TO BED	11:30 PM	

Clean Food

It's hard to believe how far we've strayed from real food. Our grocery stores overflow with foods that can last on the shelves for months. So much of our food supply is stripped of its goodness and pumped full of man-made taste, color and nutrients. It's no wonder our health continues to deteriorate.

I find that my youngest students grasp the concept of clean food the best. Together we examine a bowl of plain brown rice and a box of quick-cooking vegetable rice pilaf. They tell me what they think is in each container. "Protein, starch, carbohydrates!" they shout. We pick up the box and start reading. The first few ingredients are identifiable. Then we get into what seems like another language – poly-this, hydrogenated-that, artificial, high-fructose, modified, mono- and di-. We consider the brown rice. There is no label – a clear sign of being closer to the source. What you see is what you get – brown rice. The conclusion is easy. If you can read it and imagine how it grows, it's clean. If you can't, neither can your body. Clean food is naturally grown and minimally processed.

The diagram below uses oats to illustrate how our foods move from a "whole" and nutritious state (on the left) to a highly processed and nutritionally depleted state (on the right). Similarly, a head of broccoli grows from the earth and becomes processed as it is cut, steamed, sautéed, dehydrated, ground and possibly even added to that very package of instant vegetable rice pilaf.

The nutritional value of that head of broccoli and its effect on our health and well-being change throughout the different stages of processing. We know that broccoli is full of chlorophyll, calcium and vitamins. Eaten raw, steamed, quick boiled, blanched or even flash frozen, broccoli retains much of its nutritional goodness. Once processed, either in a processing plant or your own microwave oven, as much as 90 percent of that goodness can be lost. That does not mean that you need to eat broccoli raw to access its nutritional value. In fact, your body may be able to assimilate more of the nutrients and digest it better if it is lightly steamed or sautéed.

What we know for sure is that the more our food is processed, the more its natural nutrients are lost. This means that the best way to nourish ourselves is with clean food eaten as close to the source as possible. No matter where your foods fall on this chart, one step to the left can yield health benefits. Smaller steps and slower change are the keys to an easy and successful transition.

Most Natural and Nutritious State					Least Nutritious State
CLEAN FOOD					HIGHLY PROCESSED FOODS

◄ ∙∙ ►

Whole Oat Groats	Steel Cut Oats	Rolled Oats	Quick Cooking Oats	Instant Oatmeal	Packaged Cold Cereal

Only you know where the foods you eat fall on the chart from clean to processed foods, and in the end, only you can make healthier choices and follow a cleaner, healthier path.

Eating for Balance

Regularly I'm asked what kind of diet I follow: vegetarian, vegan, macrobiotic, raw foods, and so on. No matter how you eat, inevitably, someone will want to put a label on you. We try diets like we try hairstyles and the possibilities are infinite, but are we well served by adhering to one defined, and perhaps limited, approach to eating?

Webster's dictionary defines diet as "food and drink regularly provided or consumed, habitual nourishment." Lasting changes and health improvements are not found in fad diets. They are achieved by listening to your body, making healthy choices in diet and exercise to achieve balance on a daily basis, eating as cleanly as possible and discovering the formula that best serves your unique composition.

For years, I thought I needed to have an advanced degree in medicine to figure out balanced nutrition. How much protein do I need? Are carbohydrates good or bad? Am I getting all my vitamins? Am I getting enough calcium and minerals? The truth is, balanced nutrition can be easy and requires just a little knowledge to start you on your way.

For most of us, eating clean is not as much a matter of learning what to eat, as it is of applying what we already know. Adults and children alike can apply the following concepts to make healthy choices, eat a balanced diet and enjoy good health all year long.

Eat…

…all the colors of the rainbow

…all five tastes*

…a varied diet

…locally grown, seasonal foods

and

Enjoy your food and mealtime.

See page 9

Ways to Improve Health and Well-being

While the concepts below may seem simple, the cumulative effect of ignoring them creates excess stress on the body, contributes to acidity and becomes the basis of imbalance and disease. I find that life has a way of pulling me away from these ideals, and an occasional review is a helpful way to get back on track.

1. Chew, Chew, Chew!

The more you chew, the slower you eat, the more digestive enzymes you secrete, the less stress on your digestive organs, the more nutrients you absorb from your food, the more easily you eliminate... I've known people to shed pounds simply by increasing their chewing.

2. Practice Good Habits

Take the time to sit down when you eat so you have more energy for proper digestion and nutrient absorption. We also need to eat regular meals to fuel our metabolism and daily activities. The more we practice good habits, the more automatic they become and the better an example we set for our children and others.

3. Stop Eating Three Hours Before Bedtime

Digestion is directly linked to movement and exercise. When we sleep, everything slows down – including our digestive functions. If you go to sleep with food in your belly, your mind may sleep, but your body works overtime all night long. Over the long term, this regimen makes the body weak, out of balance and less able to maintain good health.

4. Don't Buy It If You Don't Want to Eat It

It's much easier to have strength and willpower once (in the grocery store) than every time you open up your cupboard. Do yourself a favor – fill your kitchen with nourishing foods so that you can't help but make a healthy choice.

5. Color + Taste = Balance

A balanced diet includes a full spectrum of color (not just white) and all five tastes: SWEET, SOUR, SALTY, PUNGENT and BITTER. Go for variety and start adding tastes and colors that have been missing from your palette. Make sure to put extra emphasis on green – the color of healing.

6. Listen To and Honor Your Body

At the end of the day, as you rummage through the kitchen looking for the perfect snack to fill that elusive need, ask yourself, "Am I hungry or thirsty, or do I need connection, touch, an emotional outlet, some pampering or sleep?" Answer these questions instead of reaching for the snack and discover how to truly nourish and nurture your inner self. Sometimes a massage, a foot bath, time alone with a journal or early to bed will do the trick; other times a bite of chocolate is simply the only answer!

7. Change Slowly

Go easy on your body, your lifestyle and even your sense of taste. Too big a jump from processed to unprocessed foods can bring uncomfortable side effects. Changes made too quickly can put added stress on the body and are more likely to backfire. Gradual changes allow your body and your life to adapt more easily and are more likely to be long lasting.

8. Make Peace with Your Food and Your Choices

Ultimately, life is just a series of choices – one at a time. Every choice nourishes some part of us – whether physical or emotional. The goal is to accurately identify the need and then nourish it as best as possible. The more ways we have to nourish ourselves, the less we use (and misuse) food, and the happier and healthier we can be.

9. Let Go

It's just food, after all. What you see isn't always what you get, and we can't make good choices unless we have good information. But overemphasis on food and diet isn't healthy either. Don't let the food control you. Put it in a healthy place, and nourish yourself lavishly with all that life has to offer.

If you've gotten this far, you've overcome the greatest hurdle of all. Holding the intention is half the battle of changing to a healthy, balanced diet. If you're unaccustomed to purchasing and preparing whole foods, you'll benefit from outfitting your kitchen with a few standard tools and familiarizing yourself with basic preparations and tips for cooking grains, legumes, vegetables, sea vegetables and more. Then you'll be able to dive into the seasonal recipes in this book with the confidence and knowledge needed to successfully prepare balanced meals rich in color, variety, taste and the nutrients essential for healthy metabolism.

Tools

Keep it simple and keep it natural. A friend once commented, "It's great to see that you don't need to have a fancy kitchen to make delicious, healthy food." She was right. Some basic tools can accomplish a variety of tasks and eliminate unwanted clutter. Shy away from single-use gadgets whose only function can be performed with a skillfully used knife. When it's time to purchase, go for quality and avoid unnatural or harmful materials such as aluminum (a known carcinogen) and plastic (a petro-chemical that leaches harmful dioxins and PCBs), as well as any surfaces coated to become nonstick.

LARGE WOOD OR BAMBOO CUTTING BOARD
At least 20 x 15 inches

THREE QUALITY KNIVES
High carbon stainless steel blades: an 8-inch chef's knife, a serrated-edge bread knife and a paring knife.

COLANDER
A large stainless steel colander works for both pasta and vegetables.

STAINLESS STEEL STRAINER
Make sure the weave is tight enough for rinsing grains.

WOODEN SPOONS
Look for a variety of sizes and long handles.

HEAT-RESISTANT SPATULAS
While I try to avoid man-made materials, heat-resistant silicone spatulas in large and small sizes are great for scraping out a food processor or mixing bowl.

GRATER AND MICROPLANE
Make sure both are designed with handles. I like the basic box grater with 4 surface options.

RICE COOKER
The fewer the parts, the easier the cleanup. Look for a stainless steel interior bowl and avoid exposed aluminum.

LARGE SAUTÉ PAN
I like cast iron by Lodge. It is naturally nonstick, reasonably priced and comes preseasoned in a variety of sizes.

DUTCH OVEN CASSEROLE
I use this pot for everything — steaming, sautéing, soups and more. My favorite is the #24 (4½ quart) pot by Le Creuset.

TWO COOKIE SHEETS
Select heavy gauge metal to conduct heat evenly. Have at least one with rims to prevent spillage.

PARCHMENT PAPER
Makes any baking surface nonstick and easy to clean.

GLASS STORAGE BOWLS AND MASON JARS
In a variety of sizes, for storing everything from grains and nuts to leftovers, frozen soups and school lunches.

HANDHELD BLENDER
Look for a stainless steel shaft that is removable and dishwasher-safe with a handle that is easy to grip and operate. Use interchangeably with food processor or standing blender.

FOOD PROCESSOR
Look for a large bowl, a strong motor and a model that is easy to clean and assemble. Add specialty blades and extra bowls as needed.

WOODEN CHOPSTICKS
Perfect for stirring nut and seed butters.

Basic Cooking Methods

How you prepare your food can have as profound an effect on your state of physical and mental balance as what you eat. Instinctively we desire warming soups and casseroles in the winter and cooling, raw salads and fruits in the summer. Foods that require longer cooking over higher temperatures help us keep warm and maintain balance in cold weather. The reverse is also true – raw fruits and vegetables cleanse away excess fat and keep us cool and refreshed when it's warm. If you are someone who tends to feel too hot or too cold, consider what you eat and your environment to discover how you might start to achieve greater balance.

In the Northeast, the variety of local produce diminishes dramatically in the winter months. Sticking to local foods such as grains, legumes, winter squash, root vegetables and dark leafy greens, all of which can survive through the colder months, helps us maintain balance. Perhaps it is not an accident that in the season of darkness and cold, Mother Earth gives us sweet and strengthening roots and grains and uplifting dark leafy greens; and in the heat of summer, we are blessed with refreshing cucumbers, tomatoes, peaches and sweet corn.

Experiment with locally grown produce and the following cooking methods throughout the seasons to discover your perfect balance.

PICKLING   SPROUTING   JUICING   RAW   BLANCHING   SAUTÉING   SIMMERING   BAKING   PRESSURE-COOKING   BROILING   ROASTING

More Cooling   **More Warming**

Moderation is key; too much of one form of preparation can be weakening. Mix it up by adding a raw salad to your winter meal or some quick-cooking grains such as quinoa and millet to your repertoire of summer salads.

Remember, every body is different. The more you pay attention to how your body reacts, the better you will become at determining the right combination of foods and the most suitable preparation for your unique constitution.

GRAINS

Many cultures consider grains to be the most complete food and look to them as the foundation of their diets. Grains are strengthening, grounding and rich in vitamins, minerals, fiber and protein. Be aware that grains also contain phytic acid (see page 21), which interferes with the absorption of zinc, calcium, iron and other essential minerals. Fortunately, phytic acid in grains is water soluble, so soak your grains for a minimum of one hour, drain, add fresh water, cook and voilà . . . the phytic acid washes away, leaving you with a significantly improved complex carbohydrate.

Even complex carbohydrates, however, create acidity in the body. To neutralize this effect and make grains more alkaline-forming, cook them together with minerals (either kombu sea vegetable or sea salt). Kombu added to grains (and legumes) during cooking also infuses them with minerals, improves digestibility, reduces gas and tenderizes. This is an easy way to amp up the nutritional value of your food.

It sounds like a lot to remember, but it quickly becomes second nature. At the end of the day, put some grain in a bowl and cover it with water. When ready to cook, simply drain, add fresh water and cook according to the instructions on page 14. (Refrigerate grains after 12 hours if you haven't yet cooked them.) The longer the grain soaks, the closer it gets to germinating (sprouting), the more nutritious and easier to digest it becomes and the less water and time are required for cooking.

When selecting a grain, remember that the smaller grains such as quinoa, millet, amaranth and teff are higher in protein and free of gluten, so choose wisely and pay attention to how your body responds. If you're planning to use grain in a salad or casserole, let it sit briefly before tossing to prevent it from becoming mushy and to keep it nice and fluffy.

GRAINS

Amaranth*	Buckwheat*	Jasmine rice*	Sushi rice*
Barley (whole hulled)	Bulgur wheat	Job's tears* (from the grass family)	Teff*
Brown rice* (includes short grain, medium grain, long grain, brown basmati and sweet brown rice)	Couscous (made from wheat or semolina pasta)	Millet*	Wheat berries
	Farro (also known as emmer, part of the wheat family)	Oats (whole)	Wild rice* (a high-protein grass that cooks up like a grain)
		Quinoa*	

* Does not contain gluten

All grains can be cooked on your stovetop, but if you are like me and tend to multitask, you might find yourself reminded of your cooking grains by the smell of your burning pot! Electric rice cookers are a great invention – they are reasonably priced, cook your grain perfectly every time and keep it warm until you are ready to use it.

Grains can be prepared and served simply as outlined below or as in any of the recipes throughout this book. Experiment with more water or stock to yield softer grains, and less for al dente grains. Leftover cooked grain can be stored in the refrigerator for approximately 3 days. To reheat, simply steam or water sauté (see page 20).

BROWN RICE AND WHOLE OATS

1 cup uncooked grain
2 cups water or vegetable stock
Thumb-size piece kombu* or pinch of sea salt

Rinse grain in strainer and place in bowl. Cover with water and soak at least 1 hour. Drain and place in pot with 2 cups fresh water or stock. Add kombu and make sure it is submerged. Cover and bring to boil. Reduce heat and simmer until liquid is absorbed (25–30 minutes). For softer texture use more water and longer cooking time. Remove from heat, remove and discard kombu, fluff and serve.

*See Sea Vegetables, page 16

WILD RICE

1 cup uncooked wild rice
2½ cups water or vegetable stock
Pinch of sea salt

Rinse wild rice in strainer and place in pot with water or stock and salt. Cover and bring to boil. Reduce heat and simmer until liquid is absorbed (40–45 minutes). For softer texture use more water and longer cooking time. Fluff and serve.

HULLED BARLEY AND WHEAT BERRIES

1 cup uncooked grain
2¼ cups water or stock
Thumb-size piece kombu or pinch of sea salt

Rinse grain in strainer and place in bowl. Cover with water and soak at least 1 hour. Drain and place in pot with water or stock. Add kombu and make sure it is submerged. Cover and bring to boil. Reduce heat and simmer until liquid is absorbed (about 55 minutes). For softer texture use more water and longer cooking time. Remove from heat, remove and discard kombu, fluff and serve.

MILLET

Millet tends to be somewhat bland, so I like to pan-roast it first to bring out its nutty flavor. You can also cook your millet following the same directions as brown rice, but because millet is not an acid-forming grain, it does not require soaking.

1 cup uncooked millet
2 cups water or vegetable stock
Pinch of sea salt

Rinse millet in strainer and place in dry sauté pan over medium heat. Gently stir millet until it starts to give off a nutty aroma. Keeping the pan on the burner, add water or stock and salt, cover, reduce heat and simmer until all liquid is absorbed (about 25 minutes). Fluff and serve.

QUINOA
(keen-wah)

I like my quinoa to pop in my mouth when I chew it, so I cook it in less water than other grains.

1 cup uncooked quinoa (ivory or red)*
1½ cups water or vegetable stock
Thumb-size piece kombu or pinch of sea salt

Rinse quinoa in strainer and place in pot with water or stock. Add kombu and make sure it is submerged. Cover and bring to boil. Reduce heat and simmer until liquid is absorbed (about 15 minutes). If you're planning to mix quinoa with vegetables, cool slightly before fluffing so it doesn't become mushy. Remove from heat, remove and discard kombu, fluff and serve.

*Cook black quinoa with 2 cups water or stock until liquid is absorbed (about 25 minutes).

VEGETABLES

Of all the food groups, the vegetable family has the most diversity and the greatest range of health benefits. If we divide this food group into several categories, we stand a better chance of getting a good variety of nutrients in our diets. Select from all of the vegetable categories regularly for maximum nutrition and good health.

DARK LEAFY GREENS

Rich in calcium, chlorophyll, iron and vitamins C and E, this food category is the most beneficial and the most underconsumed in our culture. Dark leafy greens lift our mood, heal our organs and counteract the damage resulting from our stressful lives. Try to add nutritionally packed greens to your diet every day. While many of these greens are part of the cabbage family, I separate them here to bring attention to what I call the heavy hitters – those that pack a big nutritional punch. Select from kale, collards, mustard greens, dandelion greens, watercress and romaine lettuce.

CRUCIFEROUS VEGETABLES

Known for their cancer-preventing nutrients and antioxidants, these vegetables break down and dissolve fats to help eliminate toxins. Here are some of the many varieties to look for: collard greens, cauliflower, broccoli, Napa cabbage, Savoy cabbage, bok choy, pac choy, tatsoi, Brussels sprouts, green and purple cabbages, kohlrabi, daikon radish, red radishes and watermelon radishes.

ROOTS AND TUBERS

These vegetables, which dig down into the ground, help us feel strong and "rooted" and provide vitamin A, beta-carotene, minerals, fiber, antioxidants and healthy sweetness to our diets. Look for parsnips, rutabagas, turnips, ginger, beets, burdock, lotus root, sweet potatoes, turmeric and yams. Also closely related are carrots, celery, celeriac and parsley.

BULBS

Known for their ability to dissolve fats and excess mucus, bulbs are particularly heart healthy. Additionally, garlic's anti-inflammatory, antibacterial and antiviral properties make it a powerful healer. Look for garlic, leeks, onions, scallions, fennel and shallots.

SQUASH

With both winter and summer varieties, you can benefit year round from the blood-alkalinizing properties of squash. I am a fan of winter squash, which contain significant amounts of carbohydrates and sugars as well as vitamin A. My favorites include acorn, butternut, kabocha, dumpling, pumpkin, buttercup, delicata, red kuri and hubbard.

HERBS

The variety of herbs on the market today warrants a separate cookbook. Herbs can heal the sick, cleanse the blood and uplift the spirit, not to mention their ability to enhance your food and delight your palate. Experiment freely with fresh herbs in the summer and dried in the winter. Keep a bouquet handy on your countertop to snip into your cooking, and don't be afraid to spice up your food and your life.

SEA VEGETABLES

The health benefits of these gems from the sea are so outstanding that you really must give them a try. Sea vegetables offer a super-rich and easily absorbable source of minerals and vitamins, including iron, calcium, vitamin B, vitamin A, potassium, magnesium, phosphorus, iodine, zinc, selenium and copper. Sea vegetables, which are highly alkaline forming, help to reduce tumors and masses and bind to radioactive substances and heavy metals to pull them from our bodies. The most widely available include wakame, kombu (kelp), nori, arame and dulse.

OTHER VEGETABLES

There are simply far too many vegetable varieties to cover them all, but some of my other favorites include shiitake, portobello and cremini mushrooms, artichokes, asparagus, avocados, corn, cucumbers, endive, escarole, green beans, jícama, peas, frisée and heirloom tomatoes.

TAKE THE VEGETABLE CHALLENGE

Try one new vegetable every week. At the end of a year you're likely to have a new vocabulary of vegetables and a whole new repertoire of clean recipes.

LEGUMES/BEANS

Legumes offer a host of health benefits that make them a highly sought after, nonanimal source of protein. While legumes, like grains, contain phytic acid *(see page 21)*, it is easily neutralized by soaking before cooking. Doing so yields an easily digestible source of protein that is rich in absorbable nutrients, supports thyroid function, balances blood sugar levels and regulates hormone activity.

A close look at legumes brings up frequently asked questions about protein – what is it and why is it so important? Popular weight loss diets have brought much attention to protein, but not always enough understanding. It's time to set the record straight: Proteins are the building blocks that allow babies to grow, young children to thrive and athletes to gain strength. The average adult requires approximately 10 percent of their diet to consist of protein. Pregnant and nursing mothers, young children, athletes and the elderly often require more.

Protein becomes a problem when it is consumed in excess, and even more so when it is largely animal based. In short, excess protein causes constipation, interferes with the absorption of calcium and minerals, and can cause serious illness over time, including weakening and even permanently damaging the liver and kidneys. Adding to these issues, a diet heavy in animal protein increases the risk of heart disease, elevated blood pressure and certain forms of cancer. Legumes are not linked to these health risks.

If you have kept away from legumes due to their negative side effects, start with the smaller varieties and follow the cooking instructions on the next page. To help reduce gas, pre-soak, rinse and skim away foam that develops during cooking. Kombu (the same sea vegetable we add to grains to increase their alkalinity) can also be added to legumes during cooking to decrease their gaseousness, to tenderize them and to provide added nutrients such as calcium, iron, B vitamins and trace minerals.

LEGUMES

Aduki beans*	Lentils*
Black beans	Mung beans*
Black-eyed peas	Navy beans
Cannellini beans	Pinto beans
Chickpeas (Garbanzo beans)	Red beans
	Soybeans
Great northern beans	Split peas
Kidney beans	

*no presoaking required

While there is no replacement for freshly cooked legumes, I do find it helpful to keep cans of prepared legumes in my pantry for last-minute or quick meals. One company in particular – Eden – offers prepared organic beans made with kombu in a BPA-free can. When using canned beans, a 30-second soak in boiling water followed by a cold rinse is a great way to freshen them up.

LEGUMES – BASIC COOKING INSTRUCTIONS

Don't be afraid to make large quantities, as extra legumes can be stored in an airtight container in the freezer. Most dried beans cook as follows:

1 cup dried beans of choice
 (yields 2¼ cups cooked beans)
Water
Thumb-size piece kombu
Pinch of sea salt

Sort through dry legumes and remove any dirt chunks and pebbles. Place legumes in pot with 3 cups water and soak overnight. Drain, rinse and return to pot with 3 cups fresh water. Cover pot, bring to boil, skim off foam and reduce heat to simmer. Add kombu and salt. Cover and cook until beans are tender (about 50 minutes). Drain remaining liquid and store cooked legumes in an airtight container in the refrigerator or freezer.

SOY

Soy falls into the legume family, but because there is so much confusion about whether soy is healthy or not, it warrants its own section. The United States produces and exports a vast amount of soy. Unfortunately, much of the soy grown in the U.S. is genetically engineered, riddled with herbicides and pesticides, unlabeled as such, and widely used in processed foods. Unless the package reads "USDA Organic" there is no way to be sure you are getting quality soy.

There is much contradictory information circulating about the health benefits and health risks of soy. Many people believe that soy products can be helpful in replacing estrogen for women, regulating thyroid and hormonal function, lowering blood cholesterol and fighting cancer. I cannot say for sure whether these claims are true, but I do know that the protein makeup of soy is particularly hard to digest and assimilate. It is high in phytic acid, which prevents our bodies from absorbing essential minerals such as calcium and iron *(see page 21)*. Soybeans also contain goitrogens (found in foods such as cabbage and cauliflower), which interfere with thyroid function by suppressing the body's use of iodine.

It is, however, widely believed that slow cooking and fermenting soy neutralizes its high acid levels, allowing us to access its health benefits with less concern over its health risks. Therefore, when it comes to managing soy intake, you can eliminate many of these concerns by sticking with organic, fermented or slowly cooked soy products prepared with kombu and consumed in medicinal quantities based on your unique constitution.

FERMENTED AND/OR
SLOW-COOKED SOY PRODUCTS

Miso	Tamari/Shoyu
Tempeh	Tofu

Of concern is the fact that non-nutritive soy in the form of highly processed isolated soy protein is used extensively in processed and packaged foods. At its core, isolated soy protein is the waste by-product of processed soy. And, like many processed preservatives, sweeteners, and emulsifiers, these additives have little nutritional value and pose significant health risks.

Soy is so overused in processed foods that it is nearly impossible to avoid unless you adhere to a strictly whole-food-based diet. It seems that every other label I read lists soy in one form or another. There are soy substitutes for many of the products we've elected to reduce or eliminate from our diets: soy cheese, soy milk, soy yogurt, soy nuts, soy hotdogs, soy butter, soy everything! The result? Excessive amounts of overprocessed soy in the American diet, causing a great deal of imbalance and disease. This is a good reason to stick with quality organic soy and reduce or even eliminate processed foods.

NUTS AND SEEDS

We now understand that protein inhibits the body from absorbing calcium. This presents a major problem for those of us who like to combine rice, beans and greens (and maybe even some pumpkin or sesame seeds sprinkled on top). In a perfect world, we would eat each food group separately for maximum absorption and minimum stress on the body and digestive system. However, that perfect world would also be quite bland! Eaten separately, nuts and seeds offer protein and fat, which convert to energy without the worry of negating calcium and mineral absorption. This makes nuts and seeds perfect snack foods.

However, not all nuts and seeds are created equal. Almonds, walnuts, pistachios, cashews and pecans offer beneficial and essential fats linked to decreased risk of heart disease. But nuts such as pine nuts, Brazil nuts and hazelnuts are full of saturated fats which can contribute to heart disease. They are difficult for the body to break down and should be eaten less frequently. Seeds, on the other hand, offer similar beneficial fats as nuts plus a host of healing properties, vitamins and minerals. Try pumpkin seeds for added zinc, sesame seeds for calcium and flax or chia seeds for essential fatty acids and lignans (cancer-fighting compounds).

Almonds	Pistachios
Cashews	Pumpkin seeds
Chia seeds	Sesame seeds
Flax seeds (must be ground)	Sunflower seeds
	Walnuts
Pecans	

If you've noticed the absence of peanuts from this list, it is because they are actually a legume, not a nut. Peanuts are a high-allergen food, have a high mold content and tend to be grown with significant amounts of pesticides. Organic peanuts however, can be a great source of protein and fat.

To prevent nuts and seeds from becoming rancid, store them in a cool, dark place and buy only as much as you will use in a short period of time. Nuts and seeds become rancid more readily when they are shelled or hulled. Refrigerating or freezing helps maintain freshness longer.

BASIC COOKING INSTRUCTIONS

PAN-ROASTING SEEDS
Place skillet over low heat and add seeds. Stir continuously until seeds become fragrant and start to brown. Remove from heat, cool completely and store in airtight container.

OVEN-ROASTING NUTS OR SEEDS
Preheat oven to 300°F. Place nuts or seeds on parchment-lined cookie sheet. Place in oven and roast – 10 minutes for seeds and 20 minutes for nuts, gently tossing every 5 minutes to prevent burning. When lightly browned and fragrant, remove from oven and lift parchment paper with nuts or seeds off cookie sheet to prevent continued roasting. Cool completely and store in airtight container.

OILS

Nut and seed oils offer beneficial fats and health benefits similar to those of whole nuts and seeds, but pay attention to how the oils are processed, packaged and stored. All nut and seed oils will break down under high heat, in the refining process and even from exposure to light. This makes it essential to buy cold-pressed, unrefined oils. Look for brands that package their oils in tinted glass bottles or cans to reduce harmful exposure to light as well as contamination from plastic bottles.

When purchasing olive oil, I always select unrefined extra virgin which comes from the first press and is never heated or exposed to chemical processing. Darker oils often have a more intense olive flavor, but color is also influenced by the region and growing conditions of the olives, so don't rely on color to determine if a particular oil is less processed or refined. Read labels carefully to make sure you are getting first pressed, unrefined oil, and experiment with different brands to find the right balance of bitterness, smoothness and aroma to please your palate.

For cooking, I recommend either extra virgin olive oil, grapeseed oil or unrefined virgin coconut oil. These oils have the highest burn thresholds and can better withstand the heat of a sauté pan with-out breaking down and becoming rancid and toxic. I often do what I call a "water sauté" where I start with a small amount of oil and then add water to achieve a sautéed texture without the negative health effects of the heated oil. Additional high-quality oil can be added after cooking to infuse dishes with more flavor and health benefits.

Toasted sesame oil is highly sensitive to heat and should not be used for frying. This aromatic oil can be added in small quantities to dishes after cooking to give exceptional flavor and aroma.

FRUIT

Rarely do people need help incorporating more fruit into their diets. Few can resist biting into a crisp apple or juicy pear in the fall, picking fresh berries or snacking on melon in the summer and enjoying oranges and grapefruits in the winter. In fact, even once-obscure fruits like pomegranates and mangoes have made their way into our diets with regularity.

Fruit offers a variety of health benefits, ranging from the soluble fiber of apples and pears to the ellagic acid (an anticancer compound) and antioxidants found in berries. But the high sugar content of fresh and dried fruit makes overindulgence – particularly in juice – a significant problem. If you are a juice drinker and you'd like to get a sense of how much fruit you consume in a day, you can either take out your vegetable juicer or make a trip to your local juice bar. The goal is to observe exactly how much fruit it takes to make a small glass of juice. You may be surprised to learn that your morning glass of juice likely contains all, if not more than, your daily fruit allowance.

When it comes to quantity, the only person who understands how your body reacts to fruit, sugar or any other food group for that matter, is *you*.

Remember, sweet is one of the essential five tastes. If we don't include it in our diets in a nutritional form, then we will be more likely to crave it nonnutritionally. The challenge is to find the sweet that best suits your delicate balance. While sweeteners may be part of your sweetness mix, you'll seldom go wrong with whole fruits and vegetables.

MINIMALLY PROCESSED SWEETENERS

Barley malt	Maple syrup
Brown rice syrup	Molasses
Honey (not vegetarian)	Stevia

See "What's That?" (*beginning page 27*) for more information on individual sweeteners and refined sugar.

Notes About Oxalic and Phytic Acids

You may notice that certain vegetables are featured much more than others in this book. Some vegetables contain oxalic acid, which makes their nutrients difficult to assimilate and can even pull important minerals such as calcium from the bones. Consumed regularly, this acid can lead to irritation of the digestive system, stomach and kidneys. For most people, it is unnecessary to eliminate these vegetables. But, if you have a family history or are concerned about arthritis, osteoporosis or mineral absorption in general, you may want to limit your intake of these vegetables in favor of the vegetables mentioned on page 15.

Another nonnutritional component, phytic acid, is found in grains, legumes and seeds. This acid binds to minerals and proteins and decreases the body's ability to absorb and utilize these nutrients. The earlier sections on these foods offer ways to eliminate or neutralize the phytic acid in them.

As you will notice, I limit the use of vegetables high in oxalic acid, and I regularly employ cooking techniques like presoaking grains and legumes to neutralize phytic acid and yield nutrients that are easier to assimilate and digest. These foods offer plenty of nutritional value and can even strengthen and heal certain constitutions, but they are not what I consider to be my daily heavy hitters. I use them for variety, but in much smaller quantities and with less frequency.

Remember, only you can feel your body's response to individual foods. This insight is provided to increase your knowledge and help you make healthy choices, but your unique in-house nutritionist – you – can best determine the right dietary mix for you. In the end, there's more to know and understand about nutrition than can be studied in a lifetime. Knowledge can empower us to make healthy choices, but it should be combined with a healthy dose of perspective so that it does not keep you from enjoying food for food's sake. **Moderation, not deprivation, is key.** Focus on filling your plate with the foods that heal you. Slowly, the foods that harm you will fall by the wayside.

VEGETABLES HIGH IN OXALIC ACID

Beets and beet greens	Rhubarb
Bell peppers	Sorrel
Chives	Spinach
Parsley	Swiss chard

OTHER FOODS CONTAINING OXALIC ACID

Chocolate	Cranberries
Cacao	Peanuts
Coffee	Strawberries

Organic, Conventional or Locally Grown?

The decision is not clear-cut and there are many factors to consider. Where is the item from and when was it picked? How was it grown? How was it packaged and shipped? Organic certification can be prohibitively expensive, especially for small local farmers. Some take The Farmer's Pledge and commit to farming with sound ecological and economic principles. Others farm ecologically, employing practices to protect the environment and produce a reliable product by using non-organic practices only on an as needed basis. And still the majority of large and small farms alike rely on non-organic crop management techniques to insure a harvest and an income.

The landscape for food production is ever changing and ever confusing, and the only true way to know what you're getting is to know the farmer. I call this **putting a face on your food.**

Buying locally grown produce is the best way to know exactly where your food comes from and how it was grown. And supporting local farmers supports not only your good health, but the health of your local environment, economy and community. As tempting as imported produce can be, choosing to buy it over locally grown can only lead to the demise of our small local farms, and greater dependence on others for our food and the petroleum that got it from the farm to the table. What's important is not that everything is organic and local, but that you as a consumer have the knowledge to make the choice that best serves you, and the awareness of how your choice contributes to the sustainability of our food and our food system.

The more you know about the source of your food, the more empowered you are to be nourished by foods rich in nutritional value, and avoid foods grown with toxins and political agendas that don't have your health in their best interest.

While organic standards are under constant scrutiny and pressure to change, today the USDA's definition of organic is: **"…the food or other agricultural product has been produced through approved methods that integrate cultural, biological, and mechanical practices that foster cycling of resources, promote ecological balance, and conserve biodiversity. Synthetic fertilizers, sewage sludge, irradiation, and genetic engineering may not be used."**

This topic warrants a separate book, but for our purposes it is important to simply clarify that organic foods have been found to retain greater nutritional value and health benefits than the same foods conventionally grown. Again, that does not mean that everything in your kitchen must be organic. However, it is a good reason to get to know your local farmer, to ask what has and has not been sprayed, to look for 'ecologically grown' fruits and vegetables that are sprayed only if and when needed, to buy seasonal produce as opposed to tropical fruits or items from other countries whose organic standards may vary from ours, and to be as aware of your food sources as possible.

To help you evaluate your options and make healthy choices, the Environmental Working Group maintains a Shoppers Guide to Pesticides in Produce that can be found at www.ewg.org. For the sake of their research, all vegetables and fruits are washed (or peeled, when appropriate) before testing. The results are "The Dirty Dozen" (the vegetables and fruits containing the highest levels of pesticides) and "The Clean 15" (the vegetables and fruits containing the the lowest levels of pesticides).

THE DIRTY DOZEN

Apples	Celery	Lettuce	Potatoes
Bell peppers	Grapes (imported)	Nectarines (imported)	Spinach
Blueberries (domestic)	Kale/collard greens	Peaches	Strawberries

THE CLEAN 15

Asparagus	Corn*	Mangoes	Pineapples
Avocados	Eggplant	Mushrooms	Sweet potatoes
Cabbage	Grapefruit	Onions	Watermelon
Cantaloupe (domestic)	Kiwi	Peas	

*Genetically modified (GMO) sweet corn is not labelled. To avoid GMO, buy organic sweet corn.

The following foods did not make it onto the Environmental Working Group's Dirty Dozen list, but also tend to be grown with high levels of pesticides: almonds, peanuts, soybeans, sunflower seeds, rapeseed (Canola) and wheat.

It is important to stress that organic standards in the United States differ from those abroad. Fruits and vegetables that are regularly sourced from out of the country may be exposed to farming practices that would not meet U.S. standards.

Additionally, many of the foods grown with high levels of pesticides (such as soy and wheat) are the very foods fed to the animals we consume. Combined with the common practice of animal farming with hormones and antibiotics, this makes a compelling case for purchasing organic dairy and meat products over conventional.

There is simply no denying – the cleaner the food, the healthier you.

Guide to Using Recipes

I am a self-taught cook with a passion for preparing healthy foods that nurture and nourish my family and friends. My greatest cooking teacher, my mother, taught me that if I use good ingredients, I am bound to get good results. These sage words have stuck with me over many years of experimenting and developing recipes. Sometimes the results are great – other times not so great. In those not-so-great instances, I often add the word *surprise* to the end of the recipe name. A failed Key lime pie, for instance, would kindly become Key Lime Surprise. Or in my mother's case, when we needed a spoon rather than a fork to enjoy it, it was dubbed "Key Lime Extravaganza."

For me, the pursuit of wholesome, organic foods is every bit as much fun as the preparation. I love to talk to farmers about what's growing well, what they're enjoying the most and how they're preparing it. There is nothing more delicious than produce grown with respect and care, as opposed to the "empty" produce that travels across the country and is featured in many grocery stores.

WASHING INGREDIENTS

When we eat food from the earth with as little processing as possible, it is natural for some of the earth to get mixed in with it – whether we buy it at the farm, off the produce shelf or from a bulk bin. It is a good idea to wash all whole grains, vegetables, legumes, fruits and sea vegetables. Unless stated otherwise, these are the methods I use.

To clean whole grains and legumes, place them in a bowl and remove any unhulled grains, pieces of grass, pebbles and chunks of dirt. Fill the bowl with water, swish it around and pour off the water and anything that floats to the surface. Repeat until the water is clean.

Most fruits and vegetables that are not peeled can be washed in salt water. This method is particularly good for leafy greens and sprouts. Fill a bowl with enough water to cover vegetables, add 2–3 tablespoons salt, swish it around, remove greens, discard the water and repeat as needed.

Leeks tend to accumulate dirt between their layers. To clean, chop off the root end, slice in half lengthwise to fan the leek open, hold it under the faucet and rinse. Chop leeks crosswise until you reach the dark outermost layer. Peel off that layer, rinse and continue chopping. Repeat to chop all light green layers (the dark outer layers are tough).

Sea vegetables, like legumes, can have dirt and other undesirable particles mixed in with them. Place them in a bowl, cover with water, swish around, drain and repeat until the water is clear.

MEASURING INGREDIENTS

I cook with my senses and hope this book empowers you to do the same. I rarely measure (except in testing these recipes) and my favorite cooking technique is "dump and stir." Whether you measure or not, your recipes are likely to come out different each time for a variety of reasons. Some vegetables (particularly dark leafy greens) will retain more water or less, which can alter the quantity once cooked. Your taste and texture preference may differ from mine, so feel free to adjust your outcome by increasing or decreasing the liquid, spice or any other ingredient. Finally, if you are drawn to a recipe but do not have all the ingredients, by all means, adapt the recipe accordingly.

COMMONLY USED INGREDIENTS

I purchase nearly all my Clean Food ingredients at my local organic farm, a natural foods store or a conventional grocery store. Hard-to-find products are often easy to find online with a simple search by brand or product.

MISO
Miso is a living food that gives recipes a salty, rich flavor. The darker the miso, the longer it has been fermented and the stronger the flavor. Good quality living miso will be in your store's refrigerated section. Look for brands that use glass containers or transfer miso to a glass container when you get home, as it is a fermented food and is adversely affected by plastic. Powdered miso lacks the health benefits of the refrigerated paste. Avoid bringing miso to a boil as it destroys its living enzymes. Experiment with different brands and types to discover the ones you like best.

OLIVE OIL
Read labels carefully to be sure you are getting first pressed, unrefined olive oil, and experiment with brands to find the right balance of aroma, bitterness and smoothness to please your senses.

PARSLEY
I prefer the stronger flavor of flat leaf parsley, also referred to as Italian parsley, but curly parsley can be substituted.

SALT
Look for sea salt, which contains more minerals than conventional table salt. When salt is listed as an ingredient use fine salt unless coarse is specified. A good rule of thumb is, the grayer the salt, the less refined and the healthier.

TAMARI AND BRAGG LIQUID AMINOS
These condiments can be used interchangeably according to your preference and health requirements. Tamari is fermented, but Bragg's is not. For more information, refer to "What's That" *(pages 34 and 28)*.

TOASTED SESAME OIL
Use cold pressed oil. Hot sesame oil can be substituted as desired.

TOFU
To guarantee quality, look for brands that use organic soy and nigari, as opposed to calcium chloride, as a natural coagulating agent, and be sure to check freshness dates. Store opened tofu for up to three days in the refrigerator in a container with water to cover and change the water daily. To make tofu easier to digest, steam it for 10 minutes before using.

VEGAN MAYONNAISE
Vegan mayonnaise is available in nearly all grocery stores. My favorite – Grapeseed Oil Vegenaise by Follow Your Heart – is found in the refrigerated section of the store.

VEGETABLE STOCK
Vegetable stock can be purchased in powder form or prepared and packaged in cartons. The infused water that remains from reconstituting dried shiitake mushrooms or sun-dried tomatoes makes a delicious stock, as does leftover water from steaming or boiling vegetables.

When it comes to Clean Food, what you see is what you get, but that doesn't mean you'll automatically know what it is. With more than 100 cooking classes under my belt, the most commonly asked question, hands down, is, "What's that?" From aduki beans and agar to wakame and wasabi, there's intention behind each ingredient. The more we understand about our food, the greater healing power we have and the more equipped and inspired we can be to add nutritional punch to all of our cooking. So fill your kitchen with foods that don't require labels, labeled foods with only natural ingredients – as few as possible and nothing else – and enjoy how delicious good health can be.

WHAT'S THAT?

ADUKI BEAN
A legume, tangy in flavor, easy to digest and known to benefit the kidneys and detoxify the body. Pairs well with sweet winter squash and root vegetables.

AGAR
Sea vegetable known for its gelling ability and high mineral content *(see* Sea Vegetables*)*.

AGAVE NECTAR
Sweetener derived from cactus. While believed to be low in sucrose with a low glycemic index, recent speculation questions these findings and leads me to use maple syrup instead.

ALMONDS
High in monosaturated fats thought to help fight heart disease by lowering cholesterol. A rich source of magnesium and the antioxidant vitamin E.

AMARANTH
High protein, non-gluten grain high in fiber, calcium, lysine and vitamins. Has a nutty flavor that mixes well with other grains, thickens soups and helps retain moisture when used for baking.

APPLE CIDER VINEGAR
Imparts a warming, sour and bitter flavor to food. As a home remedy, it can be helpful for everything from sore throats and digestive issues to elevated blood pressure, sinus problems and weight loss.

ARAME
Sea vegetable with a very mild taste. Needs only to be soaked, not boiled, before eating (making it an easy addition to salads and grain dishes). A good place to start if you're new to cooking with sea vegetables *(see* Sea Vegetables*)*.

ARROWROOT
Natural thickening agent made from a tropical root. Comes in powdered form and is used as a more nutritious substitute for cornstarch.

ASIAN GREENS
Members of the cabbage family with a mild taste. Can be eaten raw in salad, or cooked in stir fry or noodle dishes. Includes bok choy, pac choy, tatsoi, Napa cabbage and Chinese broccoli.

ASPARAGUS
Particularly high in folate, which helps prevent birth defects if consumed in the first trimester of pregnancy. Supports cardiovascular health, and is a natural diuretic.

AVOCADO
An excellent source of the monosaturated fatty acids that protect against elevated cholesterol, blood pressure and even some forms of cancer.

BAKING POWDER
Look for brands that are aluminum- and gluten-free, like Rumford or Featherweight.

BALSAMIC VINEGAR
Traditional Italian vinegar made from the juice of grapes. It is fermented and aged and has a sweet, rich and woody taste.

BARLEY
Whole hulled barley has significantly greater nutritional value than pearl barley and is known for its ability to soothe digestion and heal and strengthen the liver, spleen, pancreas and intestines. Barley's taste is nutty and chewy.

BARLEY MALT
Naturally processed, low-sucrose grain sweetener derived from whole barley.

BLACK BEANS
Also known as black turtle beans, a high-protein legume beneficial to the kidneys and liver. Can help relieve symptoms of menopause.

BRAGG LIQUID AMINOS
Condiment that tastes like soy sauce with a hint of maple. Provides essential building blocks of complete protein.

BROWN RICE
Full of vitamins, brown rice can bring the body into a deep state of balance. Popular varieties include short grain, long grain, medium grain (golden rose) and basmati, all made more healthy by soaking before cooking (see page 13).

BROWN RICE SYRUP
Naturally processed sweetener derived from fermented brown rice. It is 50 percent maltose as opposed to white, brown and raw sugars, which are 96+ percent sucrose. At the time of publication, high levels of naturally occurring arsenic were found in brown rice syrup. Be sure to purchase syrup from a manufacturer who tests for arsenic regularly and produces a clean product.

BROWN RICE VINEGAR
Imparts a sweet flavor and is commonly used in Asian cooking. Stimulates circulation and removes stagnation from the body.

BURDOCK
Root vegetable that cleanses the blood and strengthens the intestines. Highly alkalinizing and helpful for reducing sweet cravings.

CANNELLINI BEANS
Also known as white kidney beans, are high in protein and lend creamy texture to recipes.

CANOLA OIL
A monosaturated oil from the rapeseed plant. "Canola" stands for Canadian Oil Low Acid. Rapeseed is often genetically modified so purchase organic if using this oil.

CHIA SEEDS
A rich source of omega 3 fatty acids, protein and fiber without the estrogen-like properties of flax.

CHICKPEAS (Garbanzo Beans)
Legume high in protein, fiber and iron. They help lower cholesterol, regulate blood sugar and increase energy.

CINNAMON
A warming spice helpful for reducing risk of heart disease, fighting systemic yeast (candida), regulating blood sugar and relieving flu and cold symptoms.

COCONUT OIL (VIRGIN)
High in healthy saturated fat and lauric acid but trans-fat free. Thought to support a healthy heart, thyroid, strong immune system and has numerous topical applications.

COCONUT MILK
Recent research shows coconut milk to be a healthy source of fat. Coconut milk has a sweet taste and a warming effect in the body. It is a complete protein and is often used as a substitute for oil.

COCONUT NECTAR
This raw, low-glycemic sweetener comes from the sap of coconut trees and can be used as a substitute for brown rice syrup.

COLLARD GREENS

These greens are nutritional heavy hitters. A rich source of calcium, manganese, chlorophyll, antioxidant vitamins A and C, minerals, cancer-fighting phytonutrients and much more. They provide strong immune support and protect, cleanse and nourish the heart, liver, colon, lungs and the cellular system in general.

CUMIN

A pungent spice that helps circulation, energy and metabolism and pairs well with legumes, winter squash and whole grains.

DAIKON

This Japanese radish tastes milder than red radishes, breaks down mucus (particularly in the lungs) and is excellent for lowering cholesterol.

DANDELION GREENS

Bitter by nature, these super cleansers are rich in purifying chlorophyll and helpful for reestablishing healthy intestinal flora. Dried dandelions are used medicinally in teas, as a diuretic, to strengthen the liver and to promote healthy digestion and circulation.

EDAMAME

Fresh soybeans that are boiled in their pods and served with salt.

EGG REPLACER

There are many options for replacing eggs in recipes. The one you select depends on what you want the eggs to accomplish. Sometimes eggs are used to bind ingredients, as a leavening agent, or for moisture. Common substitutes include applesauce or ground flax seeds. To replace one egg, combine 1 tablespoon ground golden flax seed with 3 tablespoons water. Let sit 10 minutes, then add to recipe.

FENNEL

A soothing vegetable from the parsley family that tastes like licorice or anise. Medicinally, fennel is thought to calm intestinal and stomach cramps, gas and stomach pain. It also contains phytoestrogens helpful during menopause.

FERMENTED BLACK BEANS

Used traditionally in Chinese and Thai cuisine, these small black beans are fermented and preserved in salt. Available in Asian food stores or the Asian food section of natural food stores.

FLAX SEEDS

The richest source of omega-3 fatty acids, flax seeds cleanse the heart and arteries, provide immune strength and support liver function. The body cannot break down flax seeds in their whole form so be sure to grind them into a meal before using. Flax oil, the processed by-product of flax seeds, can be purchased in liquid or capsule form. Flax is thought to emulate estrogen in the body which should be considered when determining if it's right for you.

GALANGAL

Closely related to ginger, but with a more yellow translucent skin and a peppery, citrus taste. Available in Asian food stores.

GARLIC

A powerful healer with a warming, sweet and pungent taste. Offers many health benefits including cardiovascular support. It has anti-inflammatory, antibacterial and antiviral properties, as well as cancer-fighting phytonutrients.

GINGER
A pungent, warming spice that helps alleviate inflammation and gastrointestinal upset, promotes circulation and digestion, strengthens immunity and fights cancer.

GOMASIO
Macrobiotic condiment made of ground toasted sesame seeds and sea salt.

GRAPESEED OIL
Excellent for cooking. Withstands high temperatures without breaking down, and is heart healthy.

HIJIKI
Recent studies have found hijiki to contain high levels of arsenic, making this one sea vegetable to avoid.

HONEY
Non-vegetarian, unprocessed sweetener highly regarded as a healer. When consumed raw, honey acts as an antibacterial, antiviral and antifungal agent. Athletes find honey to be a pure source of the energy, carbohydrates and glycogen needed to fuel and heal muscle tissue. Local honey can be helpful for treating seasonal allergies.

JÍCAMA
This root looks like a turnip, but tastes like a cross between an apple, pear and potato. Peel away and discard its fibrous skin and use the white flesh raw in Mexican dishes or with crudités. Cooked, jícama takes on the flavor of the other ingredients used.

JOB'S TEARS
A highly nutritious cereal grass commonly used as a gluten-free substitute for barley. Readily found in Asian food stores.

KAFFIR LIME
Citrus leaves traditionally used in Thai cooking. Can be minced and added to soups and sauces or added whole and removed before serving.

KALE
Offers a rich supply of vitamins A and C, calcium, fiber, phytonutrients and chlorophyll. A powerful detoxifier, healer and ally in fighting cancer, heart disease, cataracts, inflammation, arthritis and diseases of the colon.

KELP
An effective digestive aid that supports kidney and thyroid function. Helps balance hormones and is useful for breaking down hardened masses in the body. Powdered kelp, available in natural food stores, is easy to add to soups, sauces, batters and even smoothies for an added nutritional punch without a seaweed taste (*see* Sea Vegetables).

KIDNEY BEANS
Like most legumes, these are particularly helpful for regulating blood sugar and providing easily absorbable protein, fiber and iron. Health benefits include reducing cholesterol and the risk of heart attack, improving brain function and providing slow burning, long-lasting energy. If gas becomes a problem when consuming kidney beans, start with smaller varieties of legumes.

KOMBU

A small piece added to grains, soups, sauces and legumes during cooking is an easy way to infuse foods with highly alkalinizing minerals, iodine and iron. Dried kombu reconstitutes and releases its nutrients into the cooking liquid that is then absorbed by your food. Also known for its ability to tenderize legumes and reduce their gaseous properties (see Sea Vegetables).

KUDZU (KUZU)

Japanese tuber that has a cooling and soothing effect on the stomach. Kudzu, most frequently found in powdered form, is a healthy and easy thickening agent. Substitute 1:1 for cornstarch.

LEEKS

Offer similar health benefits as garlic and onions, with a milder and sweeter taste. An excellent blood sugar stabilizer and blood pressure regulator. They look like huge scallions.

LEMONGRASS

An aromatic herb used in Thai cuisine that imparts a light citrus flavor and bouquet. Commonly used to flavor soups.

LENTILS

Share many of the same health benefits of other legumes, but particularly high in iron.

MAPLE SYRUP

Known as liquid gold in my home, this naturally processed sweetener from maple trees is only 65 percent sucrose and much less destructive to the body's natural mineral balance than processed sweeteners like white, brown or raw sugar. When substituting for white sugar, use 1¼ cups maple syrup per cup of sugar.

MILLET

Sweet, nutty grain that combines well with sweet winter squash and root vegetables. Has a settling effect on the stomach and is healing to the spleen and pancreas. Because millet is naturally alkalinizing, it is not necessary to cook it with kombu.

MIRIN

Sweet Japanese cooking wine made from fermented brown rice, rice koji for fermenting, water and salt. Avoid brands with added corn syrup or alcohol.

MISO

Most commonly made from fermented soy beans, this paste comes in many varieties, offering different tastes and colors. Contains living enzymes that aid digestion and help maintain healthy intestinal flora. Miso is a rich source of minerals. It tones and cleanses the body of toxins and metals such as radiation and mercury, and it helps the body assimilate good cholesterol and break down the bad. For non-soy varieties, look for chickpea, aduki bean and sweet brown rice miso.

MOCHI

Made from pressed sweet brown rice, mochi is easy to digest, warming and strengthening. To use, cut blocks into squares, bake and serve plain or with filling.

MUNG BEANS

Highly cooling legumes thought to aid the liver and gallbladder and to cleanse the cardiovascular system. Can be eaten cooked or sprouted.

MUSTARD GREENS

Greens with a pungent and peppery taste. Can be eaten raw or cooked. Help break down and cleanse the body of mucus, prevent cancer, promote heart and lung health, provide absorbable calcium and phytonutrients, fight inflammation and even help reduce hot flashes during menopause.

NORI

Similar benefits to those of kelp. Has the highest mineral content of all sea vegetables. Particularly helpful for lowering cholesterol and blood pressure and for breaking down and flushing away cysts and mucus.

OATS (Whole Oat Groats)

Powerhouse of a grain most noted for its ability to flush cholesterol from the arteries. Incredibly soothing, healing and restorative to the reproductive, nervous and digestive systems. Provides abundant antioxidants and lignans, which protect against cancer and help stabilize blood sugar levels. Rolled oats, which are only minimally processed, are slightly less beneficial than steel cut or whole oat groats.

OLIVE OIL

A rich source of polyphenols and essential fats that lubricate organs, cleanse and support nearly every bodily system. Look for first cold pressed extra virgin varieties for maximum health benefits.

PARCEL

A leafy herb that looks much like parsley and tastes like celery. A great addition to soups and salads without the bulk of a stalk.

PARSLEY

High in antioxidants and vitamins C and A, this blood purifier makes a great condiment on whole grains, legumes, vegetables, tofu, chicken and fish. Bring it home, wash it in salty water, pat it dry and arrange it in a vase with the roots covered in water so you remember to use a bit each day.

PARSNIP

This sweet root vegetable is a winter favorite and becomes sweeter in frosty weather. Parsnips look like white carrots. They are particularly healing to the stomach and cleansing to the liver and gallbladder.

PICKLED GINGER

Pickles aid digestion. Add to that ginger's stomach-calming ability and great flavor, and you've got a great healing combination.

PINTO BEANS

Like other legumes, these are high in fiber and protein, stabilize blood sugar and lower cholesterol. A rich source of vitamin B1, iron, magnesium, copper and potassium.

PISTACHIO NUTS

A great source of protein, vitamin E and antioxidants, and beneficial to the liver, kidneys and heart.

POMEGRANATE

Thought to have mystical powers, the edible seeds of this ancient fruit are cleansing and cooling. They benefit the cardiovascular system and help stabilize blood sugar. For more juice, select larger fruit with reddish brown firm skin.

PUMPKIN SEEDS
Also known as pepitas, these seeds are a rich source of zinc, iron, and omega-3 fatty acids. They support immune strength and offer essential monosaturated fats and protein.

QUINOA
High protein, non-gluten grain from the Incas. It is a complete protein with significant amounts of lysine, helpful for repairing tissue. Like other whole grains, quinoa helps fight cancer, prevents heart disease and lowers the risk of type 2 diabetes. Has a slightly bitter taste that pairs well with dark leafy greens like collards and kale, sweet root vegetables, corn and onions.

REFINED SUGAR
I call this filler food because it sneaks into your diet and takes the place of foods that can strengthen, nourish and heal you. Refined sugar negatively affects the nervous system, kidney function, mood and nutrient absorption. It is linked to imbalances in the body and brain as well as the depletion of nutrients necessary for healthy metabolism.

RUTABAGA
Sweet, strengthening and warming root vegetable that lends itself well to roasting, puréeing or adding to soups and stews. Often dipped in wax to preserve over the winter. Look for firm, smooth and unblemished skin.

SEA SALT
Usually slightly gray in color, sea salt is minimally processed, retains much of its natural mineral content and is highly alkalinizing. It has many benefits, including neutralizing acidity, tenderizing and enhancing flavors. On the other hand, conventional table salt is highly processed, nutritionally empty and can pose health risks.

SEA VEGETABLES
No other foods offer such a rich supply of minerals. They also provide significant amounts of iodine, iron, calcium, magnesium, B vitamins and lignans (cancer-fighting compounds). Used medicinally to prevent and fight cancer, regulate the thyroid, promote heart health, relieve symptoms of menopause and reduce inflammation. For information on specific varieties, see Agar, Arame, Kelp, Kombu, Nori and Wakame.

SEITAN
This high protein "wheat meat" is made from wheat gluten.

SESAME OIL (Toasted)
When unrefined and cold pressed, it is monosaturated and a healthy source of essential fats. Heating destroys its beneficial qualities and makes it toxic, so be sure to add sesame oil and other aromatic oils to food *after* cooking.

SESAME SEEDS
A rich source of calcium. Black sesame seeds have stronger medicinal value than light.

SHIITAKE MUSHROOMS
A powerful healer and delicious addition to many dishes. They protect the body from cancer, decrease fat and cholesterol in the blood and flush the body of stagnating toxins. Dried shiitakes are stronger medicinally than fresh ones, and can be soaked in hot water to reconstitute. Use the soaking liquid as a healing stock for soups and teas.

SHOYU
Soy sauce made from soybeans, water, sea salt and wheat.

SUCANAT

Minimally processed sugar made by pressing the juice from the cane, clarifying, filtering and evaporating it, then crystallizing the resulting sugar. Sucanat retains many of the minerals, vitamins and trace elements found in sugar cane.

SUMMER SQUASH

Much more delicate than their winter counterparts, summer squash is cooling, refreshing and versatile. Try serving squash raw and shredded in salads, grilled, roasted or sautéed. Look for crookneck, straightneck, zucchini and pattypan varieties.

SUNFLOWER SEEDS

Warming in nature and a rich source of protein, vitamins D, B1 and E. For people with tree-nut allergies, try sunflower butter as a substitute for peanut or almond butters.

SUSHI RICE

Traditional Japanese short grain rice that grows white and pearl-like naturally. Lighter texture than brown rice. To make it less sticky and more manageable, brown rice vinegar and brown rice syrup are often added.

SWEET BROWN RICE

High in protein and good fats, easy to digest and more glutinous in texture than regular brown rice, although still gluten-free.

TAHINI

Rich and warming butter made from sesame seeds. Comes in both regular (slightly more bitter) and roasted varieties.

TAMARI

Soy sauce made from soybeans, water and sea salt. Traditionally wheat-free, but not all manufacturers follow this guideline. Has a high sodium content, but reduced sodium tamari is available at most natural food stores.

TAMARIND

Fruits from this tree are commonly used in Asian, Indian and Mexican cuisines. Tamarinds have a tangy sweet-and-sour taste and consist of a pit surrounded by a red flesh. They are similar in texture to dates.

TEFF (Ivory and Dark)

A high protein, non-gluten grain, high in iron, calcium and zinc. Because it is such a small grain, it is impossible to hull before milling, making teff flour nearly identical in nutritional value to the whole grain. Dark teff is higher in iron, while ivory teff is higher in protein.

TEMPEH

Made from pressed and fermented soybeans. Comes in many varieties based on added ingredients such as grains and vegetables. It is 19.5 percent protein, rich in unsaturated fat, and highly alkalinizing, strengthening and easy to digest.

TOFU

Made from soybean curd. Regular tofu holds its shape and texture, and silken is used for whipping in dressings and puddings. It is high in protein, calcium, B-vitamins, potassium and iron and low in saturated fat and sodium. Tofu is rich in isoflavones thought to reduce women's risk of breast cancer, and phytoestrogens which block harmful estrogens from being absorbed by the cells.

TOMATILLO

Also known as a husk tomato, tomatillos are commonly used in Mexican cuisine and add a crisp tartness to dishes. Look for fruits with brown husks and smooth green skin.

UDON/SOBA NOODLES

Wheat or buckwheat noodles commonly used in Asian cooking. Look for varieties made with wild yam and/or mung bean.

UMEBOSHI PLUMS

Quite sour and salty, these Japanese plums are pickled and used to aid digestion and help treat liver imbalances. Highly alkalinizing to the blood and antibiotic in nature. Similar health benefits can be gained from umeboshi paste and vinegar, but be mindful of sodium content.

WAKAME

Sea vegetable most commonly served in miso soup. Add a small amount of dried wakame to hot water and let steep 3–4 minutes before stirring in the desired amount of dissolved miso (see Sea Vegetables).

WALNUTS

Super-rich in omega 3 fatty acids, these nuts benefit the heart and brain and heal imbalances caused by inflammation. Also a rich source of ellagic acid, an antioxidant that boosts immune strength and helps prevent cancer.

WASABI

Spicy Japanese mustard usually made from horseradish root and often colored with nutrient-rich spirulina (blue-green algae). Look for paste or powdered varieties packaged without preservatives.

WATERCRESS

Slightly more pungent than other bitter greens. Effective blood purifier that helps remove toxins from the body. High in vitamin A, chlorophyll and calcium. Can be eaten cooked or raw. Mix with lettuce to amp up the nutritional value of your salad.

WATERMELON RADISH

This radish looks like a turnip and should be bought when smooth and firm. Peel and discard the fibrous skin to reveal a beautiful deep pink flesh. If you can't find watermelon radishes, substitute red radishes, jícama or even red bell pepper.

WHEAT BERRIES

The whole wheat grain. Comes in two varieties – hard, which has more gluten, and soft, which has less gluten but more starch. Can be cooked and used like rice in recipes. Has a nutty taste and requires much chewing power to ensure healthy digestion.

WILD RICE

Not a grain, but a water grass. Grows along streams and swamps and is high in protein and low in fat.

WINTER SQUASH

A rich source of vitamins A, C, B1, folate, fiber and omega-3 fatty acids, these gems of the fall are sweet, warming, easy to digest, helpful for improving circulation and are mood enhancing. Look for acorn, buttercup, butternut, delicata, hubbard, kabocha, pumpkin and red kuri.

Oh, give us pleasure in the flowers today;
And give us not to think so far away
As the uncertain harvest; keep us here
All simply in the springing of the year.

ROBERT FROST

Spring

The very sight of overflowing baskets of tender baby greens that adorn the farmers market each spring lifts my spirit and heals my soul. The spinach and arugula melt in your mouth and there are enough varieties of Chinese cabbage and lettuce greens to enjoy a new one each day. Spring's increased sunshine and longer days start a natural gentle cleansing that prepares me for warmer days ahead. As everything starts to blossom and temperatures rise, I feel a renewed sense of community, connection and hope. Each conversation at the farm has a recipe involved. I listen as I wander around baskets of tender asparagus, artichokes, pac choy, fennel, watermelon radishes and green beans. My basket fills with tastes and textures all begging to come home with me. Whether you are looking to lighten up, gain mental clarity, energize or simply take advantage of spring's delicious bounty, it's time to get cooking.

SPRING

DIPS AND DRESSINGS

Lemony Artichoke Dip 40
Creamy Miso Dressing 41
Basic Balsamic Vinaigrette 43
Ginger Sesame Vinaigrette 43
Maple Mustard Vinaigrette 43
Garlic Scape and Walnut Pesto 44

SOUPS

Lettuce Soup with Cilantro and Hot Sesame Oil 45
Cream of Asparagus Soup 46
My Favorite Miso Soup 47

VEGETABLES

Baby Spinach Salad with Mustard Vinaigrette 48
Spring Greens with Apricot Vinaigrette 49
Fennel and Orange Salad 50
Watercress, Daikon and Avocado Salad
    with Mustard Seed Dressing 51
Chopped Salad with Shallot Poppy Seed Dressing 52
Caesar Salad 53
Grilled Vidalia Onions with
    Wild Mushrooms and Lemon Zest 54
Carrot Raisin Salad 56
Crispy Sesame Carrots 57
Seared Fennel with Meyer Lemon 58
Sautéed Fennel and Asian Greens
    with Ginger and Apricot 59
Mango Sesame Tatsoi 60
Seared Artichokes with Red Pepper Aioli 61
Asparagus with Mustard Vinaigrette
    and Toasted Pecans 62
Bok Choy and Chickpeas with Cashews 63
Roasted Portobello Sandwich
    with Sun-dried Tomato Aioli 65
Artichokes, Fennel and Olives over Penne 66
Swiss Chard with Roasted Golden Beets
    and Sweet Peas 67
Sweet and Sour Stir-Fry 68

SEA VEGETABLES

Arame and Sunflower Seeds 69
Seaweed and Cabbage Sauté 70
Gingered Arame with Snow Peas 71
Quinoa with Arame, Toasted Nuts and Seeds. 72

LEGUMES

Multibean Salad with Fresh Herbs 73
French Lentil Salad with Lemon, Radish and Cilantro . . . 74
Marinated Aduki Beans 76
Tempeh Salad 77
Crispy Chickpea Fritters 78

GRAINS

Mochi Dumplings 79
Brown Rice with Ginger and Umeboshi Plums 80
Inca Red Quinoa with Currants 81
Millet Black Bean Patties with Corn 83
Barley with Lemon and Herbs 84
Wild Rice Pilaf 85

DESSERTS

Blueberry Kanten with Cashew Cream 86
Mixed Berry Couscous Cake 87
Banana Coconut Chocolate Chip Cookies 88
Chocolate Coconut Granola Bites 90
Lemon Almond Cookie Tart with Strawberry Topping . . 91

Lemony Artichoke Dip

FRESH ARTICHOKES ARE A TREAT, but also a lot of work. Canned artichoke hearts, available in most grocery stores, allow you to enjoy the delicious taste of artichokes anytime without the fuss. I like to serve this dip with rice crackers or Pita Chips *(page 317)*.

1	garlic clove, peeled
1	shallot, peeled
2	tablespoons lemon juice
½	cup vegan mayonnaise
1	tablespoon apple cider vinegar
¾	cup great northern beans
¼	teaspoon sea salt
½	teaspoon powdered mustard
¼	teaspoon ground white pepper
1	4-ounce can chopped green chiles
2½	cups canned artichoke hearts, drained

With food processor running, drop in garlic clove and process until minced. Turn off processor, scrape down sides of bowl, add remaining ingredients except artichokes and process until well combined. Add artichokes and process briefly so that small chunks remain. Season to taste with additional salt and serve.

MAKES 3 cups

Creamy Miso Dressing

IN WINTER WE DRINK PIPING HOT MISO SOUP to cleanse the digestive system, replenish healthy intestinal flora, regulate cholesterol and flush away toxins. In spring we can gain the same health benefits from miso by using it in salad dressings or dips, as I've done here.

1	shallot, minced
1	garlic clove, minced
3	tablespoons lemon juice
2	tablespoons mellow white miso
2	tablespoons tahini
½	cup extra virgin olive oil
¼	cup water

Place all ingredients in food processor and pulse to combine. Store in airtight container in refrigerator for up to 5 days.

MAKES 1 cup

Salad Dressings

WHEN I FIRST STARTED EATING WHOLE FOODS, someone suggested that I combine any cooked grain with legumes and vegetables, and toss them with my favorite salad dressing. Whether being used to spice up grains, legumes or a traditional salad, these dressings are sure to become staples in your refrigerator. I use a handheld blender for salad dressings to keep ingredients from separating, to blend flavors and to eliminate any chopping. If using a whisk, mince garlic and shallots first and then add to bowl with other ingredients. A sealable glass pitcher makes a perfect container for mixing and storing.

BASIC BALSAMIC VINAIGRETTE

1   garlic clove,
    peeled and minced
1   small shallot,
    peeled and minced
1   teaspoon lemon juice
2   tablespoons maple syrup
¼   cup balsamic vinegar
½   cup extra virgin olive oil
Sea salt and freshly ground
    black pepper to taste

Place all ingredients in bowl and whisk to combine or emulsify with handheld blender.

MAKES about 1 cup

GINGER SESAME VINAIGRETTE

1   small shallot,
    peeled and minced
1   tablespoon grated
    fresh ginger
2   tablespoons tahini
¼   cup toasted sesame oil
¼   cup brown rice vinegar
¼   cup grapeseed oil
1   tablespoon freshly
    squeezed orange
    or lime juice
1   teaspoon orange zest
2   tablespoons toasted
    hulled sesame seeds

Place all ingredients except sesame seeds in bowl and whisk to combine or emulsify with handheld blender. Stir in sesame seeds.

MAKES about 1 cup

MAPLE MUSTARD VINAIGRETTE

1   garlic clove,
    peeled and minced
1   heaping teaspoon
    prepared mustard
2   tablespoons maple syrup
1   tablespoon lemon juice
3   tablespoons red wine
    vinegar
½   cup extra virgin olive oil
Sea salt

Place all ingredients in bowl and whisk to combine or emulsify with handheld blender.

MAKES about 1 cup

Garlic Scape and Walnut Pesto

JUST BEFORE THE HARDNECK GARLIC IS READY to harvest, it sends out curly flower stems that are tender, mellow and delicious. Cutting the scapes sends necessary energy back into the maturing garlic, forcing it to grow, and provides us with this special spring delicacy.

10	garlic scapes, cut into 1-inch pieces (about 1 cup)
1	cup cilantro, lightly packed
½	cup extra virgin olive oil
½	cup walnuts
2	tablespoons lemon juice
1	teaspoon lemon zest
¼	teaspoon sea salt

Place all ingredients in food processor and process until smooth. Refrigerate in airtight container or freeze until ready to use.

MAKES 1½ cups

SERVING SUGGESTION
Toss this pesto with pasta, roasted golden beets, steamed vegetables, white beans or whatever you'd like.

Lettuce Soup with Cilantro and Hot Sesame Oil

I ONCE HEARD A FAMOUS CHEF TALKING about making soup out of leftover salad greens. My initial reaction was not positive, but each spring as salad greens became abundant the idea started to intrigue me. It didn't take much experimentation to create this delicious soup that offers a surprising combination of light and refreshing taste with an added touch of heat.

6	dried shiitake mushrooms
6	cups water
1	leek, sliced into thin rounds
1	cup bamboo shoots
2	cups corn, fresh or frozen
¼	cup chopped fresh cilantro
2	cups thinly sliced romaine lettuce (or other variety)
5	dashes hot sesame oil
7	dashes ume plum vinegar

Place mushrooms in pot with water, bring to boil, reduce heat and simmer 20 minutes. Remove mushrooms, discard stems, thinly slice caps and return to pot. Add leek, bamboo shoots and corn. Simmer 3 minutes. Add cilantro and lettuce, stir and continue to cook until greens have wilted (about 3 minutes). Add hot sesame oil and vinegar and serve. Refrigerate leftovers in airtight container for up to 4 days.

SERVES 6

Cream of Asparagus Soup

ALL WINTER LONG I SUSTAIN MYSELF with hearty soups that I can practically eat with a fork. By early spring, I transition to more delicate soups like this one. This nondairy soup has the richness of a cream soup without the fat and guilt, and is surprisingly easy to make. If you're preparing this soup for guests, do so in advance, chill for 3–4 hours to allow flavors to blend, then reheat, garnish and serve.

2–3 bunches asparagus
(about 6 cups chopped)

2 tablespoons
extra virgin olive oil

2 garlic cloves, minced

3 leeks, white parts
only, chopped

½ cup rolled oats

3 cups rice milk or soy milk

½ teaspoon dried dill

Water as needed

White pepper

1 teaspoon mellow
white miso per serving

Chopped fresh parsley
for garnish

Bend each piece of asparagus near the tough dried end until it snaps off at its natural breaking point. Discard ends, wash remaining asparagus, cut into 2-inch pieces and set aside.

In large pot over medium heat, sauté garlic and leeks in olive oil until soft (2–3 minutes). Add asparagus, oats, milk and dill, then add enough water to just cover asparagus. Bring to boil, reduce heat, cover and simmer until asparagus is soft (about 10 minutes). Remove from heat and cool slightly.

Purée soup using a handheld blender. Add water if thinner soup is desired. Season to taste with white pepper. Dissolve miso in just enough water to make it liquid. Stir into each serving. Garnish with parsley and serve.

Note: Miso is added to individual servings rather than to the full pot so you can reheat leftover soup without destroying miso's living enzymes.

SERVES 6

My Favorite Miso Soup

I CALL THIS WATER SOUP! Because miso is a living food and boiling destroys its beneficial enzymes, I prepare the ingredients in water and then add miso to the individual servings. That way I can save any leftover soup in the refrigerator, and reheat it without worrying about harming miso's living enzymes. This easy-to-make soup combines the medicinal benefits of sea vegetables, miso and tofu.

6⅓ cups water

3   carrots, chopped

12   ounces extra firm silken
     tofu, diced

1   3-inch strip wakame,
     broken into small pieces

Dash of tamari or shoyu

¼   cup miso (I like traditional
     barley, chickpea or mellow
     white)

2–3 scallions, chopped

In large pot over high heat bring 6 cups water to boil. Add carrots, tofu, wakame and tamari, reduce heat and simmer 10 minutes. Remove from heat.

In separate bowl, dissolve miso in remaining ⅓ cup water. Ladle soup into individual bowls and stir 1 generous tablespoon of dissolved miso into each serving. Top with chopped scallions and serve.

SERVES 4

Baby Spinach Salad with Mustard Vinaigrette

THIS SALAD BURSTS WITH FLAVOR AND COLOR and makes a perfect complement to grilled fish or chicken. For a quick and easy lunch, try tossing with half a cup of great northern or navy beans.

6 cups loosely packed baby spinach

1 cup stemmed and sliced strawberries

¼ cup toasted pumpkin seeds

VINAIGRETTE

2 tablespoons red wine vinegar

¼ cup extra virgin olive oil

1 teaspoon maple syrup

1 teaspoon Dijon mustard

Pinch of sea salt

Place spinach and ½ cup strawberries in salad bowl. In small bowl, whisk together all vinaigrette ingredients. Pour over salad and toss to coat. Top with remaining strawberries and pumpkin seeds and serve.

SERVES 4

Spring Greens with Apricot Vinaigrette

TO BE APPEALING AND DELICIOUS, a tossed salad does not need to be decorated with fancy fixings, nor do hearty greens need to be sautéed or steamed. These greens and herbs fall into both categories. Experiment with different combinations and don't be afraid to try something new. A trip to your local farm or farmers' market can fill your salad bowl with all sorts of unusual findings. You might also enjoy this salad with some sliced avocado and pumpkin seeds.

6 cups spring greens and herbs of choice (try bok choy, baby chard, chives, dill, escarole, fennel, fennel fronds, garlic scapes, mustard greens, parcel,* pea shoots, romaine lettuce or other)

VINAIGRETTE

1 garlic clove, minced

1 small shallot, minced

Juice of 2 Meyer lemons

¼ cup apricot juice

¼ cup balsamic vinegar

½ cup extra virgin olive oil

1 tablespoon maple mustard

2 tablespoons maple syrup

Pinch of sea salt

Tear greens into pieces and place in large bowl. In separate bowl, whisk together vinaigrette ingredients. Pour vinaigrette over greens, toss and serve.

*See "What's That?" *(page 32) for information on this leafy herb.*

SERVES 6

Fennel and Orange Salad

THE COMBINATION OF CRISP FRESH FENNEL with cool refreshing citrus is a treat. The coriander adds just a bit of savory flavor to give this dish even more depth and interest. Be sure to tear your mint leaves rather than cut them to keep the edges from turning brown.

---

4   navel oranges
½   small red onion, very thinly sliced
1   fennel bulb, halved, cored and thinly sliced
¼   cup fresh mint leaves, torn

DRESSING
1   teaspoon ground coriander
2   tablespoons fresh orange juice
2   tablespoons red wine vinegar
¼   teaspoon sea salt
3   tablespoons extra virgin olive oil

Remove zest from 2 oranges and set aside. Remove and discard orange peels and white outer skins from all 4 oranges. Slice oranges into rounds, or separate into segments.

Bring 2 cups water to boil. Place sliced onion in small bowl, cover with boiling water, let sit 30 seconds, then drain well.

In large bowl, toss together orange segments, red onion, fennel and mint leaves. In separate bowl, whisk together all dressing ingredients. Add zest, whisk to combine and pour over salad. Toss to coat evenly and serve.

SERVES 6

Watercress, Daikon and Avocado Salad with Mustard Seed Dressing

WATERCRESS AND DAIKON MAKE THIS SALAD super cleansing and heart healthy, and their bitter flavors and crisp textures are balanced perfectly by the smooth richness of avocado and mustard. I like to use the stems and leaves of watercress and remove only the dried stem ends (or the wet root ball if it is hydroponically grown).

1	large bunch watercress, chopped
1	large daikon, peeled and julienned
1	avocado, peeled, pitted and diced

DRESSING

1	tablespoon yellow mustard seeds
1	tablespoon lemon juice
1	teaspoon light miso
2	tablespoons maple syrup
1	tablespoon prepared mustard
2	tablespoons extra virgin olive oil

GARNISH

½	cup toasted pumpkin seeds

In large bowl, combine watercress, daikon and avocado.

In dry pan, over medium heat, toast mustard seeds until they start to pop. Remove from heat and let cool slightly. In medium bowl, whisk together remaining dressing ingredients. Stir in mustard seeds.

Pour dressing over vegetables and fold gently to coat evenly. Top with pumpkins seeds and serve at room temperature.

Note: If you prefer salad chilled, refrigerate watercress, daikon, avocado and dressing all separately. Toss together and top with pumpkin seeds just before serving.

SERVES 4

Chopped Salad with Shallot Poppy Seed Dressing

THIS COLORFUL AND COOLING SALAD features a variety of tastes, including fresh asparagus, bitter greens, creamy avocado and salty olives to yield a delightful dish that is always a crowd pleaser. It pairs nicely with grilled chicken or fish.

8	stalks asparagus
1	avocado
1	tablespoon lemon juice
2	heads endive, chopped
2	bunches watercress, chopped
1	head radicchio, chopped
1	cup halved cherry tomatoes
1	orange bell pepper, chopped
½	cup kalamata olives, pitted
3	stalks celery, chopped
½	red onion, chopped

DRESSING

1	cup extra virgin olive oil
⅓	cup red wine vinegar
1	small shallot, minced
½	teaspoon sea salt
¼	cup maple syrup
2	tablespoons poppy seeds

GARNISH

1	cup toasted pumpkin seeds

Bend each piece of asparagus near the tough dried end until it snaps off at its natural breaking point. Discard ends, wash asparagus and cut into 1-inch pieces. Place in bowl. Bring 3 cups water to boil. Pour over asparagus, let sit 1 minute, the drain.

Cut avocado in half and remove pit. Scoop out flesh, cut into chunks and toss with lemon juice to prevent browning.

In large bowl, combine asparagus, avocado and all remaining salad ingredients. Set aside.

In separate bowl, combine all dressing ingredients except poppy seeds and whisk by hand or with handheld blender. Stir in poppy seeds.

Pour dressing over salad and toss to combine. Top with toasted pumpkin seeds and serve.

SERVES 8 as a side salad

Caesar Salad

I LOVE A TRADITIONAL CAESAR SALAD, so it was absolutely essential that I develop this heart-healthy version. If you are not opposed to fish, the addition of one anchovy or two tablespoons of dried bonito to the dressing makes this already delicious faux-Caesar taste even more like the real deal.

2   heads romaine lettuce

½   cup kalamata olives, pitted

1   cup sourdough croutons (or gluten-free variety of choice)

DRESSING

6   ounces soft silken tofu

1   tablespoon apple cider vinegar

2   tablespoons lemon juice

1   tablespoon mellow white miso

2   garlic cloves, minced

1   teaspoon grated fresh ginger

½   cup extra virgin olive oil

1   tablespoon chopped fresh parsley

Water

Tear lettuce into bite-size pieces and place in large salad bowl. Top with olives and croutons.

In food processor, whip tofu until smooth. Add remaining ingredients except water and process until combined. Add water one tablespoon at a time to thin to desired consistency. Pour desired amount of dressing over salad, toss and serve.

SERVES 6 (makes about 1 cup of dressing)

Grilled Vidalia Onions with Wild Mushrooms and Lemon Zest

THIS DISH LITERALLY MELTS IN YOUR MOUTH and is a sweet and savory addition to any meal, whether served over grilled fish or tofu, or simply on its own. While it's easy to prepare in advance, you may find it irresistible and difficult to save for your meal.

---

4   Vidalia onions

1½ pounds mixed variety mushrooms (chanterelles, maitake, shiitakes...)

2   tablespoons extra virgin olive oil, plus more for drizzling

Mirin

Zest and juice of 1 lemon

Coarse sea salt

Preheat grill to medium. Place whole, unpeeled onions directly on grate, close cover and grill. Time will vary according to size of onions. When onions are charred black on the outside and soft throughout, remove from heat and set aside until cool enough to touch.

Peel and discard charred outer layer from onions. Remove and discard root end and slice remaining bulb into wedges. Place wedges in mixing bowl and set aside.

Prepare mushrooms as follows: for shiitake, remove stems and slice caps thinly; slice chanterelles thinly; crumble maitakes; and thinly slice most other varieties. In large cast iron skillet over medium heat, sauté mushrooms in olive oil until translucent. Add mirin 1 teaspoon at a time to deglaze pan and encourage caramelization. Sauté for a total of 10–12 minutes or until mushrooms are evenly browned. Remove from heat, add to bowl with onions and drizzle with olive oil. Add zest, lemon juice and coarse sea salt to taste, toss and serve.

SERVES 8

VARIATION
Onions can be roasted in an oven-proof casserole at 400°F until soft throughout.

Carrot Raisin Salad

THIS RECIPE TAKES A DELI COUNTER FAVORITE and spices it up with orange zest and grated fresh ginger. To prevent the nuts from getting soggy, add them just before serving this dish.

¼ cup nuts or seeds (I like pine nuts or sunflower seeds)

3 cups grated carrots

½ cup raisins

Zest and juice of ½ lemon

Juice of 2 oranges

Zest of 1 orange

1 teaspoon grated fresh ginger

Pinch of sea salt

Preheat oven to 250°F.

Place nuts or seeds on parchment-lined baking sheet and roast until fragrant and lightly browned (watch closely to avoid burning). Remove from oven and set aside.

In large bowl, combine carrots and raisins. Cover with 4 cups boiling water, let sit for 30 seconds, drain, rinse with cold water and drain completely. Press out excess water, stir in juices, zests, ginger and salt. Refrigerate until cold. Sprinkle with toasted nuts or seeds and serve.

SERVES 4

Crispy Sesame Carrots

THESE LIGHT AND CRISPY CARROTS WERE A BIG HIT with my family from the start and are a far cry from my grandmother's plain steamed carrots! If you have a food processor, the slicing disc will make your prep time minimal. It will feel like you are preparing an enormous amount of carrots, but they shrink dramatically in the oven. In fact, you may want to make extra to compensate for all the ones you and your family members will sneak before you get this dish to the table.

---

1   tablespoon
     extra virgin olive oil

2   pounds carrots,
     sliced into thin rounds

2   tablespoons
     toasted sesame oil

Coarse sea salt

2   tablespoons
     toasted sesame seeds

2   tablespoons toasted
     black sesame seeds

Preheat oven to 350°F.

In large sauté pan over medium-high heat, sauté sliced carrots in olive oil until just soft (about 6 minutes). Remove from heat and toss with toasted sesame oil and sea salt. Spread out carrots in a single layer on two cookie sheets and bake for 30 minutes, or until brown on the edges and orange in the center. Remove from oven, toss with sesame seeds and let set 5 minutes to allow carrots to crisp up before serving.

SERVES 4

VARIATION
Use different colored carrots if available for an extra-beautiful presentation.

Seared Fennel with Meyer Lemon

MEYER LEMONS ARE A SPRING DELICACY and infuse this dish with a sweet citrus tang. If Meyer lemons are not available, substitute regular lemons plus a dash of orange juice. Use a cast-iron skillet to sear this dish to perfection.

---

3   fennel bulbs
    (save fronds)

2   tablespoons
    extra virgin olive oil

1   shallot, thinly sliced

Zest and juice of
    1 Meyer lemon

Pinch of coarse sea salt

Cut fennel bulbs into wedges and steam until just soft. Remove from heat and set aside.

In large skillet over medium-high heat, sauté shallot in olive oil for 2 minutes. Add fennel wedges and sear 1–2 minutes per side. Add lemon zest and juice, chopped fennel fronds and a pinch of salt. Sauté 1 more minute. Remove from heat and serve.

SERVES 6

Sautéed Fennel and Asian Greens with Ginger and Apricot

WHILE I AM A NUT FOR KALE AND COLLARD GREENS most of the year round, I am every bit as nutty for the Asian greens that are so bountiful at the farm in early spring. Bok choy, pac choy, tatsoi, Napa cabbage, Chinese broccoli … the selection is overwhelming, and all of the varieties work in this recipe, so have fun experimenting.

2	tablespoons extra virgin olive or grapeseed oil
2	tablespoons grated fresh ginger
½	fennel bulb, halved, cored and thinly sliced
3	tablespoons apricot all-fruit jam
1	tablespoon tamari
8	cups sliced Asian greens

In large skillet or Dutch oven over medium heat, sauté ginger in oil 1 minute. Add fennel and sauté 5 minutes or until fennel is soft and translucent. Stir in apricot jam and tamari, add greens and gently fold until greens are bright green. Remove from heat and serve.

SERVES 4

Mango Sesame Tatsoi

LOOK FOR THIS TENDER SPRING SPECIALTY Chinese cabbage at your local organic farm or Asian grocery store. If you can't find it, you can substitute baby bok choy or pac choy instead.

6   heads tatsoi (whole)

2   tablespoons water

1   tablespoon toasted sesame seeds

DRESSING

½   mango, peeled, pitted and finely chopped

1   shallot, minced

2   tablespoons brown rice vinegar

2   tablespoons toasted sesame oil

¼   cup grapeseed oil

Sea salt

In medium bowl, whisk together all dressing ingredients and set aside.

Rinse tatsoi, keeping heads together (do *not* trim off ends or separate leaves). Heat water in large skillet over medium-high heat. Add greens and toss until just soft and bright green (1–2 minutes). Remove from heat, arrange greens on serving dish and top with mango dressing. Sprinkle with sesame seeds and serve.

SERVES 6

Seared Artichokes with Red Pepper Aioli

ARTICHOKES ARE REASONABLY PRICED AND PLENTIFUL in the spring. For years I would stuff each leaf with herbed bread crumbs. Many hours (and pounds) later, I switched to this light and easy approach. Marinating the artichokes infuses them with flavor and the aioli makes for an impressive finish.

4	whole artichokes
¼	cup extra virgin olive oil
1	tablespoon lemon juice
2	tablespoons chopped fresh herbs of choice (tarragon, dill, lemon balm, marjoram or rosemary)

Sea salt and freshly ground black pepper

RED PEPPER AIOLI

1	garlic clove, peeled
2	tablespoons extra virgin olive oil
1½	cups grapeseed oil mayonnaise
3	roasted red peppers, skins and seeds removed

Sea salt and freshly ground black pepper

PREPARING ARTICHOKES

Bring large pot of water to boil.

Remove tough lower leaves from artichokes, and trim and peel the stems. Snip off sharp ends of leaves, and cut off top ½-inch where leaves are tight. Place artichokes in pot, reduce heat, cover and cook until cores are just soft (about 20 minutes). Drain cooking water, rinse with cold water and set upside-down to drain completely.

Once artichokes have cooled, gently squeeze out remaining water and carefully cut in half from stem to tip. Scoop out and discard fuzzy choke.

In medium bowl, whisk together olive oil, lemon juice, herbs and salt and pepper to taste. Place prepared artichokes in sealable container, pour in marinade, seal, shake gently and refrigerate at least 1 hour, shaking container occasionally to redistribute marinade.

PREPARING AIOLI

With the food processor running, drop in garlic clove and process until minced, scraping down sides as needed. Add remaining ingredients and purée until smooth. Transfer to separate container, cover and refrigerate until ready to use.

FINISHING

Preheat griddle, grill or cast-iron skillet to high and sear artichokes until grill lines show (1–2 minutes per side). Serve hot with aioli on the side.

SERVES 8

Asparagus with Mustard Vinaigrette and Toasted Pecans

VINAIGRETTES ARE A SIMPLE WAY to season fresh steamed vegetables, and toasted pecans finish this dish with an extra-special touch. Toasting the nuts and preparing the vinaigrette in advance will allow you to put this dish together in no time.

¾   cup pecans
2   pounds asparagus

VINAIGRETTE

½   cup extra virgin olive oil
1   clove garlic, minced
¼   cup red wine vinegar
1   tablespoon prepared
     mustard
⅛   teaspoon sea salt
Freshly ground black pepper

Preheat oven to 300°F.

In small bowl, whisk together vinaigrette ingredients and set aside.

Place pecans on parchment-lined cookie sheet and toast until fragrant and lightly browned. Remove from oven and set aside to cool.

To prepare asparagus, bend each piece near the tough dried end until it snaps off. Discard ends and steam asparagus until it turns bright green (about 3 minutes). Remove from heat and place on a serving dish. Drizzle with vinaigrette, top with toasted pecans and serve.

SERVES 4

Bok Choy and Chickpeas with Cashews

THIS IS ONE OF MY FAVORITE BREAKFAST DISHES! No, that is not a typo. I love the uplifting energy of greens first thing in the morning, and the addition of chickpeas and cashews makes this dish one that satisfies me and keeps me energized for hours.

---

1 tablespoon extra virgin olive oil

1 tablespoon grated fresh ginger

1 tablespoon Bragg Liquid Aminos

1 tablespoon mirin

1 cup cooked chickpeas

6 heads baby bok choy, chopped into large pieces

½ cup toasted cashews

In large skillet over medium heat, sauté ginger in olive oil 1 minute. Add liquid aminos, mirin and chickpeas and sauté 2 minutes. Add bok choy and sauté another 2–3 minutes or until greens are just tender. Remove from heat, top with toasted cashews and serve.

SERVES 4

Roasted Portobello Sandwich with Sun-dried Tomato Aioli

BITING INTO A PORTOBELLO MUSHROOM is about as far as you can get from the sprouts and shaved-carrot vegetarian sandwich of the past. Not only is this sandwich delicious, it really gives you something to sink your teeth into. The aioli will last five days in the refrigerator, so you may want to make extra to enjoy with crudités after your sandwiches are gone.

Portobello mushrooms
(1–2 per serving)

Extra virgin olive oil

1   tablespoon minced fresh Italian herbs of choice (oregano, basil, thyme or parsley)

Sea salt and freshly ground black pepper

Sourdough or gluten-free bread (2 slices per serving)

Roasted red peppers, sliced into ½-inch strips

Avocado, thinly sliced

Romaine lettuce

Spicy honey mustard

AIOLI

6   sun-dried tomatoes

1   garlic clove, peeled

1½ cups grapeseed oil mayonnaise

2   tablespoons fresh Italian herbs of choice

Pinch of sea salt

PREPARING AIOLI

Soak dried tomatoes in hot water 15 minutes or until soft. With the food processor running, drop in garlic. Process until minced. Squeeze excess water from tomatoes and add them along with mayonnaise to processor. Scrape down sides of the bowl as needed and process until smooth. Add herbs and salt and process lightly. Transfer to container and refrigerate to allow flavors to blend.

ROASTING PORTOBELLOS

Preheat oven to 400°F.

Line cookie sheet with parchment paper. Wipe mushrooms with a damp towel to clean. Discard stems and rub smooth side of mushroom caps with olive oil. Place caps smooth side down on cookie sheet and sprinkle insides with Italian herbs, pepper and a pinch of salt. Roast for 8–10 minutes until soft. Remove and set aside.

ASSEMBLING

Slice bread and lightly toast. Spread aioli on toast and top with roasted portobello, roasted red pepper, avocado and lettuce. Spread mustard on second piece of toasted bread, top sandwich and serve warm.

MAKES enough aioli for 6 sandwiches

Artichokes, Fennel and Olives over Penne

THE STRONG FLAVORS OF THIS DISH demand pasta for balance and to hold it all together. This is one of those recipes that simply cannot fail. Don't worry if you don't have all of the ingredients – any bitter greens (try dandelion greens, mustard greens or watercress) will substitute beautifully for the arugula. For an even bigger change, serve over polenta.

1	pound penne pasta
3	tablespoons extra virgin olive oil
1	onion, diced
2	garlic cloves, minced
1	cup canned artichoke hearts, quartered
½	cup kalamata olives, pitted
1	fennel bulb, halved, cored and thinly sliced
1	bunch arugula
1	cup chopped tomatoes, fresh or canned
¼	cup chopped fresh parsley
1	tablespoon lemon juice
Sea salt and freshly ground black pepper	

Cook penne according to directions on package. Rinse, drain and return to pot. Drizzle with 1 tablespoon olive oil and set aside.

Meanwhile, in large pot over medium heat, sauté onion and garlic in remaining 2 tablespoons olive oil until soft (about 3 minutes). Add artichokes, olives, fennel and arugula. Sauté until heated through (about 5 minutes). Add tomatoes and sauté another 2 minutes. Add parsley and lemon juice. Season to taste with salt and pepper. Remove from heat and serve over pasta.

SERVES 4

Swiss Chard with Roasted Golden Beets and Sweet Peas

THIS RECIPE WILL WORK with any of your favorite dark leafy greens. In spring and early summer we devour peas right out of their shells. They are as sweet as candy and a wonderful addition to any salad or vegetable dish. During the cooler months, try frozen sweet peas or edamame beans. To make this dish a complete meal, serve it over couscous or try French lentils if you prefer to keep it gluten-free.

3–4	golden beets
2	tablespoons extra virgin olive oil
1	Vidalia onion (or other sweet variety), diced
3	bunches Swiss chard
1	cup fresh peas removed from their shells
	Coarse sea salt and freshly ground black pepper

Preheat oven to 425°F.

Wrap beets loosely in foil, place in baking dish and bake 45 minutes or until soft throughout. Remove from oven and set aside. When cool enough to touch, open foil and gently peel away skins by pressing them firmly with your thumb. Trim away blemishes and cut beets into bite-size pieces.

In large skillet over medium heat, sauté onion in 1 tablespoon olive oil until soft (about 3 minutes). Add chard and toss gently until it starts to wilt (1–2 minutes). Add beets and peas and sauté another minute until peas are heated through and bright green. Remove from heat and toss with remaining tablespoon olive oil. Season to taste with salt and pepper and serve.

SERVES 6

Sweet and Sour Stir-Fry

THE SECRET TO MAKING NOODLES that stand up to stir-frying is to cook your noodles and then chill them before using. This is one of the first stir-fry combinations I ever made, and it has endured the test of time. It's colorful, simple and full of flavor.

½ pound udon, soba or rice noodles

1–2 heads broccoli

3 carrots, diced

1 tablespoon grapeseed oil

3 garlic cloves, minced

1 tablespoon grated fresh ginger

1 cup snow peas, ends trimmed and strings removed

1 cup pineapple chunks

2 tablespoons brown rice vinegar

2 tablespoons mirin

2 tablespoons Bragg Liquid Aminos

2 tablespoons toasted sesame oil

4 scallions, chopped

¼ cup toasted sesame seeds

Cook noodles according to directions on package. Drain in colander and rinse thoroughly under cold water. Place colander on a plate and refrigerate.

PREPARING VEGETABLES

Bring 2–3 cups water to boil. Cut broccoli florets into bite-size pieces. Peel and discard tough outer stems and cut remaining stems into chunks. Place prepared carrots and broccoli in heatproof bowl, cover with boiling water and let sit 2 minutes. Drain, rinse with cold water and set aside.

STIR-FRYING

Heat wok or skillet over medium-high heat. Add grapeseed oil, garlic and ginger and cook 1 minute. If anything starts to stick, add water 1 tablespoon at a time. Add broccoli, carrots and snow peas, stir and cook 2–3 minutes. Add pineapple, 1 tablespoon vinegar, 1 tablespoon mirin and 1 tablespoon liquid aminos and cook 1 minute longer. Remove vegetables from wok and set aside.

Pour remaining tablespoon of vinegar, mirin and liquid aminos into empty wok. Fold in chilled noodles until evenly coated and heated through. Drizzle with 1 tablespoon sesame oil. Transfer noodles to serving dish. Toss vegetables briefly in hot wok to reheat, drizzle with remaining tablespoon toasted sesame oil and spoon vegetables over noodles. Top with chopped scallions and sesame seeds and serve.

SERVES 6

Arame and Sunflower Seeds

I TEND TO EAT MORE ARAME than other sea vegetables because it is so easy to prepare and goes so nicely with everything from carrots and salad greens to brown rice and aduki beans. Sunflower seeds are a rich source of protein, vitamins D, B-complex and E and make a nutritionally packed crunchy addition to this recipe. If you don't plan to finish eating this dish in one sitting, add seeds only to individual servings so that the sunflower seeds don't get soggy as leftovers.

1	cup dried arame
2	teaspoons grapeseed oil
¼	cup shredded carrot
1	tablespoon mirin
½	cup roasted salted or tamari-roasted sunflower seeds
1	tablespoon chopped fresh parsley
½	teaspoon ume plum vinegar

Soak arame in 4 cups of water for 20 minutes and drain.

In large skillet over medium heat, sauté arame in oil for 3 minutes. Add carrot and mirin and sauté 2 minutes more. Remove from heat, fold in sunflower seeds and parsley, and drizzle with ume plum vinegar. Toss to evenly distribute ingredients and serve warm.

SERVES 2

Seaweed and Cabbage Sauté

I CRAVE THIS POWERHOUSE COMBINATION in the spring for its incredible cleansing and healing properties. Sea vegetables are loaded with easily absorbable calcium. Cabbage is a tonic for the stomach and digestive system, a blood alkalinizer, and a rich source of antioxidants, vitamins and minerals. Now that's strong medicine! This recipe doubles easily and keeps 4–5 days.

1	cup dried arame
1	teaspoon grapeseed oil
1	red onion, cut into wedges
3	carrots, cut into matchsticks
½	small cabbage (green or Napa), thinly sliced
2	tablespoons tamari
2–3	dashes ume plum vinegar
1	tablespoon toasted sesame oil

Soak arame in 4 cups of water for 20 minutes, drain well and set aside.

In large skillet over medium heat, sauté onion in grapeseed oil until translucent (3 minutes). Add carrots and sauté another 2–3 minutes. Add cabbage and tamari and sauté until all vegetables have softened. Add arame and cook to heat through. Remove from heat, add vinegar and toasted sesame oil and serve warm or chilled.

SERVES 6

Gingered Arame with Snow Peas

FEW FOODS PROVIDE THE NUTRITIONAL PUNCH and cleansing ability of sea vegetables. Chock-full of calcium and minerals, alkalinizing to the blood, and highly regarded for its ability to break down tumors and support thyroid function, arame is a powerful ally to health and well-being.

1   cup dried arame
2   tablespoons tamari
½   red onion, cut into wedges
1½ cups snow peas,
    cut into matchsticks
8   radishes,
    cut into matchsticks

DRESSING

1   tablespoon
    grated fresh ginger
2   teaspoons
    apple cider vinegar
2   teaspoons maple syrup
1   teaspoon tamari
2   tablespoons
    toasted sesame oil

Soak arame in 4 cups of water for 20 minutes. Drain and place in pot with enough fresh water to cover plus 2 tablespoons tamari. Bring to boil, reduce heat and simmer uncovered 15 minutes. Drain well and set aside.

In medium bowl, combine onion, snow peas and radishes. Bring 4 cups water to boil, pour over vegetables, let sit 1 minute then drain. Rinse vegetables under cold running water and drain completely. Combine with arame and set aside.

PREPARING DRESSING

In small sauté pan, combine ginger, vinegar, syrup and tamari. Cook over medium heat 1–2 minutes until blended and heated through. Remove from heat and stir in sesame oil. Pour over arame mixture, toss to combine and serve.

SERVES 6

Quinoa with Arame, Toasted Nuts and Seeds

THIS RECIPE COMES TOGETHER QUICKLY whether you're making it from scratch or doctoring up leftover quinoa (which is how this recipe originally came to be). Marinated onions are available in many natural food and gourmet stores and are even starting to make regular appearances in the cheese department of many conventional grocery stores. If you can't find them, substitute red onions. For variety, add fresh herbs, your favorite roasted vegetables or soaked and drained arame.

1	cup quinoa
1½	cups water or vegetable stock
½	cup dried arame
¼	cup currants
½	cup marinated or roasted cipollini onions, quartered (or chopped red onion)
¼	cup diced fennel
¼	cup toasted pumpkin seeds
¼	cup toasted sunflower seeds
¼	cup toasted sliced almonds
¼	cup chopped fresh cilantro or flat parsley
¼	cup extra virgin olive oil
2	teaspoons ume plum vinegar

Rinse and drain quinoa and place in pot with water or stock. Bring to boil, cover, reduce heat to low and simmer until all water is absorbed (about 15 minutes). Remove from heat and set aside to cool for a few minutes. Fluff with wooden spoon.

Place arame in bowl with enough water to cover. Soak 20 minutes, rinse, drain and fold into quinoa. Gently fold in currants, onions, fennel, pumpkin and sunflower seeds, almonds and cilantro or parsley. Drizzle with olive oil and vinegar and stir to combine. Serve warm or at room temperature.

SERVES 6

Multibean Salad with Fresh Herbs

THIS RECIPE IS A PERFECT WAY TO EXPERIMENT with a variety of fresh herbs – whether from your garden, the farm or the grocery store. Look for one of the many different varieties of basil, or perhaps fennel, dill, chervil, lemon balm or lovage. This one salad can provide a whole education on herbs and herb combinations. It did for me!

1   cup green beans, trimmed
1   cup cooked black beans
1   cup cooked chickpeas
1   cup cooked kidney beans

VINAIGRETTE

½   small red onion,
    finely chopped
¼   cup extra virgin olive oil
1   tablespoon
    red wine vinegar
1   teaspoon lemon juice
1   teaspoon
    chopped fresh rosemary
1   tablespoon
    chopped fresh basil
1   teaspoon
    chopped fresh chives
1   tablespoon
    chopped fresh parsley
1   tablespoon
    prepared mustard
Freshly ground black pepper

Cut green beans in half and place in bowl. Add black beans, chickpeas and kidney beans. Bring 4 cups water to boil, pour over beans and let sit 1 minute. Drain, rinse under cold running water and drain completely.

In separate bowl, whisk together all vinaigrette ingredients. Pour over beans, toss to coat and serve.

SERVES 6

French Lentil Salad with Lemon, Radish and Cilantro

CREAMY LENTIL SOUP CAN SUSTAIN ME all winter long, but come spring I prefer my lentils in salads like this one. Featuring delicate spring radishes and herbs, this high-protein salad is refreshing and satisfying – whether served on its own, as a side dish, or on a bed of fresh arugula, my personal favorite.

1½ cups French lentils

3   cups water

1   thumb-size piece kombu

1   cup thinly sliced French Breakfast radishes (or other variety)

1   cup chopped orange bell pepper

½   cup finely chopped red onion

½   cup coarsely chopped cilantro

⅓   cup chopped mint

3   tablespoons extra virgin olive oil

Zest and juice of 1 lemon

Sea salt and freshly ground black pepper

Place lentils in pot or rice cooker with water and kombu. Bring to boil, reduce heat, cover and simmer until lentils are soft and liquid is absorbed. Remove from heat and cool slightly before fluffing.

Place radishes, bell pepper and onion in large mixing bowl. Fluff lentils and add to radish mixture. Fold in cilantro and mint. Add olive oil, lemon zest and juice and fold to combine. Season to taste with salt and pepper and serve.

SERVES 6

Marinated Aduki Beans

ADUKI BEANS ARE ONE OF THE EASIEST LEGUMES to digest, but their tangy flavor makes them a challenge to pair with other foods. Some of my favorite matches for these beans include millet, sweet brown rice, winter squash, root vegetables and collard greens. I'm always looking for new ways to get aduki beans into my diet so I can take full advantage of their ability to detoxify the body and support the kidneys. Serve this recipe with Ginger Sesame Greens *(page 180)* and pan-roasted millet *(page 14)*, or enjoy it chilled for lunch or a snack.

2	cups cooked aduki beans
2	carrots, cut into matchsticks
½	red onion, thinly sliced
2	tablespoons toasted sesame seeds

MARINADE

2	teaspoons toasted sesame oil
1	tablespoon grated fresh ginger
1	teaspoon tamari
1	teaspoon apple cider vinegar
1	teaspoon maple syrup

Rinse cooked beans in colander and drain well. Place carrots and onion in bowl. Bring 2 cups water to boil, pour over carrots and onion, let sit 1 minute, then drain. Add carrots and onions to beans. Toss to combine.

In separate bowl, whisk together all marinade ingredients. Pour over bean mixture and stir to coat evenly. Let sit 10–15 minutes to allow flavors to combine. Stir again, sprinkle with sesame seeds and serve.

SERVES 4

Tempeh Salad

I LOVED TUNA AS A CHILD AND I STILL DO, but as an adult I worry about the high levels of mercury and other toxins found in large fish like tuna and swordfish. I enjoy this tuna-inspired salad every bit as much as tuna from the can, if not more. Your body will appreciate the significant health benefits from the addition of kelp – known for its rich supply of minerals and its ability to dissolve masses in the body, balance hormones and support thyroid function.

1	8-ounce package tempeh
1	carrot, shredded
½	red onion, minced
2	tablespoons sweet pickle relish
½	fennel bulb, chopped
1	tablespoon capers
1	tablespoon chopped fresh parsley
2	tablespoons grapeseed oil mayonnaise
1	tablespoon powdered kelp
Sea salt and freshly ground black pepper	

Cut tempeh into 3–4 large pieces and steam 10 minutes. Remove from heat and cool slightly. Crumble or chop tempeh into small pieces. Add remaining ingredients and stir to combine. Adjust seasoning to taste with salt and pepper. Serve at room temperature or chilled.

SERVES 4

VARIATIONS
Serve on a bed of romaine lettuce, in a wrap or even in a grilled soy or rice cheese sandwich.

Crispy Chickpea Fritters

THESE RICH AND TASTY FRITTERS ARE SURPRISINGLY VERSATILE. Each combination highlights them in a completely different way. Enjoy them alongside Sautéed Garlic Greens *(page 179),* Chopped Salad with Shallot Poppy Seed Dressing *(page 52)* or Caesar Salad *(page 53).* Or serve them as an appetizer with a bowl of tomato sauce for dipping. Whichever pairing you choose, you won't be disappointed.

---

2 cups chickpea flour

3 cups water

1 tablespoon coarse sea salt

¼ red onion, minced

1 carrot, grated

2 tablespoons minced fresh rosemary

2 tablespoons extra virgin olive oil

Grapeseed or extra virgin olive oil for frying

In large pot over no heat, whisk together chickpea flour, water, salt, onion, carrot, rosemary and olive oil. Turn heat to medium and continue to whisk until mixture becomes quite thick (about 15 minutes). Remove from heat and either whisk by hand or process with a handheld blender to smooth out any lumps.

Oil 9 x 12-inch glass casserole and spread mixture evenly across the bottom. Cool slightly, cover and refrigerate until firm (about 2 hours).

Preheat oven to 250°F.

Cut chilled chickpea mixture into thin strips and gently remove strips from casserole. Heat large sauté pan (cast-iron gives a nice crispy outer crust), cover the bottom with grapeseed oil and fry strips 2–3 minutes per side. Transfer fritters to a paper towel-lined plate or keep warm in the oven while you fry the remaining strips. Serve immediately.

SERVES 6–8

Mochi Dumplings

THIS RECIPE GREW OUT OF my children's addiction to dumplings from one of our favorite Chinese restaurants. It simply wasn't realistic to order in dumplings every night, so I came up with this quick and easy version. This traditional dumpling filling is a perfect complement to baked mochi. Plus, we all love watching the mochi puff in the oven and stuffing our own squares.

1	tablespoon extra virgin olive oil
½	onion, diced
1	tablespoon grated fresh ginger
1	carrot, grated
1	cup cabbage, thinly sliced
¼	cup thinly sliced shiitake mushroom caps
1	tablespoon tamari or shoyu
1	tablespoon mirin
1	12.5-ounce block mochi, cut into 2-inch squares

DIPPING SAUCE

2	tablespoons tamari
1	tablespoon toasted sesame oil
1	teaspoon brown rice vinegar
	Sesame seeds and scallions for garnish

Preheat oven to 400°F.

In large skillet over medium heat, sauté onion and ginger in olive oil for 2–3 minutes. Add carrot, cabbage, mushrooms, tamari and mirin and sauté 5–7 minutes or until vegetables are soft. Remove from heat and set aside.

In small bowl, combine all dipping sauce ingredients and set aside.

Place mochi squares 2 inches apart on parchment-lined cookie sheet. Bake 10–12 minutes (until squares puff and lightly brown). Remove from oven, cool slightly, slice open mochi puffs and fill with stuffing. Serve warm with dipping sauce.

MAKES 10–12 dumplings

Brown Rice with Ginger and Umeboshi Plums

WHEN I FIRST DISCOVERED high-protein, non-gluten grains like quinoa and millet, I soon completely forgot about brown rice. Yet there is something so basic and simple about brown rice that recently I have found myself craving it, not only for its health benefits, satisfying taste and texture, but also for a return to pure and simple goodness.

---

1   cup short grain brown rice

2   cups water

1   thumb-size piece kombu

6   umeboshi plums

3   tablespoons brown rice vinegar

2   tablespoons brown rice syrup or coconut nectar

¼   cup pickled ginger, minced

1   cup snow peas, trimmed, blanched and julienned

Soak rice for at least 1 hour in bowl with enough water to cover. Drain, rinse and place in pot with 2 cups water and kombu. Bring to boil, then reduce heat, cover and simmer for 25 minutes or until water is absorbed. Remove from heat, discard kombu and set rice aside.

To prepare umeboshi plums, remove pits and finely dice fruit. In small skillet over low heat, whisk together brown rice vinegar and syrup. Fold into rice along with plums, pickled ginger and snow peas and serve.

SERVES 6

Inca Red Quinoa with Currants

THIS DEEP RED VARIETY OF QUINOA has every bit as much protein as traditional ivory quinoa, plus a nuttier taste, more texture and less bitterness. I eat quinoa year-round and prefer it to other grains because it is so light. You may also like the red variety mixed with black quinoa, the traditional ivory, or both. Pair with Spring's bitter greens or stuff into Fall's sweet winter squashes.

---

1   cup Inca red quinoa
2   cups water
Pinch of sea salt
2   tablespoons extra virgin olive oil
1   small yellow onion, chopped
½   cup currants
2   tablespoons dried summer savory
Ume plum vinegar

Rinse quinoa well and drain. Place quinoa in pot or rice cooker with water and salt and bring to boil. Cover, reduce to simmer and cook until water is absorbed (about 15 minutes). Remove from heat, cool slightly, then fluff with fork.

In large skillet, heat 1 tablespoon olive oil over medium heat, add onion and sauté until soft (about 3 minutes). Add currants and savory and sauté another 3 minutes or until currants soften. Add cooked quinoa and fold to combine all ingredients. Add remaining tablespoon of olive oil and 3–4 dashes of vinegar, toss and serve.

SERVES 6

Millet Black Bean Patties with Corn

THIS IS ANOTHER FAMILY FAVORITE AND WEEKLY STAPLE. I keep organic frozen corn in my freezer year-round just for recipes like this one. Try these patties with salsa, ketchup or the accompaniment of your choice. We like them with sweet potato fries and a salad. Leftovers are great stuffed into a pita with lettuce and tomato.

1   cup millet
2½   cups water
Grapeseed oil for frying
1   medium onion, minced
¼   teaspoon sea salt
¼   teaspoon chile powder
1   tablespoon paprika
2   teaspoons ground cumin
1½   cups cooked black beans
1   cup corn, fresh or frozen
Freshly ground black pepper
     or hot pepper sauce
½   cup cornmeal
     or corn flour

PREPARING MILLET

Rinse millet, place in sauté pan over medium heat and toast for 3–4 minutes, stirring continuously. When millet begins to take on a nutty aroma, add water, cover, reduce heat to low and cook until all water is absorbed (about 25 minutes). Remove from heat and set aside to cool slightly.

PREPARING PATTIES

In large skillet or Dutch oven over medium heat, sauté onion in 2 tablespoons grapeseed oil until soft (about 3 minutes). Add salt, chile powder, paprika and cumin and stir to combine. Add black beans and corn and remove from heat. Add cooked millet and mash together. Season to taste with pepper, then stir in cornmeal a little at a time until batter is stiff.

Preheat large skillet over medium heat (I use cast-iron to yield a nice crispy crust) and add 2 tablespoons of oil. Scoop and form mixture into 2-inch balls. Working in batches and adding more oil as needed, place balls in skillet and press down to form patties. Repeat until skillet is full. Fry 3–4 minutes per side. Place cooked patties on a baking sheet, cover with foil and keep warm in the oven until ready to serve.

Note: To reheat leftovers, wrap in foil and bake at 350°F for 15 minutes.

MAKES 10 hearty patties

Barley with Lemon and Herbs

BARLEY IS PARTICULARLY STRENGTHENING and easy to digest. It also helps to lower cholesterol and tone the liver and stomach. Whole barley is minimally processed and nutritionally far superior to pearl barley. Barley is particularly acidic, so be sure to allow time for presoaking. For a gluten-free version of this recipe, substitute Job's tears for the barley.

---

1   cup whole barley
    or Job's tears

2¼ cups vegetable stock

1   thumb-size piece kombu

DRESSING

¼   cup extra virgin olive oil

¼   cup lemon juice

1   garlic clove, minced

1   tablespoon
    chopped fresh parsley

½   teaspoon minced
    fresh rosemary

1   tablespoon fresh
    lemon thyme leaves

2   teaspoons
    dried summer savory

Sea salt and freshly ground
    black pepper

Soak grain at least 1 hour and drain. Place grain in pot or rice cooker with stock and kombu and bring to boil. Reduce heat and simmer covered until liquid is absorbed.

While grain is cooking, in medium bowl whisk together dressing ingredients and set aside for flavors to blend.

Remove cooked grain from heat and discard kombu. Fluff with fork, toss with dressing and serve.

SERVES 6

Wild Rice Pilaf

WILD RICE IS ACTUALLY A GRASS, not a grain, and is extremely high in protein. I like this recipe in the fall and winter, too, but in spring it provides a nice transition away from winter's heavier, more warming grain dishes. This sweet and savory recipe complements a variety of flavors and dishes and is perfect for holiday entertaining.

1   cup wild rice

½   cup brown basmati rice

3   cups vegetable stock
     or water

Pinch of sea salt

2   tablespoons
     extra virgin olive oil

6   shallots, diced

2   tablespoons mirin

3   stalks celery, diced

½   pound cremini
     mushrooms, diced

1   tablespoon
     minced fresh rosemary

½   cup dried cranberries

½   cup toasted slivered
     almonds

¼   cup chopped fresh parsley

Sea salt and freshly ground
     black pepper

Place wild and basmati rice together in pot or rice cooker with stock or water and pinch of salt. Bring to boil, cover, reduce heat and simmer until liquid is absorbed (about 40 minutes). Remove from heat and set aside.

In large skillet over medium heat, sauté shallots in olive oil and mirin until translucent. Add celery, mushrooms and rosemary and sauté 2–3 minutes. Mix in cranberries. Fluff rice with fork and fold into vegetable mixture. Cook another 2 minutes to heat through. Remove from heat, fold in almonds and parsley, season to taste with salt and pepper and serve.

SERVES 6

Blueberry Kanten with Cashew Cream

A KANTEN IS A VEGETARIAN JELLED DESSERT made with fruit and agar. It's hard to believe that these delicate little flakes can have such tremendous healing and alkalinizing power, but agar is loaded with minerals and is particularly detoxifying. Agar is also cooling and calming to the gastrointestinal tract. Hardly sounds like dessert anymore!

KANTEN

3 cups apple or pear juice
3 tablespoons agar flakes
Pinch of sea salt
1 tablespoon lemon juice or apple cider vinegar
2 cups frozen blueberries

CASHEW CREAM

2 cups apple juice
2 cups lightly toasted cashews
3 tablespoons maple syrup

TOPPING

Cookie crumbs of choice

PREPARING KANTEN

In large pot over medium-high heat, bring juice to boil. Reduce heat to low and stir in agar flakes, salt and lemon juice or cider vinegar. Continue stirring until flakes have dissolved. Remove from heat, add blueberries and transfer to 9 x 13-inch glass casserole. Refrigerate until firm (about 45 minutes). Remove from refrigerator and purée with handheld blender until texture is similar to mousse.

PREPARING CASHEW CREAM

In small pot over medium-high heat, bring apple juice to boil. Remove from heat and cool slightly. Place cashews and syrup in food processor and process 10–15 seconds. With the processor running, slowly add juice a little at a time until you have the desired texture (you may not need all the juice).

ASSEMBLING

Fill bottom of 6–8 parfait glasses with a layer of kanten, add a layer of cashew cream, top with cookie crumbs and serve.

SERVES 6–8

Mixed Berry Couscous Cake

THIS CAKE IS NOT THE LIGHT AND FLUFFY KIND, but you're going to love it anyway. When chilled, couscous remains quite moist, dense and cool, making for a cake that's refreshing and guilt-free. Enjoy it as a dessert, snack or even for breakfast.

---

7   cups apple juice
1   tablespoon vanilla extract
1   cup maple syrup
3   cups couscous
3   tablespoons agar powder or flakes
3–4 cups berries of choice
Fresh mint leaves for garnish

In medium pot over no heat, whisk together 6 cups apple juice, vanilla and ½ cup maple syrup. Bring to boil, add couscous and stir until thick. Remove from heat, rinse 9-inch springform pan with cool water (to prevent sticking) and pour in cooked couscous. Smooth top and set aside.

In small pot over medium heat, dissolve agar in remaining cup of apple juice. Add remaining ½ cup maple syrup and stir until agar dissolves. Fold in berries and remove mixture from heat. Place couscous cake on large plate or cookie sheet (to catch fruit drippings), and immediately pour berry mixture over couscous. Refrigerate at least 1 hour to chill and to allow fruit topping to set. Before serving, remove cake from pan by cutting around the edge of the cake to break the seal with the pan. Garnish with fresh mint leaves and serve.

GLUTEN-FREE OPTION
Substitute 2 cups quinoa for couscous and cook in 4 cups apple juice, vanilla and ½ cup maple syrup for 20 minutes covered. Remove cover and simmer 20 minutes more or until liquid is absorbed. Remove from heat, transfer to rinsed springform pan and continue with recipe as described above.

MAKES ONE 9-inch cake

Banana Coconut Chocolate Chip Cookies

FINALLY A RECIPE FOR THOSE OVERRIPE BANANAS other than banana bread! Gluten is the protein in wheat that is quite sticky and helps hold baked goods together. In this wheat-free recipe, bananas bind the ingredients and also add significant sweetness so that only a small amount of maple syrup is needed.

2	bananas, mashed
¼	cup virgin coconut oil, melted
¼	cup maple syrup
½	teaspoon vanilla extract
1	cup rolled oats
⅔	cup brown rice flour
¼	teaspoon baking soda
½	cup shredded unsweetened dried coconut

Pinch of sea salt

¼	cup semi-sweet or dark chocolate chips

Preheat oven to 350°F.

In medium bowl, combine bananas, oil, syrup and vanilla. In separate medium bowl, combine oats, flour, baking soda, coconut and salt. Add the banana mixture to the dry ingredients and blend until just combined (do not overstir). Fold in chocolate chips.

Line cookie sheet with parchment paper and drop batter by the heaping teaspoon onto sheet. There is no need to roll, flatten or shape the mounds. Place in oven and bake 14 minutes or until lightly browned. Remove from oven and place directly on wire rack to cool.

MAKES 1½ dozen cookies

Chocolate Coconut Granola Bites

THESE TREATS ARE TO DIE FOR! They're made from all healthy ingredients, but they're far from innocent. Even my children refer to them as Mom's "dirty food!"

2½ cups Maple Nut Granola *(page 324)*, or other type of granola

½ cup shredded unsweetened dried coconut

½ cup dried cranberries

1½ cups semi-sweet or dark chocolate chips

1 tablespoon virgin coconut oil

Line baking sheet with parchment paper.

Place granola in mixing bowl with shredded coconut and cranberries and set aside. In small pot over low heat, melt chocolate chips until smooth. Add coconut oil and stir to combine. Drizzle over granola mixture and fold to coat. Spread evenly over prepared baking sheet and refrigerate for one hour. Remove from refrigerator, break into bite-size pieces and serve. Store in airtight container in refrigerator.

MAKES about 36 bites

VARIATIONS
Experiment with your favorite dried fruits, nuts and seeds to discover your own unique combination.

Lemon Almond Cookie Tart with Strawberry Topping

I'D CHOOSE COOKIES OVER CAKE ANY DAY, and this cake-size cookie is like a dream come true. It's also the perfect complement to the strawberries we pick at the farm down the street.

DRY INGREDIENTS

2   cups almond flour
¾   cup millet flour
¼   teaspoon sea salt
¼   teaspoon ground nutmeg

WET INGREDIENTS

½   cup maple syrup
2   tablespoons
      extra virgin olive oil,
      plus more to grease tin
2   tablespoons applesauce
2   tablespoons lemon juice
½   teaspoon lemon extract
      or flavor

TOPPING

2   cups apple juice
1   cup maple syrup
Zest and juice of 1 lemon
2   cups strawberries,
      stemmed and chopped
2   teaspoons arrowroot
2   tablespoons water

Preheat oven to 350°F.

Grease 10½-inch tart tin with oil. In medium mixing bowl, whisk together all dry ingredients. In separate bowl, whisk together all wet ingredients. Pour wet ingredients into the dry and fold until combined. Pour into prepared tart tin, spread to fill tin and smooth top with spatula. Bake 23 minutes or until lightly browned around edges. Remove from heat and set aside to cool and set.

Combine apple juice, maple syrup, zest and lemon juice in pot and bring to boil. Reduce heat and simmer until liquid reduces by half. Stir in strawberries and simmer 5 minutes, stirring continuously to break up berries. In separate bowl, whisk together arrowroot and water until dissolved. Add to syrup, whisk continuously until topping thickens (about 2 minutes), and remove from heat.

Spoon sauce over individual servings of cookie and serve.

SERVES 10

SERVING SUGGESTIONS
Substitute raspberries, blueberries or chopped peaches for the strawberries to take this dessert from spring through summer.

Love is to the heart what the summer
is to the farmer's year – it brings to harvest
all the loveliest flowers of the soul.

AUTHOR UNKNOWN

Summer

The selection and taste of freshly picked organic produce is never more exciting than in summer and it appeals to my every sense. Everywhere I look are infinite varieties of heirloom tomatoes, beets in every color, potatoes as small as pebbles and seemingly bottomless baskets filled with green beans. The berries are sweeter than sugar, and herbs and flowers fill the air with their aromatic bouquet. Food artisans of all kinds display their specialty breads, oils, cheeses, vinegars and relishes, giving me a glimpse into their kitchens and a taste of new flavors and ideas to spice up my own menu. Eating seasonally helps me maintain balance with the environment, and purchasing local organic produce allows me an even greater sense of harmony and supports a sustainable approach to farming and nutrition. A conversation with the farmer directs me to unusual varieties, freshly harvested picks and the "cream of the crop." There is no better way to get to know your food – from seed to table.

SUMMER

DIPS, DRESSINGS AND MORE

Herbal Iced Tea 96
Fruity Balsamic Vinaigrette 97
Jícama Strawberry Guacamole 98
Traditional Guacamole 100
Mango Salsa 101
Black Bean, Corn and Tomato Salsa 102
Herbed Aioli 103
Tofu Sour Cream 104

SOUPS

Gazpacho 105
Honeydew Cucumber Soup 107
Carrot Fruit Soup 108

VEGETABLES

Heirloom Tomato Salad 109
Tangy Tomato and Tomatillo Salad 110
Traditional Coleslaw 111
Asian Coleslaw 112
Baby Greens with Grilled Balsamic Pears 114
Fresh Herb Salad with Lemon and Olive Oil 115
Grilled Cipollini Onions 116
Green Beans and Sweet Corn
    with Summer Vinaigrette 117
Cucumber Noodles with Bok Choy
    and Peanut Sauce 119
Golden Beet and Snap Pea Salad 120
Grilled Vegetables with Pasta 121
Fingerling Potato Salad with Fresh Herbs 122
Fingerling Potatoes and Green Beans
    with Lemon Dill Dressing 124
Zucchini with Garlic and Oregano 125
Summer Rolls with Lemon Basil Pesto 127
Pad Thai Summer Rolls
    with Tamarind Dipping Sauce 128
Arame Sauté 129

LEGUMES

Cucumber, Mango and Chickpea Salad 130
Chickpea and Cherry Tomato Salad
    with Cilantro Dressing 131
Black Bean Salad 132
Black Bean Patties with Pineapple Guacamole 133
White Bean Salad
    with Roasted Tomatoes and Arugula 134

TOFU AND TEMPEH

Tofu Salad 135
Tempeh Quesadillas 136
Pineapple Tempeh Kebabs 137
Curry Tempeh Salad with Raisins and Cashews 139

GRAINS

Sprouted Quinoa Tabbouleh 140
Quinoa and Black Bean Salad
    with Apricot Lime Vinaigrette 141
Wheatberry Salad 142
Sprouted Quinoa with Strawberries and Lime 143
Pesto Pasta Salad 144
Grilled Polenta with Mushroom Ragoût 145

DESSERTS

Nuts Over Strawberry Rhubarb Pie 146
Fresh Fruit Tart with Almond Crust 147
Strawberry Custard
    with Fresh Berries and Lemon Peel 148
Peach, Fresh Fig and Bourbon Crisp
    with Pecan Topping 149
Strawberry Rhubarb Compote
    with Cashew Cream 150
Lemon Berry Cream Pie 152
Chocolate Pudding with Fresh Berries 153
Mixed Berry Tart 154
Fresh Berries with Tofu Cream 155

Herbal Iced Tea

YEARS AGO, MY NATUROPATH PRESCRIBED a concoction of herbs for me to brew that I quickly coined "dirt tea." Over the years, this much more pleasant brew evolved. Not only does it replenish my adrenals, but it is refreshing and satisfying too. Feel free to experiment with other herbs to make your own unique brew.

---

10 cups water

¼ cup dried nettles

1 tablespoon
dried red clover flowers

2 tablespoons
dried rosemary

3 tablespoons chamomile

2 tablespoons
dried peppermint leaves

1 tablespoon maple syrup

In large pot, bring water to boil. Remove from heat, stir in herbs and maple syrup, and set aside to brew and cool for at least 1 hour. Pour tea through fine mesh strainer into pitcher. Discard herbs, chill tea and enjoy.

MAKES 10 cups

Fruity Balsamic Vinaigrette

THERE ARE SO MANY DIFFERENT JUICES AND NECTARS available in stores these days. You can achieve completely different vinaigrettes by substituting mango, cranberry or even carrot juice for the apricot juice in this recipe.

---

1 garlic clove, peeled

1 small shallot

Juice of 2 Meyer lemons
or 1 large regular lemon

¼ cup apricot juice

¼ cup balsamic vinegar

½ cup extra virgin olive oil

1 tablespoon maple mustard
or honey mustard

2 tablespoons maple syrup

Pinch of sea salt

Combine all ingredients in food processor or with handheld blender. Vinaigrette will keep refrigerated for up to one week.

MAKES 1½ cups

Jícama Strawberry Guacamole

IF YOU'VE NEVER TASTED A WATERMELON RADISH, you've been missing out. Its sweet taste and vibrant pink flesh will have you hooked in no time. If watermelon radishes aren't available, don't deprive yourself of this guacamole. Tomatillos, cipollini onions or even peaches make great substitutes.

---

1   cup diced strawberries

½   cup peeled and diced jícama

1   watermelon radish, peeled and diced

2   avocados, peeled, pitted and diced (save the pits)

1   jalapeño, seeded and minced

Juice of 2 limes

¼   teaspoon sea salt

¼   teaspoon garlic powder

2   tablespoons extra virgin olive oil

In large bowl, combine strawberries, jícama, watermelon radish, avocados and jalapeño. In separate bowl, combine lime juice, salt, garlic powder and olive oil. Pour over strawberry mixture, stir until combined and serve.

If you do not plan to serve guacamole immediately, place pits on top of mixture to keep it from turning brown. Cover and refrigerate. Before serving, remove pits and stir briefly.

MAKES 3 cups

Traditional Guacamole

I'M NOT SURE WHAT MAKES RECIPES "TRADITIONAL." Perhaps it means that they've been passed from generation to generation, or maybe there is simply no dispute about the ingredients. What I do know is that there is a little Mexican restaurant in Chicago where they make the most outstanding guacamole right at your table, and ever since tasting their fresh guacamole I've been making this one.

3   large avocados, peeled, pitted and chopped (save the pits)

2   garlic cloves, minced

¼   cup chopped red onion

2   tomatoes, diced

2   jalapeños, seeded and minced

¼   cup chopped fresh cilantro

3   tablespoons lime juice

Sea salt to taste

Place all ingredients in medium bowl, gently mash to the desired texture and serve.

If you do not plan to serve guacamole immediately, place pits on top of mixture to keep it from turning brown. Cover and refrigerate. Before serving, remove pits and stir briefly.

MAKES 2 cups

Mango Salsa

THIS SALSA ADDS ZEST TO A VARIETY OF DISHES and is a great accompaniment to baby bok choy, asparagus and grilled fish. I also serve it solo with chips for a refreshing change from its more ordinary cousins tomato salsa and guacamole. If you don't care for mango, try preparing this salsa with peaches, nectarines or papaya.

1   mango, pitted, peeled and diced

1   avocado, peeled, pitted and diced (save pit)

1   tomato, diced

¼   cup peeled and diced jícama

1   jalapeño, seeded and minced

1   small red onion, minced

¼   cup chopped fresh cilantro

Juice of 1 lime

1–2 tablespoons extra virgin olive oil

Sea salt

In large bowl, combine mango, avocado, tomato, jícama, jalapeño, onion and cilantro. Fold in lime juice. Add olive oil (1 tablespoon at a time) until desired consistency is reached. Season with sea salt to taste, place pit on top of mixture to keep avocado from turning brown, cover and set aside (or chill) to allow flavors to blend. Remove pit before serving.

MAKES 3 cups

Black Bean, Corn and Tomato Salsa

SERVE THIS SUMMER SALSA with corn chips, tacos, rice and beans or grilled chicken or fish. The delicate texture and sweet taste of fresh native tomatoes are compromised by refrigeration, so I serve this salsa at room temperature.

¾ cup cooked corn, fresh or frozen

2 garlic cloves, minced

¾ cup cooked black beans

1½ cups chopped fresh tomatoes

¼ cup chopped green bell pepper

¼ cup chopped fresh cilantro

2 jalapeños, seeded and minced

2 tablespoons lemon juice

1 tablespoon extra virgin olive oil

Sea salt and freshly ground black pepper

Hot pepper sauce

If using frozen corn, place in strainer and run under hot water to thaw.

In large bowl, combine corn, garlic, beans, tomatoes, bell pepper, cilantro and jalapeños. Add lemon juice and olive oil. Season to taste with salt, pepper and hot pepper sauce. Set aside for 1 hour to allow flavors to blend.

MAKES 3 cups

Herbed Aioli

THIS DIP IS A SPRING AND SUMMER MUST. Serve it with crudités or steamed artichokes, or wrap it up in a sheet of nori with avocado, smoked salmon, carrot and cucumber. Create a whole new dip simply by substituting different seasonal herbs. The possibilities are endless.

---

1   garlic clove, peeled
1½ cups grapeseed oil mayonnaise
¼   cup fresh chives
¼   cup fresh basil

With food processor running, drop in garlic and mince. Turn off processor, scrape down sides, add remaining ingredients and pulse until herbs are chopped. The goal is a white dip with green flecks — not a green dip. Serve immediately or refrigerate for up to 5 days.

MAKES 1½ cups

Tofu Sour Cream

IF YOU HAVE ELIMINATED DAIRY from your diet, there are certain basic recipes, like this one, that you want to make sure you have when you need them. This simple nondairy sour cream whips up in a snap and is a great addition to tacos, burritos, refried beans and so much more. For a more traditional sour cream, eliminate the jalapeño.

---

12 ounces firm or extra-firm silken tofu

3 tablespoons lemon juice

2 tablespoons extra virgin olive oil

1 tablespoon apple cider vinegar

½ teaspoon sea salt

½ jalapeño, stem and seeds removed

Wrap tofu in towel and press to remove excess liquid.

In food processor, whip tofu until smooth. Add remaining ingredients and process until jalapeño is minced and ingredients are well combined. Chill before serving.

MAKES 1 cup

Gazpacho

I ONCE READ THAT THE EASIEST WAY to make gazpacho was to put the previous night's leftover salad in a blender with tomato juice, lemon juice, salt and pepper. I've yet to try it, so if you're feeling daring, please let me know how it comes out! Meanwhile, I'll stick to this tried-and-true recipe that gets rave reviews every time.

4–6 tomatoes

1   small red onion, minced

1   green bell pepper, minced

1   cucumber, diced

1   garlic clove, minced

2   tablespoons
     chopped fresh parsley

2   tablespoons
     chopped fresh basil

2   tablespoons
     chopped fresh cilantro

4   cups tomato juice

2   tablespoons lemon juice

2   tablespoons
     balsamic vinegar

Dash of hot pepper sauce

¼   cup extra virgin olive oil

Sea salt and freshly ground
     black pepper

Fresh parsley and lemon
     for garnish

Bring large pot of water to boil. Drop in tomatoes, let sit 30 seconds, drain and set aside. When cool, peel away skins by applying pressure and pushing them off with your thumbs. Dice and return to empty pot.

Add remaining ingredients and adjust seasoning to taste with hot pepper sauce, salt and pepper. Stir until evenly combined. Cover and refrigerate. Serve cold with a wedge of lemon and a sprig of parsley.

SERVES 6

Honeydew Cucumber Soup

MY GARDEN PRODUCES MORE CUCUMBERS than we can possibly eat. We put them in everything, which is how this recipe came to be. My family had refused to eat even one more cucumber, so I snuck them into this cool, refreshing and totally raw soup. They loved the soup and were never the wiser about the cucumbers.

1   honeydew melon

2   medium cucumbers, peeled and seeded

2   tablespoons champagne vinegar

Zest and juice of 1 lime (about 2 tablespoons juice)

Sea salt

Extra virgin olive oil

Fresh mint leaves

Blueberries

Halve honeydew, scoop out and discard seeds and remove melon from rind. Place melon in food processor and process until smooth. Transfer to medium pot or bowl. Place cucumbers in food processor, process until smooth and add to pot with melon. Add vinegar, zest and lime juice, and salt to taste, and stir to combine. Stir in a drizzle of olive oil and served topped with mint leaves and blueberries.

SERVES 6

SERVING SUGGESTION

Add some kick to this soup by adding one jalapeño. After preparing cucumber, halve jalapeño, remove and discard seeds and drop into running food processor to mince. Stir into soup and continue with instructions above.

Carrot Fruit Soup

SIMPLE, REFRESHING AND BEAUTIFUL! This sweet soup is a perfect way to start any summer barbecue.

1   cantaloupe

2   peaches, peeled and cut into chunks

1   mango, peeled and cut into chunks

1½   cups carrot juice

1   tablespoon fresh lemon juice

¼   teaspoon ground cloves

Pinch of sea salt

Blueberries for garnish

Halve cantaloupe, scoop out seeds, remove outer skin and cut melon into chunks. Place in large pot and add peaches, mango, carrot juice, lemon juice, cloves and sea salt. Bring to simmer and cook 3 minutes to soften fruit. Purée with handheld blender and refrigerate for 1 hour or longer. Garnish with blueberries and serve.

SERVES 6

Heirloom Tomato Salad

THE KEY TO ENJOYING DELICIOUS NATIVE TOMATOES is never to refrigerate them as doing so makes their flesh mealy. There are so many varieties of heirloom tomatoes that I feel bad leaving some out. Reds, yellows, oranges, stripes, ringed plums…it's a veritable symphony of tomatoes!

---

5 cups heirloom tomatoes of choice

2 small cucumbers

1 avocado, peeled and pitted

¼ red onion, finely chopped

¼ cup chopped fresh basil

1 tablespoon red wine vinegar

2 tablespoons extra virgin olive oil

Sea salt and freshly ground black pepper

Chop tomatoes, cucumbers and avocado into bite-size pieces and combine in serving dish. In separate bowl, combine onion, basil, vinegar, oil, and salt and pepper to taste. Pour over tomatoes and serve.

Note: Combine green and purple varieties of basil for an especially beautiful presentation.

SERVES 6

Tangy Tomato and Tomatillo Salad

TOMATILLOS AND LIME JUICE GIVE this tomato salad a surprising and refreshing twist, and minced jalapeño gives it some extra zip. For a spicy yet refreshing summer meal, serve this with burritos, corn on the cob, fresh guacamole and chips.

---

4 cups small heirloom tomatoes (yellow peach variety are my favorites)

4 tomatillos, husked and quartered

½ watermelon radish, peeled and julienned

¼ cup chopped fresh cilantro

2 tablespoons lime juice

2 tablespoons extra virgin olive oil

1 jalapeño, seeded and minced

Coarse sea salt

Cut tomatoes into half-moons and place in serving dish with prepared tomatillos, radish and cilantro. In separate bowl, whisk together lime juice, olive oil and jalapeño. Pour over salad, sprinkle with coarse sea salt and serve.

SERVES 6

Traditional Coleslaw

OKAY, SO MAYBE THIS COLESLAW isn't 100 percent traditional, but it's a cinch to make and one of my favorite ways to enjoy greens in the summer. Everyone who tries it ends up asking for the recipe. Ume plum vinegar wilts the vegetables perfectly and makes them easier to digest as well. Feel free to add your favorite vegetables for color and variety.

1   large green cabbage

Ume plum vinegar

1   fennel bulb, thinly sliced

3   carrots, julienned

½   red onion, finely chopped

1   watermelon radish, julienned (or 6 small radishes cut into matchsticks)

¼   cup grapeseed oil mayonnaise

Cut cabbage in half, core and slice into thin strips. Place in large bowl and sprinkle generously with ume plum vinegar to coat. Cover and let sit for at least 2 hours. Stir cabbage every 30 minutes to redistribute vinegar. Cabbage will break down considerably.

When done, transfer cabbage to a large colander, rinse and drain well to remove excess vinegar. Dry and return to bowl. Add fennel, carrots, onion and radish and toss to combine. Fold in mayonnaise to evenly coat, then serve. Store leftovers for up to 5 days refrigerated in airtight container.

Note: Drain excess water from leftovers before serving each day, as cabbage will continue to break down.

SERVES 6

Asian Coleslaw

CHINESE CABBAGE MAKES THIS SLAW SOMETHING SPECIAL, and I just love the added zip of fresh ginger in this cool and refreshing salad. Because these cabbages are more delicate than regular green cabbage, there's no need to wilt them first. Just slice up your vegetables, add your dressing and chill. This salad is a great complement to grilled salmon.

3	cups thinly sliced bok choy or pac choy
4	cups thinly sliced Napa cabbage
1	carrot, julienned
2	cups julienned snow peas
1	cup julienned red bell pepper
2	tablespoons toasted black sesame seeds
2	tablespoons toasted white sesame seeds

DRESSING

1	tablespoon extra virgin olive oil
1	tablespoon toasted sesame oil
2	teaspoons ume plum vinegar
1	tablespoon tamari
2	teaspoons grated fresh ginger

In large bowl, combine cabbages, carrot, peas and bell pepper. In separate bowl, whisk together all dressing ingredients. Pour over cabbage mixture and toss to coat evenly. Refrigerate 10–20 minutes to help flavors blend. Before serving, toss again and top with toasted sesame seeds.

SERVES 8

Baby Greens with Grilled Balsamic Pears

THIS SALAD REQUIRES SOME ADVANCE PLANNING to marinate and grill the pears, but it's worth the effort, especially once that first bite of balsamic pear melts in your mouth. Add tender baby greens and rich toasted walnuts and you'll be wishing you had made extra.

3   ripe pears, cored and thinly sliced

¼   cup balsamic vinegar

2   tablespoons maple syrup

Pinch of sea salt

Extra virgin olive oil for grilling

6   cups baby salad greens or mesclun mix

1   cup chopped toasted walnuts

1   avocado, peeled, pitted and thinly sliced

VINAIGRETTE

¼   cup walnut oil

2   tablespoons balsamic vinegar

2   shallots, minced

1   tablespoon maple syrup

1   teaspoon Dijon mustard

Sea salt and freshly ground black pepper

PREPARING PEARS

Place pears in shallow dish. In separate bowl, whisk together vinegar, maple syrup and a pinch of sea salt. Pour mixture over pears and marinate 15 minutes.

Heat grill or grill pan to medium, brush cooking surface with olive oil and place pears on grill. Grill each side 3 minutes or until soft. Remove from heat and set aside.

PREPARING VINAIGRETTE

In small bowl, whisk together all vinaigrette ingredients.

ASSEMBLING SALAD

Place greens in large bowl, drizzle with vinaigrette and toss to coat. Compose individual servings of greens on each plate and top with nuts, avocado slices and grilled pears. Serve immediately.

SERVES 6

VARIATION

Grilled pineapple completely changes this recipe, but is equally tasty. Prepare pineapple by cutting away the outer skin, slicing into rounds and grilling 3 minutes per side. Place on plate, top with baby greens and avocado slices (no walnuts), drizzle with vinaigrette and serve.

Fresh Herb Salad with Lemon and Olive Oil

LEMON IS A POWERFUL ALLY when it comes to maintaining balance, increasing alkalinity and cleansing. This simple salad features fresh greens, abundant herbs and lemon, which means it's quick and easy to prepare and big on flavor and texture – supporting the theory that less is often more.

2	heads romaine lettuce
2	cups mixed fresh herbs (such as parsley, cilantro, fennel, dill, basil or mint)
¼	cup chopped scallions

DRESSING

¼	cup extra virgin olive oil
¼	cup lemon juice
1	tablespoon lemon zest
⅛	teaspoon sea salt
	Plenty of freshly ground black pepper

Tear lettuce into pieces and place in large salad bowl with fresh herbs and scallions. In separate bowl, whisk together dressing ingredients. Pour over salad and toss to coat evenly. Serve immediately.

SERVES 4

Grilled Cipollini Onions

THESE ONIONS ARE ONE OF THE MANY GREAT DISCOVERIES passed on to me by my organic farmers. They are juicy, succulent and irresistible just off the grill. Serve them tossed with other grilled vegetables like zucchini and eggplant, with baby field greens in a salad, with steamed beans or potatoes, sliced over grilled chicken or fish, or as a simple yet elegant side dish as presented here.

As many cipollini onions
  as you like

Extra virgin olive oil

Lemon zest and juice

Coarse sea salt

Preheat grill to medium-high.

Place whole unpeeled onions directly on grill and cook until charred on the outside and soft throughout. Remove from heat and set aside until cool enough to handle, then gently squeeze the root end of each onion so that the burnt outer peel slips off and the inside of the onion pops out. Discard the outer skins and place the onions in a bowl. Season to taste with olive oil, lemon juice, lemon zest and coarse sea salt. Serve warm.

Green Beans and Sweet Corn with Summer Vinaigrette

THIS SIDE DISH WHIPS UP IN AN INSTANT and adds beautiful color, sweetness and a bit of crunch to any meal. I lengthen the season for this recipe with fresh-frozen organic sweet corn. To maintain the full flavor and texture of your tomatoes, refrain from refrigerating them.

1½ cups corn, fresh or frozen

2 pounds haricots verts or green beans, trimmed

1 cup orange pear-shaped or cherry tomatoes, halved

VINAIGRETTE

2 tablespoons extra virgin olive oil

2 tablespoons red wine vinegar

1 garlic clove, minced

2 tablespoons chopped fresh basil or lemon thyme

Splash of fresh lemon juice

Sea salt and freshly ground black pepper

If using fresh corn, steam until tender (about 5 minutes). Remove from steamer and set aside until cool enough to handle. Cut off kernels and set aside. If using frozen corn, add to pot with green beans for last minute of steaming.

In large pot, steam or boil green beans for 3 minutes or until bright green and just tender. Drain water, add corn and set aside. In small bowl, whisk together all vinaigrette ingredients and pour over beans and corn. Add tomatoes, toss and serve.

SERVES 6

Cucumber Noodles with Bok Choy and Peanut Sauce

I SIMPLY DON'T HAVE ENOUGH NEIGHBORS to give away all of the cucumbers harvested from my garden. This is yet another recipe that I created out of desperation to use up cucumbers that nobody was eating. The result was so delicious that it quickly became a summer staple.

2 medium cucumbers, peeled

1 medium baby bok choy

PEANUT SAUCE

¼ cup peanut butter

3 tablespoons vegetable stock or water

1 tablespoon brown rice vinegar

1 tablespoon grated fresh ginger

1 tablespoon tamari

1 clove garlic

Zest and juice of 1 lime (about 2 tablespoons juice)

2 teaspoons maple syrup

2-3 dashes hot sesame oil

TOPPING

¼ cup chopped fresh cilantro

3–4 scallions, chopped

¼ cup roasted peanuts

Slice cucumbers in half lengthwise and remove seeds (a melon baller works well for this task). Julienne cucumber into long strips and place in a mixing bowl. Thinly slice bok choy crosswise, add to bowl with cucumber and set aside.

Place all peanut sauce ingredients in a separate mixing bowl. Whisk or process with handheld blender until smooth. Pour sauce over cucumber mixture and toss to evenly coat. Transfer to serving dish and top with cilantro, scallion and peanuts and serve.

SERVES 4

Golden Beet and Snap Pea Salad

I LOVE FRESH BEETS IN THE SUMMER, but dread working with red beets that stain my hands and kitchen. These golden beets leave you stain-free and are even sweeter than their red cousins. Believe me, nobody else likes cooking with beets either, so you'll get big points for preparing this dish for family and friends.

4–5 golden beets
2   cups snap peas
2   cups frisée

DRESSING

¼   cup extra virgin olive oil
3   tablespoons
     chopped fresh dill
1   tablespoon maple syrup
Juice of 1 lemon
Coarse sea salt and freshly
     ground black pepper

Place whole beets in large pot of boiling water and cook until tender throughout when pierced with knife (about 20 minutes). Drain water and set aside until cool enough to handle. Holding beets under cold water, gently push away outer skins. Cut away root ends and any blemishes, slice into wedges and set aside.

To prepare snap peas, pinch stems and pull down to remove ends and strings. Place in mixing bowl and blanch with boiling water for 30 seconds. Drain and rinse with cold water. Return to mixing bowl, combine with beets and set aside.

In small bowl, whisk together all dressing ingredients, pour over beets and peas and toss to combine.

Arrange beets and peas on bed of frisée and serve.

SERVES 6

Grilled Vegetables with Pasta

THIS RECIPE IS A FEAST FROM THE FARM. Select whatever looks best to you, grill it on a skewer or in a grilling basket and toss it with pasta and herbs. You simply can't go wrong.

1	orange bell pepper
1	zucchini
3	small Japanese eggplants
12	cremini mushrooms
8	cipollini onions
12	cherry tomatoes
3	tablespoons extra virgin olive oil

Sea salt

1	pound pasta (fusilli or penne)
1	garlic clove, minced
¼	cup chopped fresh basil

Freshly ground black pepper

Preheat grill to medium-high. If you have a grilling basket, place on grill to heat. If using wooden skewers, pre-soak them in water for 15–20 minutes.

Cut pepper, zucchini and eggplants into 1-inch pieces. Wipe mushrooms clean with damp towel and remove stems. Peel onions and trim away root ends. Place tomatoes and all vegetables in large bowl, drizzle with 1 tablespoon olive oil and sea salt to taste. If using skewers to grill, place tomatoes and vegetables on them now.

Lower heat to medium and grill vegetables 5–7 minutes or until tender and slightly charred on the outside. Remove vegetables from grill, cover to keep warm and set aside.

Cook pasta according to directions on package. Drain cooked pasta, return to pot and add garlic, remaining 2 tablespoons olive oil and basil. Add vegetables, season to taste with salt and pepper, toss and serve.

SERVES 6

Fingerling Potato Salad with Fresh Herbs

THIS RECIPE SATISFIES THOSE IN MY FAMILY who crave traditional potato salad, and the fresh herbs make me feel like I've added my own special touch and a little extra love. The first time I made it was with the most beautiful purple carrots from the farmers market. When I sliced them into rounds, I discovered that their insides were orange. What a gorgeous potato salad that was!

1   pound French fingerling potatoes (or small potato variety of choice)

3   carrots (vary color if possible), peeled and cut into ¼-inch slices

2   large garlic cloves, minced

¼   cup minced red onion

3   tablespoons chopped chives

2   tablespoon minced sage

2   tablespoon thyme leaves (or lemon thyme leaves)

3   tablespoons grapeseed oil mayonnaise

Sea salt and freshly ground black pepper

Extra virgin olive oil

Fill Dutch oven or medium pot half way with water. Wash potatoes, cut into bite-size pieces and place immediately in pot of water (to prevent browning). Place pot on stove over high heat, cover partially and bring to boil. Reduce heat and simmer 15 minutes. Add carrots and simmer 5 minutes longer or until potatoes are tender (time will vary according to size of potatoes). Drain potatoes and carrots in a colander and rinse with cold water to stop vegetables from cooking further. Set aside to cool slightly.

In large bowl, combine garlic, onion, chives, sage and thyme. Add cooled potato mixture and mayonnaise and fold to combine all ingredients. Season to taste with plenty of salt and pepper and drizzle with olive oil as desired. Toss one more time and serve at room temperature or chilled slightly.

SERVES 4

Fingerling Potatoes and Green Beans with Lemon Dill Dressing

THESE POTATOES HIT THE FARM STANDS IN AUGUST in the Northeast and come in shades of red, purple and yellow. I like to comb through the bin and find the smallest ones – some even as small as marbles! Combined with haricots verts or regular green beans, they make a beautiful addition to any summer meal. For a colorful vegetarian feast that's sure to please, serve this dish with corn on the cob and Heirloom Tomato Salad *(page 109)*.

2   pounds fingerling potatoes

2   pounds haricots verts or green beans, trimmed

DRESSING

1   lemon

1   garlic clove, minced

¼   cup extra virgin olive oil

3   tablespoons chopped fresh dill

1   tablespoon chopped fresh parsley

Sea salt and freshly ground black pepper

In large pot, steam potatoes until nearly cooked through. Add green beans and steam 2–3 minutes longer, until bright green and al dente. Remove from heat and drain water.

Remove zest from lemon and set aside. Juice lemon into separate bowl and whisk together with remaining dressing ingredients. Drizzle over the potatoes and beans and fold gently to combine. Top with zest and serve warm or at room temperature.

SERVES 8

Zucchini with Garlic and Oregano

MY CHILDREN NEVER LIKED ZUCCHINI...until I made it like this. Now they simply can't get enough. You can use any variety of garlic, but the fresh hard-neck garlic available in early summer makes this dish especially delicious.

---

1 tablespoon extra virgin olive oil

2 tablespoons minced garlic

4 cups thinly sliced zucchini

2 teaspoons coarsely chopped oregano

Coarse sea salt and freshly ground black pepper

In large cast iron skillet over medium heat, sauté garlic in olive oil for 2 minutes or until soft. Add zucchini and sauté 5 minutes. Add oregano and sauté until zucchini is as soft as desired (time will vary depending on thickness of slices). Season to taste with sea salt and black pepper, remove from heat and serve.

SERVES 4

SERVING SUGGESTIONS
This dish complements most summer barbeque menus and even makes a simple and delicious meal when combined with cannellini beans and served over a bed of millet.

Summer Rolls with Lemon Basil Pesto

MY DAUGHTER CAME HOME FROM SCHOOL one day with a bag full of lemon balm and the expectation that I would turn it into something spectacular – and so this recipe was born. Wrappers made with tapioca flour will soften more quickly and yield a more delicate tasting finished product. If you don't have wrappers, enjoy this refreshing pesto on grilled vegetables.

2	cups sprouts of choice, rinsed and patted dry
2	avocados, peeled, pitted and sliced lengthwise
1	large red beet, peeled and julienned
3	carrots, julienned
8–10	rice or tapioca spring roll wrappers
	Shallow bowl or plate of hot water and towels

LEMON BASIL PESTO

1	cup fresh lemon balm
1	cup fresh basil leaves
½	cup fresh mint leaves
1	cup toasted pine nuts
½	cup extra virgin olive oil
½	teaspoon sea salt

Prepare all vegetables and lay everything out ready for assembly in the following order: wrappers, bowl of water, sprouts, avocados, beets, carrots.

PREPARING PESTO

In food processor, blend all pesto ingredients until fairly smooth. Place in bowl and add to the line-up between the sprouts and avocados.

ASSEMBLING

Place a towel in front of you. Put one wrapper in bowl with hot water until soft (about 45 seconds). Remove and place on towel and pat dry. Place sprouts centered along the edge closest to you. Spread pesto over sprouts. Top with avocado, beet and carrot. Wrap by folding up the edge closest to you, folding in the sides, then rolling toward the far edge. Leave rolls whole or slice in half and place on serving dish. Continue with remaining wrappers and filling and serve chilled or at room temperature.

MAKES 8–10

Pad Thai Summer Rolls with Tamarind Dipping Sauce

A TASTY TWIST ON A TRADITIONAL ASIAN ROLL. I like to play with different sauces and stuffings in my rolls and hope you'll feel inspired to do the same. For variety, try making these rolls with Peanut Sauce *(page 308),* a favorite among the women in my book club.

8   ounces rice noodles

8   rice or tapioca spring roll wrappers

Shallow bowl or plate of hot water and towels

8   Bibb lettuce leaves

4   scallions, thinly sliced

1   cup snow peas, thinly sliced

2   cups mung bean sprouts

1   cup chopped fresh cilantro, leaves and stems

½   cup chopped roasted peanuts

TAMARIND SAUCE

2   tablespoons tamarind concentrate

¼   cup hot water

4   garlic cloves, minced

1   teaspoon red chili paste

2   tablespoons sucanat

2   tablespoons lime juice

2   tablespoons peanut butter

3   tablespoons toasted sesame oil

Cook rice noodles according to directions on package, drain and set aside. Lay out ingredients for assembly into rolls in the following order: wrappers, bowl of water, lettuce, noodles, scallions, snow peas, bean sprouts, cilantro, peanuts.

PREPARING SAUCE

In medium bowl, dissolve tamarind in ¼ cup of hot water and remove any seeds. Add remaining ingredients. Purée with handheld blender until thick and smooth. Add to line-up of ingredients after the noodles.

ASSEMBLING

Lay out towel in front of you. Put one wrapper in bowl of hot water until soft (about 45 seconds). Remove and place on towel and pat dry. Place lettuce leaf centered along the edge closest to you. Add ingredients on top of lettuce as they are arranged – noodles, sauce, scallions, snow peas, bean sprouts, cilantro and peanuts. Wrap by folding up the edge closest to you, then folding in the sides and rolling tightly toward the far edge. Place on serving dish and continue with remaining wrappers and filling. Serve with extra sauce for dipping.

MAKES 8

Arame Sauté

ARAME'S MILD FLAVOR makes it easy to add to a variety of recipes. This dish can be served fresh off the stove, at room temperature or chilled. Try it with a piece of grilled fish, with vegetable nori rolls or with marinated and grilled tofu or tempeh.

1	cup dried arame
1	teaspoon grapeseed oil
2	small cipollini onions, thinly sliced
4	carrots, julienned
1	cup peeled and julienned jícama
1	cup snow peas, trimmed
2	tablespoons mirin
1	tablespoon brown rice syrup or coconut nectar
1	teaspoon tamari
½	teaspoon ume plum vinegar
2	tablespoons water
¼	cup toasted sesame seeds

Place arame in bowl with enough water to cover. Soak 20 minutes. Rinse, drain and set aside.

In large skillet or Dutch oven over medium heat, sauté onions in grapeseed oil until soft (about 5 minutes). Add carrots, jícama, snow peas and mirin and cook 3 minutes longer until vegetables are al dente.

In small bowl, whisk together brown rice syrup, tamari, vinegar and water. Pour over vegetables and bring to simmer. Fold in arame and sauté 4 minutes to combine flavors and heat through. Remove from heat, top with sesame seeds and serve.

SERVES 4

Cucumber, Mango and Chickpea Salad

MY KIDS MADE UP THIS COMBINATION ONE NIGHT when my own creativity was running dry. I insisted that they needed to eat something green, and they opted for the cucumber with mango. I threw in the chickpeas for protein, and together we rummaged through the refrigerator (and garden) to find ingredients for our dressing. The rest is history!

2	medium cucumbers, peeled and diced
1	mango, peeled, pitted and diced
2	cups cooked chickpeas
¼	cup currants
¼	cup dried apricots, minced
½	cup fresh mint, chopped (orange mint or lemon balm are also nice)

DRESSING

2	tablespoons extra virgin olive oil
3	tablespoons lemon juice
1	small shallot, minced
	Sea salt and freshly ground black pepper

In large bowl, combine cucumbers, mango, chickpeas, currants, apricots and mint. In separate bowl, whisk together all dressing ingredients. Pour over salad, toss and serve.

SERVES 6

Chickpea and Cherry Tomato Salad with Cilantro Dressing

SUN GOLD CHERRY TOMATOES are super-sweet and provide a wonderful contrast in flavor and texture to chickpeas. Look for these and other heirloom varieties to make this simple salad extra-special. To maintain the delicious flavor and texture of your tomatoes, be sure *not* to refrigerate them.

2 pounds cherry tomatoes (mix varieties when possible)

3 cups cooked chickpeas

4–5 scallions, chopped

DRESSING

1 garlic clove, peeled

1 large bunch cilantro (about 1 cup)

½ cup extra virgin olive oil

2 tablespoons lemon juice

Sea salt and freshly ground black pepper

Cut cherry tomatoes in half and place in large bowl with chickpeas and scallions.

With food processor running, drop in whole garlic clove and mince. Turn off processor, scrape down sides, add cilantro, olive oil, lemon juice, salt and pepper. Pulse to combine. Drizzle dressing over salad, toss to coat and serve.

SERVES 6

Black Bean Salad

THIS SALAD IS A SUMMER STAPLE IN MY HOME. It adds a splash of color to any meal, travels well for outings, hits the spot on the beach and tastes great alone or rolled into a burrito with avocados and salsa. Even if you don't have all the ingredients, go ahead and toss together what you have. With flavors like these, it's hard to go wrong!

4 cups cooked black beans

4 tomatillos, husked and diced

1 red bell pepper, diced

½ red onion, diced

1½ cups corn, fresh or frozen

2 jalapeños, seeded and minced

⅓ cup chopped fresh cilantro

1 teaspoon ground cumin

Juice of 1 lime

2 tablespoons extra virgin olive oil

Sea salt and freshly ground black pepper

Combine all ingredients in large bowl. Season to taste with salt and pepper. Set aside or refrigerate to allow flavors to blend, then serve cold or at room temperature. Store refrigerated in airtight container for up to 5 days.

SERVES 8

Black Bean Patties with Pineapple Guacamole

THESE DELICIOUS PATTIES can be made in advance and reheated in the oven before serving. For a complete meal, serve with a salad of mixed greens.

GUACAMOLE

1	cup diced fresh pineapple
1	cup peeled and diced jícama
1	roasted red pepper, minced
1	jalapeño, seeded and diced
2	avocados, peeled, pitted and diced (save pits)
½	red onion, minced
½	cup chopped fresh cilantro
2	tablespoons lime juice
1	tablespoon extra virgin olive oil
⅛	teaspoon sea salt

PATTIES

1	tablespoon ground golden flax seeds
3	tablespoons water
2	garlic cloves, peeled
1	jalapeño, halved and seeded
¼	onion, peeled
½	cup chopped fresh cilantro
1½	teaspoons ground cumin
4	cups cooked black beans
⅔	cup cornmeal or gluten-free bread crumbs
	Sea salt and freshly ground black pepper
	Extra virgin olive oil or grapeseed oil for frying

PREPARING GUACAMOLE

Combine all ingredients in large bowl. Place pits on top of guacamole to keep avocados from browning. Cover and refrigerate to allow flavors to develop.

PREPARING PATTIES

Soak ground flax in bowl with 3 tablespoons water for 20 minutes.

With the food processor running, drop in garlic cloves, then jalapeño and then onion. Turn off processor, scrape down sides and process again until minced. Add cilantro and cumin and pulse briefly. Add 2 cups black beans and cornmeal or bread crumbs and process until just combined. Overprocessing will make your mixture too mushy. Transfer mixture to large bowl. Fold in soaked flax and remaining 2 cups of black beans and season to taste with salt and pepper.

Form bean mixture into 8 patties. Heat skillet over medium-high (I use a cast-iron skillet to yield a crisp patty), and add 2 tablespoons oil. Working in batches, fry patties 3–4 minutes on each side adding more oil to the skillet as needed. Transfer to paper towels or place in 200°F oven to keep warm.

Remove guacamole from refrigerator, discard pits and serve with patties.

Note: Patties can be made in advance, refrigerated and reheated. Simply wrap in foil and heat in 300°F oven for 10–15 minutes.

MAKES 8 patties

White Bean Salad with Roasted Tomatoes and Arugula

EVERY TIME I MAKE THIS RECIPE I am reminded of the August morning I spent at the farmers market in Waitsfield, Vermont, with my friend Pam. Together we selected local organic produce until our arms could carry no more. We returned home and got to work. The kitchen hummed as delicious aromas filled the house. It was a meal and a day to remember.

5 garlic cloves, peeled

2 sweet onions, cut into wedges (look for Walla Walla or Vidalia)

1 fennel bulb, halved, cored and chopped

5 carrots, chopped

Extra virgin olive oil

½ teaspoon coarse sea salt

Freshly ground black pepper

8 tomatoes, halved or quartered depending on size

3 cups cooked great northern or navy beans

6 cups arugula leaves

Preheat oven to 400°F.

In glass baking dish, combine garlic, onions, fennel and carrots. Drizzle with just enough olive oil to coat vegetables evenly. Toss with sea salt and plenty of pepper. Roast uncovered 20 minutes or until just tender. Remove from oven, fold in tomatoes and beans and return to oven to roast an additional 10 minutes or until tomatoes are soft.

Remove from oven, cover individual plates or large platter with fresh arugula, top with bean and vegetable mixture and serve.

SERVES 4

Tofu Salad

THIS SALAD IS SURE TO SATISFY even your meat-eating friends. For a special lunch or light dinner, serve it on a bed of salad greens surrounded by slices of cantaloupe, fresh tomatoes and avocado.

---

24 ounces extra firm silken tofu, cut into ½-inch slices

½ cup Bragg Liquid Aminos

3 tablespoons mirin

2 tablespoons brown rice vinegar

1 cup water

2 stalks celery, diced

½ red onion, diced

1 roasted red pepper, diced

1 cup halved grapes

2 tablespoons chopped fresh parsley

1½ teaspoons dried sage

¼ cup grapeseed oil mayonnaise

Freshly ground black pepper

Preheat oven to 425°F.

Place tofu slices side by side in large glass casserole. In small bowl, whisk together aminos, mirin, vinegar and water and pour over tofu. Marinate 20 minutes, then transfer tofu slices to a lightly oiled cookie sheet and roast 15 minutes. Remove from oven, flip tofu and roast another 10 minutes, or until firm throughout and crisp on the outside.

When tofu is cool enough to handle, cut into ½-inch randomly shaped pieces. Place in large bowl and toss with celery, onion, roasted red pepper, grapes, parsley and sage. Fold in mayonnaise, season to taste with pepper and serve room temperature or chilled.

SERVES 4

Tempeh Quesadillas

I DISCOVERED RICE TORTILLAS when I started cutting down on gluten in my diet. I first used them to make a wrap, but they were simply too firm to roll without splitting. When I grilled them for these hearty quesadillas, they stood up beautifully. If you're looking for something to sink your teeth into, this is it.

1   8-ounce package tempeh
1   cup prepared salsa
Grapeseed oil or
    extra virgin olive oil
4   rice tortillas
2   cups shredded rice cheese
1   cup chopped
    romaine lettuce

Cut tempeh into pieces and steam 5 minutes. Remove from heat and set aside. When cool enough to handle, crumble into large bowl and stir in salsa.

Lightly oil griddle or skillet and place over medium heat. Place 1 tortilla in skillet, sprinkle with ½ cup shredded cheese, top with half of the tempeh mixture, ½ cup chopped lettuce, ½ cup cheese and another tortilla. Grill 3–4 minutes, carefully flip and grill another 3–4 minutes. Remove from heat. Repeat with remaining tortillas and filling. Slice into wedges and serve.

Note: Experiment with the different salsa and guacamole recipes in this book to discover your favorite combination.

SERVES 6–8

Pineapple Tempeh Kebabs

THESE KEBABS ARE SWEET AND SAVORY and a great main course for a summer barbeque. Serve them on their own or over basmati or Chinese forbidden black rice. For maximum flavor, leave yourself plenty of time to marinate the tempeh.

KEBABS

2   8-ounce packages tempeh, cut into squares

1   red onion, cut into wedges

2   green bell peppers, cut into triangles

½   fresh pineapple, cut into triangles

MARINADE

¾   cup pineapple juice

2   tablespoons extra virgin olive oil

1   tablespoon tamari

1   tablespoon maple syrup

2   garlic cloves, minced

1   tablespoon grated fresh ginger

1   tablespoon chopped fresh mint

1   tablespoon minced red onion

In medium pot, steam tempeh for 5 minutes. Remove from heat, cool slightly and place squares in large sealable container.

Add onion, green pepper and pineapple to container with tempeh. In small bowl, whisk together all marinade ingredients, pour into container, seal and shake. Refrigerate at least 1 hour, flipping container several times every 15–20 minutes to redistribute marinade.

If using wooden skewers, soak in water for 15 minutes before assembling kebabs. Place ingredients on skewers in an alternating pattern, leaving room to grab ends of skewers.

Heat grill to medium-high and cook kebabs 3–4 minutes per side until cooked through. Remove from heat and serve.

SERVES 4

Curry Tempeh Salad with Raisins and Cashews

THIS IS THE PERFECT LUNCHEON SALAD. You can enjoy it over a bed of greens with rice crackers on the side, with a wedge of cantaloupe, wrapped in a burrito with arugula or spinach, or straight out of the mixing bowl as I often do.

½ pound tempeh, any variety

¼ cup finely chopped red onion

¼ cup finely chopped red bell pepper

1 stalk celery, finely chopped

¼ cup raisins

2 tablespoons chopped roasted cashews

2 tablespoons chopped fresh cilantro

3 tablespoons vegan mayonnaise

2 teaspoons curry powder

1 teaspoon cumin

¼ teaspoon sea salt

Cut tempeh into 4 large pieces, place in steamer basket over boiling water and steam 10 minutes. Remove from heat and cool slightly. Chop into small pieces and place in medium mixing bowl. Add onion, bell pepper, celery, raisins, cashews and cilantro and fold to combine. In separate small mixing bowl, combine mayonnaise, curry powder, cumin and sea salt. Add to tempeh mixture and fold to incorporate all ingredients. Serve chilled or at room temperature.

SERVES 4

Sprouted Quinoa Tabbouleh

IF YOU LIKE TABBOULEH AS MUCH AS I DO, but can't eat gluten, you no longer have to do without. Don't forget to leave yourself 24 hours to sprout your quinoa before assembling this high-protein, low-fat, non-gluten tabbouleh. I like to start soaking my quinoa at night just before I go to bed, rinse it when I wake up and then assemble my salad just before dinner.

½   cup quinoa

½   cup chopped fresh mint

½   cup chopped fresh parsley

1   cup diced cucumber

1   cup halved cherry tomatoes

2   tablespoons extra virgin olive oil

2   garlic cloves, minced

¼   cup lemon juice

Sea salt to taste

SPROUTING QUINOA

Rinse quinoa thoroughly and place in bowl with enough water to cover. Allow quinoa to absorb water, about 4 hours. Place quinoa in fine-mesh strainer, rinse and place the strainer on plate on counter. Rinse two more times during the day. Quinoa will sprout within 24 hours.

PREPARING SALAD

In large bowl, combine sprouted quinoa with remaining ingredients. Serve chilled or at room temperature.

SERVES 6

VARIATION

Leftover cooked quinoa works equally well and is a quick and easy alternative to sprouted quinoa.

Quinoa and Black Bean Salad with Apricot Lime Vinaigrette

THIS SALAD HAS A FRUITY TWIST that makes it particularly light and refreshing and provides an interesting change from my more traditional black bean salad. Much of this salad can be prepared in advance, but hold off on adding the tomatoes, seeds or dressing until you're ready to serve.

1¼ cups water

¾ cup quinoa

Pinch of sea salt

3 cups cooked black beans

½ cup chopped red onion

1 mango, peeled, pitted and diced

1 cup peeled and diced jícama

1 cup halved cherry tomatoes

¼ cup toasted sunflower seeds

¼ cup toasted pumpkin seeds

VINAIGRETTE

¼ cup extra virgin olive oil

2 tablespoons lime juice

¼ cup apricot nectar or juice

2 jalapeños, seeded and minced

½ cup chopped fresh mint

Sea salt and freshly ground black pepper

Bring water to boil and add quinoa and salt. Cover, reduce heat and simmer until all water is absorbed (about 15 minutes). Remove from heat and set aside to cool.

Place beans, onion, mango and jícama in large bowl. Fluff cooled quinoa with fork, add to bowl and gently fold to combine.

In small bowl, whisk together all dressing ingredients. Pour dressing over salad and toss to coat. Fold in tomatoes, sunflower seeds and pumpkin seeds just before serving.

SERVES 8

Wheatberry Salad

THIS SALAD IS A SNAP TO PREPARE and makes a great side dish or main dish for breakfast, lunch or dinner. Wheatberries can be hard to digest, so make sure to take the time to soak them first. For a change, substitute your favorite vinaigrette for the sesame oil and lime juice.

1½ cups wheatberries

3¼ cups water

Pinch of sea salt

4–5 scallions, chopped

1   cup chopped peaches (apples are a nice substitute in fall)

½   cup currants

¼   cup toasted sunflower seeds

Juice of 1 lime

3   tablespoons toasted sesame oil

Rinse wheatberries, soak in bowl with enough water to cover for at least 1 hour, then drain. In large pot, bring 3¼ cups water to boil. Add wheatberries and pinch of salt, reduce heat, cover, and simmer until all water is absorbed (35–45 minutes). Set aside to cool, then fluff with fork.

In large bowl, combine cooked wheatberries with scallions, peaches, currants and toasted sunflower seeds. Toss with lime juice, toasted sesame oil and pinch of salt. Serve at room temperature or chilled.

GLUTEN-FREE OPTIONS

Instead of wheatberries, use wild rice or certified gluten-free whole oat groats.

SERVES 8

Sprouted Quinoa with Strawberries and Lime

QUINOA IS ONE OF JUST A FEW GRAINS that I find light enough to enjoy in the summer, and sprouting it makes it even more cooling and nutritious. Watermelon radishes, with their vibrant pink flesh, are a sweet and colorful addition to this salad, and they seem to be getting easier to find each year. If you can't get your hands on them, substitute red radishes or make this salad with no radishes at all.

1   cup quinoa

½   cup peeled and diced jícama

2   avocados, peeled, pitted and diced

4   apricots (fresh or dried), diced

3   tomatillos, husked and diced

1   cup quartered strawberries

1   yellow bell pepper, diced

½   watermelon radish, peeled and diced

DRESSING

¼   cup extra virgin olive oil

3   tablespoons lime juice

Zest and juice of 1 orange

1   jalapeño, seeded and minced

2   tablespoons chopped fresh cilantro

2   tablespoons fresh mint

Sea salt

SPROUTING QUINOA

Rinse quinoa thoroughly and place in bowl with enough water to cover. Allow quinoa to absorb water, about 4 hours. Place quinoa in fine-mesh strainer, rinse and place the strainer on plate on counter. Rinse two more times during the day. Quinoa will sprout within 24 hours.

PREPARING SALAD

In large bowl, combine sprouted quinoa, jícama, avocado, apricots, tomatillos, strawberries, yellow pepper and watermelon radish. In separate bowl, whisk together all dressing ingredients. Pour over salad, toss to combine and refrigerate. Serve cold.

SERVES 8

Pesto Pasta Salad

THIS PASTA SALAD HAS BEEN TO MORE FAMILY PICNICS than I can count. Freshly made pesto turns this basic salad into something special. For variety, experiment with lemon basil or even lemon balm instead of traditional basil for another light and wonderful pesto. I've also been known to make a more heart-healthy version with walnuts or pumpkin seeds instead of pine nuts. Experiment freely to discover the combination you like best.

1½	pounds rice pasta (fusilli or tortellini)

Extra virgin olive oil

3	cups broccoli florets
4	carrots, sliced into ¼-inch rounds
1	yellow bell pepper, diced
10	cherry tomatoes, halved
1½	cups black olives, pitted

PESTO

3	garlic cloves, peeled
2½	cups fresh basil or lemon basil leaves
1	cup toasted pine nuts
½	cup extra virgin olive oil

Lemon juice

Cook pasta according to directions on package. Drain, rinse, then drain again and return to pot. Drizzle with olive oil and set aside.

PREPARING PESTO

With food processor running, drop in garlic cloves and process until minced. Add basil, pine nuts and olive oil and process until smooth, scrapping down sides of bowl as needed. Add lemon juice 1 tablespoon at a time as desired.

PREPARING SALAD

Bring 4 cups of water to boil. Place broccoli florets and carrots in medium bowl. Cover with boiling water and let sit for 1 minute. Drain, rinse with cold water and drain again. Add to pasta along with bell pepper, tomatoes and olives. Fold in pesto. Serve warm or chilled.

SERVES 8

Grilled Polenta with Mushroom Ragoût

POLENTA IS NOT DIFFICULT TO MAKE, but it does require time to cool and firm. To enjoy this dish without the fuss, look for prepared polenta in your natural food store. Either way, this dish is a snap to whip up, and the fresh mushrooms add rich, complex flavor.

POLENTA

5½ cups water

1 teaspoon sea salt

1½ cups polenta

12 sun-dried tomatoes, reconstituted in hot water, drained and chopped

MUSHROOM RAGOÛT

2 tablespoons extra virgin olive oil, plus more for grilling

2 garlic cloves, peeled

1½ pounds wild mushrooms (shiitake, cremini, portobello and/or mitake varieties)

4 teaspoons chopped fresh marjoram

2 tablespoons chopped fresh parsley

Sea salt and freshly ground black pepper

½ cup vegetable stock

1 cup chopped fresh tomatoes

PREPARING POLENTA

In large sauté pan, bring water to boil over medium-high heat. Add salt. Reduce heat and, whisking continuously, slowly pour in polenta. Add sun-dried tomatoes and stir constantly until polenta is thick and a spoon can stand straight up in it. Pour into 8 x 8-inch square glass baking dish, cool and place in refrigerator to set.

PREPARING RAGOÛT

In large saucepan over medium heat, sauté oil and garlic until fragrant (2–3 minutes). Add mushrooms, marjoram and parsley. Season to taste with salt and pepper and sauté 4–5 minutes. Add vegetable stock and chopped tomatoes and simmer until mushrooms are soft and sauce has started to reduce. Remove from heat, cover and set aside.

FINISHING

Remove polenta from refrigerator and cut into 6 squares. Heat grill pan or griddle over medium-high heat, brush with olive oil and grill each polenta square 3–4 minutes per side. Place patties on individual plates or serving tray, top with mushroom ragoût and serve.

SERVES 6

Nuts Over Strawberry Rhubarb Pie

OH, THE RECIPES THAT COME TOGETHER when your children are allergic to wheat. This savory and gluten-free crust brings out the tartness of the rhubarb more than a traditional strawberry rhubarb pie, making this quite a favorite in my home.

CRUST

1¼ cups almonds

1¼ cups pecans

1¼ cups walnuts

1 cup brown rice flour

½ cup maple syrup

½ cup virgin coconut oil, melted

Pinch of sea salt

FILLING

¾ cup apple juice

2 tablespoons maple syrup

1 teaspoon agar powder or flakes

3 tablespoons arrowroot or kudzu, dissolved in 2 tablespoons water

5 stalks rhubarb, cut into 1-inch pieces

4 cups strawberries, stemmed and cut into large chunks

Preheat oven to 350°F.

PREPARING CRUST

Place all nuts in food processor and pulse until mixture resembles coarse meal. Add rice flour, syrup, oil and salt and pulse to combine. Place two-thirds of mixture in lightly oiled 9-inch pie plate, press down to form crust, and bake 15–20 minutes until lightly browned. Remove from oven and set aside on wire rack to cool. Keep the oven on.

PREPARING FILLING

Combine apple juice and maple syrup in large pot over medium heat, bring to boil and reduce to simmer. Slowly whisk in agar. Cook 2 minutes or until agar dissolves. Stir in arrowroot mixture and cook until sauce thickens. Add rhubarb and strawberries and cook until rhubarb just starts to fall apart. Remove from heat and cool 2–3 minutes.

FINISHING

Pour filling into prepared pie crust and sprinkle with remaining nut mixture. Place in oven and bake 40 minutes. Remove from oven and set aside for 5–10 minutes to set. Serve warm.

MAKES ONE 9-inch pie

Fresh Fruit Tart with Almond Crust

THIS ELEGANT, EASY AND HEALTHY PRESENTATION for summer fruit and berries is sure to become your go-to dessert for entertaining.

CRUST

1   cup almonds

1½ cups rolled oats

Pinch of sea salt

3   tablespoons maple syrup

3   tablespoons virgin coconut oil, melted

1   teaspoon almond extract

FILLING

4   kiwis, peeled and thinly sliced

3   peaches, thinly sliced

3   cups berries of choice

1   cup apple juice

¼   cup fruit nectar or juice of choice

2   tablespoons maple syrup

1   tablespoon agar powder or flakes

1   tablespoon arrowroot or kudzu, dissolved in 1 tablespoon water

1   teaspoon vanilla extract

PREPARING CRUST

Preheat oven to 350°F.

Place nuts in food processor and pulse to chop coarsely. Add rolled oats and salt and process until mixture resembles coarse meal. In small bowl, whisk together maple syrup, oil and almond extract. Add to almond-oat mixture and process to combine. Transfer to 9-inch oiled tart pan or springform pan and press down to form crust. Pierce several times with fork and bake 15 minutes or until lightly browned. Remove from oven and set aside on wire rack to cool.

ASSEMBLING TART

Arrange sliced kiwis and peaches around outside edge of tart and fill center with berries. In medium pot over no heat, combine apple juice, fruit nectar, syrup and agar. Turn heat to medium-high and whisk continuously until agar dissolves. Add arrowroot mixture and continue whisking until thick. Add vanilla, remove from heat and set aside to cool 5 minutes. Spoon evenly over tart and refrigerate at least 1 hour before serving.

MAKES ONE 9-inch tart

Strawberry Custard with Fresh Berries and Lemon Peel

THIS SWEET AND REFRESHING DESSERT is the perfect choice after your annual strawberry-picking outing.

---

2   pounds fresh strawberries, stemmed

24 ounces firm silken tofu

½   teaspoon vanilla extract

⅔   cup maple syrup

⅓   cup ivory teff or white rice flour

1   cup mixed berries

2   tablespoons lemon peel

Purée strawberries in food processor and press through a fine sieve into separate bowl. Discard seeds and set liquid aside.

Clean food processor and whip tofu until creamy (make sure all chunks get whipped). Add vanilla, syrup, strawberry liquid and ivory teff or white rice flour. Process to combine. Pour into serving bowl or individual parfait or martini glasses. Refrigerate at least 1 hour. Top with mixed berries and lemon peel. Serve cold.

SERVES 8

Peach, Fresh Fig and Bourbon Crisp with Pecan Topping

THIS TOPPING CAN BE PRESSED INTO A PIE SHELL or crumbled over fruit for a quick and delicious dessert as I've done here. If fresh figs aren't available, either leave them out or turn this into a completely new dessert by using berries and no bourbon. The skins of organic peaches add nice texture and color.

FILLING

8–10 peaches, pitted and cut into wedges

6–8 fresh figs, cut into wedges

2 tablespoons maple syrup

1 teaspoon vanilla extract

3 tablespoons bourbon

3 tablespoons brown rice flour

Pinch of sea salt

TOPPING

4 cups pecans

½ cup brown rice flour or ivory teff flour

⅓ cup virgin coconut oil, melted

¼ cup maple syrup

Pinch of sea salt

Preheat oven to 350°F.

PREPARING FILLING

Place peaches and figs in large bowl. In separate bowl, combine maple syrup, vanilla and bourbon. Pour over fruit, sprinkle with flour and salt and gently fold to combine. Transfer to casserole and set aside.

PREPARING TOPPING

Chop nuts in food processor until mixture resembles coarse meal. Add flour and process to combine. Add oil, maple syrup and salt. Process until mixture is moist enough to stick together when pressed, but still crumbly.

FINISHING

Spread nut mixture evenly over fruit, cover loosely with foil and bake 30 minutes. Remove foil and bake another 20 minutes or until fruit is soft. Remove from oven, cool slightly and serve warm.

GLUTEN-FREE OPTION

Look for gluten-free bourbon made from corn as opposed to wheat.

SERVES 8

Strawberry Rhubarb Compote with Cashew Cream

THERE'S SOMETHING ABOUT FRESHLY PICKED RHUBARB at the farm stand that I simply can't pass up. This may be one of the simplest ways to use rhubarb, and the finished product is a smooth and sweet complement to the rich cashew cream. For an even quicker dessert, serve the compote over chocolate or vanilla ice cream.

CASHEW CREAM

2   cups apple juice

2   cups lightly roasted cashews

3   tablespoons maple syrup

COMPOTE

2   cups chopped rhubarb

½   cup apple juice

1   teaspoon agar powder

3   tablespoons arrowroot or kudzu, dissolved in 2 tablespoons water

4   cups stemmed and halved strawberries

Fresh mint or lemon balm sprigs for garnish

PREPARING CASHEW CREAM

In small pot, bring apple juice to boil and remove from heat. Place cashews and syrup in food processor. Turn on machine and slowly add juice to cashews and syrup until you achieve the desired texture (you may not need all of the juice). Refrigerate for 1 hour.

PREPARING COMPOTE

In saucepan over medium heat, combine rhubarb and apple juice and simmer until rhubarb starts to fall apart. Add agar and whisk until it dissolves. Add arrowroot mixture and whisk until sauce starts to thicken. Add strawberries and remove from heat. Set aside to cool slightly.

ASSEMBLING

Layer compote and cashew cream in glasses or glass bowl. Top with sprigs of fresh mint or lemon balm and serve.

SERVES 6

Lemon Berry Cream Pie

I WAS ABSOLUTELY OBSESSED WITH CREATING THIS PIE! I could taste exactly what I was craving, but simply couldn't achieve it. After far too many attempts, it finally came together as I hoped it would, and it has been my all-time favorite summer pie ever since. It's creamy, sweet, tart and refreshing, and the use of store-bought lemon snaps allows the crust to come together in no time. I hope you love it as much as I do.

CRUST

2	heaping cups gluten-free lemon snaps
3	tablespoons virgin coconut oil, melted
3	tablespoons maple syrup

FILLING

1	cup apple juice
¼	cup lemon juice
1	tablespoon agar powder
2½	tablespoons arrowroot
12	ounces extra firm silken tofu
¾	cup maple syrup
2	tablespoons lemon extract
1	tablespoon lemon zest
1	tablespoon vanilla extract

Pinch of sea salt

2–3 cups fresh blueberries

PREPARING CRUST

Preheat oven to 350°F.

Place lemon snaps in food processor and process until they resemble coarse flour. Add oil and syrup and process to combine. Place in 9-inch pie plate and press down to form crust. Bake 12 minutes, then remove from oven, press down any bubbles with the back of a wooden spoon and set aside on wire rack to cool.

PREPARING FILLING

In small pot over no heat, whisk together apple juice, lemon juice, agar powder and arrowroot until there are no lumps. Place over medium heat and stir continuously until mixture thickens and starts to look translucent. Remove from heat and set aside to cool.

In food processor, whip tofu until smooth. Add maple syrup, lemon extract and zest, vanilla and salt, and process briefly. Add apple juice mixture and pulse to just combine.

FINISHING

Pour tofu mixture into pie shell and completely cover top of pie with berries. Refrigerate to chill and set at least 2 hours before serving.

MAKES ONE 9-inch pie

Chocolate Pudding with Fresh Berries

THIS PUDDING IS ONE OF MY MOST VERSATILE dessert recipes. I serve it as a pudding; I take out the bananas and use it to frost cakes; and sometimes I take out the bananas, add roasted nuts and pour it into a pie crust for chocolate cream pie.

---

25 ounces extra firm or firm silken tofu

1 teaspoon vanilla extract

Pinch of sea salt

2–3 ripe bananas

1 cup semisweet or dark chocolate chips

2 cups strawberries, raspberries and/or blackberries

Wrap blocks of tofu in towels and press to remove excess liquid. In food processor, blend tofu, vanilla and salt. Scrape sides of bowl and blend again until there are no lumps. Add bananas and blend until smooth.

In small saucepan, melt chocolate, immediately add to tofu mixture and process until combined. Pour mixture into large serving bowl or individual parfait glasses and refrigerate at least 1 hour to firm and chill. Remove from refrigerator, top with fresh berries and serve.

SERVES 6

Mixed Berry Tart

SIMPLE, ELEGANT, GLUTEN-FREE, LOW CALORIE AND SATISFYING.
Who could ask for more?

CRUST

1⅓ cups ivory teff flour

¼ teaspoon sea salt

½ cup maple syrup

¼ cup virgin coconut oil, melted

FILLING

5 cups fresh mixed berries

1½ cups clear apple juice

2 tablespoons maple syrup

1 tablespoon agar powder or flakes

2 tablespoons arrowroot, dissolved in 1 tablespoon water

1 teaspoon vanilla extract

PREPARING CRUST

Preheat oven to 350°F.

Place all crust ingredients in food processor and pulse to combine. Pour mixture into 9-inch oiled tart or springform pan. Press down to form crust. Pierce several times with fork and bake 15 minutes until lightly browned. Remove from oven and set aside on wire rack to cool.

ASSEMBLING TART

Fill tart with berries. In medium pot over medium-high heat, combine apple juice, syrup and agar. Whisk continuously until agar dissolves. Add arrowroot mixture and continue whisking until glaze thickens. Add vanilla, remove from heat and set aside to cool 5 minutes. Spoon evenly over tart and refrigerate 1 hour or until set.

MAKES ONE 9-inch tart

Fresh Berries with Tofu Cream

THERE ARE A FEW BASIC RECIPES that are not only delicious on their own, but also helpful for making a variety of other recipes. This tofu cream is one of them. You can serve it on top of fresh berries, top it with granola for dipping sliced fruit, spread it between two layers of cake or serve it over pie. No matter how you use it, you just can't go wrong!

3   cups fresh berries of choice

Mint leaves for garnish

TOFU CREAM

18 ounces extra firm silken tofu

¼ cup apple juice

¼ cup cashew butter

⅓ cup maple syrup

1   teaspoon vanilla extract

Pinch of sea salt

3   tablespoons rice milk

2   teaspoons arrowroot

Drain tofu, wrap in towels and press out excess water. Place in food processor and whip until perfectly smooth, scraping down sides of bowl so that all pieces get whipped. Add apple juice, cashew butter, maple syrup, vanilla and sea salt and process until smooth.

Combine rice milk and arrowroot in small pot. Place over medium heat and whisk continuously until thick (3–4 minutes). Remove from heat, add to tofu and process to combine.

Transfer tofu cream to bowl and refrigerate 1 hour or until cold. Divide berries, place in individual bowls and top with tofu cream and mint leaves.

SERVES 6

Autumn is a second spring when every leaf is a flower.

ALBERT CAMUS

Fall

It's hard to say good-bye to summer's bright and colorful palette, but by mid-September I am ready for cool crisp mornings, apple-picking excursions, pumpkin carving and hayrides. A colorful blanket of foliage drapes over New England. Farms sell bunches of fresh herbs for drying, bags of basil for making pesto, boxes of tomatoes for canning and gourds for decorating. Apples and pears come in reds, yellows and greens, reflecting the changing leaves around them, and the winter squash are so tasty that my children devour them, skin and all. There's nothing like the sweetness of kale and collard greens after fall's first frost. While most of my family reserve dark leafy greens for dinner, these greens are often my breakfast of choice. I enjoy starting my day with their uplifting, long-lasting energy. It's a great way to keep positive and balanced while transitioning into the darker, colder months ahead.

FALL

DIPS, DRESSINGS AND MORE
Spiced Kukicha Iced Tea 160
Ginger Pear Sauce 161
Cranberry Chutney 163
Apple Chutney 164
Lentil Walnut Pâté 165

SOUPS
Apple Squash Soup 166
Autumn Harvest Soup 167
Sweet Potato, Corn and Kale Chowder 168
Corn Chowder 170
Carrot Ginger Soup 171
Creamy Shiitake and Chickpea Soup 172
Savory Black Bean Soup 173

VEGETABLES
Marinated Bitter Greens 174
Warm Greens with Citrus Dressing and Pomegranate . . 175
Julienned Beet, Broccoli Stem and Carrot Salad 176
Quick Boiled Broccoli and Stems
    with Toasted Sesame Seeds 178
Sautéed Garlic Greens 179
Ginger Sesame Greens 180
Kale with Caramelized Shallots 181
Kale with Pine Nuts and Currants 182
Tamari-Braised Mustard Greens 183
Raw Kale Salad with Great Northen Beans
    and Kalamata Olives 185
Curried Parsnips 186
Roasted Root Vegetables with Truffle Oil 187
Spiced Sweet Potato Fries 188
Sautéed Yams with Ginger and Lime 189
Root Veggie Fries 190
Three Sisters Deep-Dish Pie 191
Sesame Brussels Sprout Sauté 192
Rutabaga Purée with Orange and Ginger 194
Roasted Squash with Fennel and Asparagus 195
Savory Stuffed Pumpkins 196
Roasted Kabocha Squash and Creminis
    with Fresh Herbs 197
Silky Sweet Potato Pie 198

SEA VEGETABLES
Stir-Fried Broccoli with Arame 199
Arame with Caramelized Shiitakes 200
Wild Rice, Barley and Arame Salad 201

LEGUMES
Millet, Aduki Beans and Corn with Lemon Dressing . . . 203
Refried Pinto Beans with Chiles 204
White Beans and Escarole 205
Sweet Potato and Black Bean Burritos
    with Cashew Cheese 206

TOFU, TEMPEH AND SEITAN
Scrambled Tofu 208
Marinated Tofu with Ginger Cashew Dipping Sauce . . . 209
Baked Maple Mustard Tempeh 210
Seitan Walnut Stuffed Collard Greens 211
Tofu Kale Lasagna 213

GRAINS
Skillet Cornbread 214
Quinoa with Sweet Corn 215
Multigrain Pilaf with Toasted Sunflower Seeds 216
Pan-Roasted Millet with Pumpkin Seeds 217
Quinoa with Almonds and Currants 218
Stovetop Barley with Sweet Vegetables 219
Kabocha Squash Stuffed with Brown Rice
    and Chickpea Pilaf 220
Sweet Dumpling Squash
    with Orange-Scented Quinoa Stuffing 222
Mediterranean Pasta with Greens 223

DESSERTS
Apple Crisp 224
Ginger Pear Crisp 225
Chocolate Lover's Tart 227
Maple Poached Pears 228
Green Tea Poached Pears
    with Pomegranate Glaze and Pistachios 229
Tofu Pumpkin Pie with Gingersnap Crust 230
Glazed Oranges with Pomegranate Seeds 231

Spiced Kukicha Iced Tea

KUKICHA TEA IS HIGHLY REGARDED for its medicinal properties. It is alkalinizing and strengthening to the body and can be consumed daily. It also has almost no caffeine, supports healthy digestion and can be helpful in treating heart disease and fatigue. Kukicha is even safe for children. You can drink it straight or with a dash of lemon juice and maple syrup, but this recipe gives you a way to create a medicine you'll love to take. Choose any combination of fruit juices to make it your own.

---

4   cups water

4   1-ounce kukicha
     tea bags

1   cinnamon stick

¾   cup orange juice
     (preferably freshly
     squeezed)

2   cups apple cider

1   cup pomegranate juice

Fresh sprigs of mint or lemon
     balm for garnish

Bring water to boil and remove from heat. Add tea bags and cinnamon stick and steep 10 minutes. With slotted spoon, remove and discard cinnamon stick and tea bags. Stir in remaining juices and refrigerate to chill. Serve with sprigs of fresh mint or lemon balm.

MAKES 7 cups

Ginger Pear Sauce

THIS IS A WONDERFUL ALTERNATIVE to applesauce and provides a nice balance and pleasant surprise when served with Seitan Walnut Stuffed Collard Greens *(page 211)* or Three Sisters Deep-Dish Pie *(page 191)*.

10   ripe pears

8   cloves

2   tablespoons grated fresh ginger

2   cups water or pear juice

1   cinnamon stick

Peel, core and slice pears and place in large pot with remaining ingredients. Bring to boil over medium-high heat, cover, reduce heat and simmer 6–8 minutes until fruit is soft. Remove from heat and let cool slightly. Discard cinnamon stick and then purée fruit with handheld blender. Serve warm or at room temperature.

MAKES 3 cups

Cranberry Chutney

AS A CHILD, I INSISTED ON STORE-BOUGHT CRANBERRY SAUCE –
no chunks, just that smooth roll, complete with indentations from the can.
When I finally tasted my mother's homemade chutney, I was converted.
I now make it in huge batches, give it as gifts around the holidays and even
freeze it to have throughout the year. It goes great on a turkey sandwich
with avocado and honey mustard or with vegetable pot pie. Once you
taste it, you'll understand why I'm addicted.

2	cups fresh cranberries
1	cup raisins
½	cup sucanat
½	cup maple syrup
1	tablespoon ground cinnamon
2	teaspoons grated fresh ginger
¼	teaspoon ground cloves
1	cup water
1	small onion, chopped
3	medium apples, cored and chopped
4	stalks celery, chopped
1	teaspoon grated lemon peel

Combine cranberries, raisins, sucanat, maple syrup, cinnamon, ginger, cloves and water in Dutch oven. Place over medium heat and cook 15 minutes. Stir in onion, apples and celery and cook 15 minutes more. Remove from heat, fold in lemon peel, and serve.

Chutney can be made in advance and stored in an airtight container in the freezer.

MAKES 4 cups

Apple Chutney

THANKSGIVING WOULDN'T BE THE SAME without cranberry chutney, but sometimes I crave a more delicate condiment – something between Mom's cranberry variety and my homemade applesauce. This recipe fills that gap perfectly and also makes a great accompaniment to Three Sisters Deep-Dish Pie *(page 191)*.

1	cup apple cider or juice
2	cinnamon sticks
5	cloves
8	large firm and tart apples (Granny Smith, Macoun or other)
1	cup golden raisins
½	cup maple syrup
1	tablespoon grated fresh ginger
1	large onion, diced
1	fennel bulb, halved, cored and diced

Pinch of sea salt

Zest of 1 lemon

Place apple cider, cinnamon sticks and cloves in small pot over medium heat and simmer 15 minutes. Turn off heat, remove cinnamon sticks and cloves and set aside. Meanwhile, peel, core and dice apples.

In 2-quart pot, combine apples, raisins, maple syrup, ginger, onion, fennel and salt. Place over medium-high heat and add spiced apple cider. Bring to boil, reduce heat and simmer 45 minutes or until chutney is thick. Remove from heat, fold in lemon zest and serve warm or cold.

MAKES 3 cups

Lentil Walnut Pâté

THIS DIP REMINDS ME of the chopped liver my mother used to make when I was a child, only better. While it works without the walnuts, they add richness and complexity that's well worth the extra fuss. Serve with Pita Chips *(page 317)*, thin rye bread rounds or rice crackers.

---

1   cup brown or
    green lentils

1   thumb-size piece kombu

2   cups water

1   cup walnut pieces

1   tablespoon
    extra virgin olive oil

2   onions, chopped

Ume plum vinegar

Water and/or extra virgin
    olive oil

Preheat oven to 300°F.

Rinse lentils and place in pot or rice cooker with kombu and water. Cover and bring to boil over high heat. Reduce heat to simmer and cook 35–40 minutes until water is absorbed. Remove from heat, discard kombu and set lentils aside.

While lentils are cooking, crush or chop walnuts and roast on a parchment-lined cookie sheet for 12 minutes or until golden brown. In medium skillet over medium heat, sauté onion in olive oil until translucent (about 5 minutes).

Place cooked lentils in food processor with roasted walnuts, sautéed onions and a few dashes of vinegar. Add water and/or olive oil a tablespoon at a time and process until smooth and desired thickness is achieved. Season to taste with vinegar and serve at room temperature or cold.

MAKES 3 cups

Apple Squash Soup

THIS SWEET, SILKY AND UPLIFTING DISH is the quintessential fall soup. I serve it to friends and family and even send it to school for my children's lunches. Pair it with a salad or some sautéed greens and grains for an easy and satisfying meal.

---

1 large butternut squash

2 tablespoons grapeseed oil

1 large yellow onion, chopped

4 large apples, peeled, cored and quartered

4 cups vegetable stock

1 cup rice milk

¼ cup coconut milk

½ teaspoon ground nutmeg

Sea salt

Peel squash, cut in half and remove seeds. Cut into 2-inch pieces.

In large pot over medium heat, sauté onion in oil until soft (about 5 minutes). Add squash, apples, stock, rice milk, coconut milk and nutmeg. Cover, bring to boil, then reduce heat and simmer 20 minutes or until squash is soft. Purée with handheld blender and remove from heat to cool slightly. Season to taste with salt and serve.

SERVES 6

Autumn Harvest Soup

THIS AUTUMN SOUP IS A NUTRITIONAL POWERHOUSE. With shiitake mushroom stock to help reduce blood cholesterol levels, dark leafy greens rich in calcium and legumes to regulate your blood sugar, support your thyroid and balance your hormones, this meal in a pot is just what the doctor ordered. For those with a bigger appetite, serve over soba noodles or brown rice.

4	dried shiitake mushrooms
6	cups water
2	tablespoons extra virgin olive oil
1	large onion, diced
3	garlic cloves, minced
1	tablespoon grated fresh ginger
3	carrots, diced
4	cups chopped kale or collard greens
2	cups cooked cannellini beans
¼	cup mirin

Splash of tamari

Splash of apple cider vinegar

4–5 dashes toasted sesame oil

Freshly ground black pepper

Place dried mushrooms in medium pot with 6 cups water. Bring to boil, then reduce heat and simmer 15 minutes. Remove from heat and set aside to cool slightly. When mushrooms are soft, remove from broth and cut off and discard stems. Dice caps and place back in pot with broth.

In large pot over medium heat, sauté onion, garlic and ginger in oil 3 minutes. Add carrots and sauté 3 minutes. Add kale or collard greens, beans and mirin and sauté until greens are deep green and tender. Pour broth and mushrooms into pot with kale, add tamari and vinegar and simmer 5–7 minutes. Season to taste with toasted sesame oil and black pepper and serve.

SERVES 6

Sweet Potato, Corn and Kale Chowder

WHEN I PREPARE DINNER, I try to make sure there's something for everyone. This chowder accomplishes that in one pot and is a colorful variation on an old favorite. It cooks up quickly and provides a balanced meal rich in nutrients all in one satisfying bowl.

---

1 tablespoon grapeseed oil

1 small onion, diced

3 stalks celery, diced

3 carrots, diced

3 medium sweet potatoes, peeled and diced

3 cups corn, fresh or frozen

2 teaspoons dried thyme

2 cups vegetable stock

2 cups rice milk, plus more if needed

2 tablespoons cashew butter, dissolved in ¼ cup hot water

1 bunch kale, chopped into small pieces

Water or stock as needed

Sea salt and freshly ground black pepper

In large pot over medium heat, sauté onion in oil until soft (about 3 minutes). Add celery, carrots, sweet potatoes, corn, thyme and stock and simmer 5 minutes. Add enough rice milk to cover the vegetables. Bring to boil, reduce heat and simmer until vegetables are soft (about 20 minutes). Remove from heat and add dissolved cashew butter. Partially purée using a handheld blender. Add kale, return to heat, thin with water or stock to achieve desired consistency and cook until kale is tender. Season to taste with salt and pepper and serve.

SERVES 6

Corn Chowder

MY DAUGHTER FELL IN LOVE WITH CORN CHOWDER at our local natural food store, but I didn't feel good about all the heavy cream and butter that was in it. I developed this completely nondairy recipe, and she loves it even more than the other. It can be put together in no time, is a welcome treat year-round, and is especially delicious with sweet corn straight off the cob.

---

1   tablespoon
    extra virgin olive oil

1   onion, chopped

4   stalks celery, chopped

2   carrots, chopped

2   medium potatoes,
    peeled and chopped

¼   cup mirin

½   teaspoon sea salt

3½ cups corn, fresh or frozen

5   cups rice milk or soy milk,
    plus more if needed

Water as needed

Sea salt and freshly ground
    black pepper

In large pot over medium heat, sauté onion in olive oil until soft (about 3 minutes). Add celery, carrots, potatoes, mirin and salt and sauté 3–4 minutes. Add corn and enough milk to just cover ingredients. Bring to boil, reduce heat, cover and simmer 20 minutes. Remove from heat and purée gently with a handheld blender. Add water as needed to achieve desired consistency. Season to taste with salt and pepper and serve.

SERVES 4

Carrot Ginger Soup

THIS NONDAIRY SOUP IS SURPRISINGLY EASY TO MAKE and is big on taste. Use this recipe as a template and experiment with different spices like cumin, turmeric or even cayenne to make it your own. When possible, prepare soups a day in advance to allow the flavors to blend. Then simply reheat, garnish and serve.

2	tablespoons grapeseed oil
1	onion, chopped
2	tablespoons grated fresh ginger
4	cups chopped carrots
½	cup rolled oats
½	cup orange juice (preferably freshly squeezed)
	Vegetable stock
3	tablespoons mellow white miso
	Chopped fresh parsley for garnish

In large pot over medium heat, sauté onion and ginger in oil 3 minutes. Add carrots, oats, orange juice and enough stock to cover carrots. Bring to boil, reduce heat, cover and let simmer until carrots are soft (about 20 minutes). Remove from heat and purée with handheld blender. Thin with stock as needed to achieve desired consistency. In small bowl, dissolve miso in ½ cup room-temperature water and stir into soup. Garnish with parsley and serve.

SERVES 4

VARIATION
Spice up this soup by adding 1 teaspoon ground cumin and 3–4 dashes hot sauce or hot sesame oil.

Creamy Shiitake and Chickpea Soup

LEGUMES ARE HIGH IN PROTEIN and are perfect for making satisfying soups. Chickpeas in particular are a great source of iron, calcium and heart-healthy unsaturated fats. Combined with dried shiitake mushrooms (known for their cholesterol-lowering properties) and calcium-rich broccoli, this soup is as healing as it is delicious.

---

4 dried shiitake mushrooms
1 large strip kombu
Water
1 tablespoon extra virgin olive oil
1 medium onion, chopped
1 garlic clove, minced
3 tablespoons lemon juice
2 tablespoons tamari
3 cups cooked chickpeas
1 tablespoon kudzu or arrowroot powder
2 cups broccoli cut into bite-size pieces
⅓ cup raisins
Sea salt and freshly ground black pepper

Soak dried mushrooms and kombu for 30 minutes in bowl with 2 cups water. Saving the soaking liquid, remove mushrooms and kombu. Discard mushroom stems and thinly slice caps. Mince kombu and return both sliced caps and kombu to soaking liquid.

In large pot over medium heat, sauté onion and garlic in oil for 3 minutes. Add mushrooms, kombu and soaking water, lemon juice, tamari and chickpeas and stir. Dissolve kudzu in ¼ cup water and stir into soup. Cover and simmer 15 minutes.

Meanwhile, place broccoli in bowl and pour in enough boiling water to cover. Let sit for 2 minutes, then drain and set aside.

Using handheld blender, lightly purée soup. Add raisins and cook 3 minutes or until soft. Add broccoli and simmer briefly to heat through. Season to taste with salt and pepper and serve.

SERVES 4

Savory Black Bean Soup

I LOVE BLACK BEANS YEAR ROUND, whether in salads, burritos, chili or this favorite soup. For a simple fall meal, serve with corn chips and a dollop of Tofu Sour Cream *(page 104)*.

1	thumb-size piece kombu
1	tablespoon extra virgin olive oil
4	garlic cloves, minced
1	onion, chopped
1	stalk celery, chopped
2	carrots, chopped
1	teaspoon ground cumin
¼	teaspoon cayenne pepper
¼	teaspoon sea salt
6	cups cooked black beans
4	cups water or vegetable stock
1	cup diced tomatoes (preferably without skins)
2	tablespoons mirin
1	tablespoon tamari
	Chopped fresh cilantro for garnish

Place kombu in bowl with enough warm water to cover and soak 10 minutes or until soft. Drain, mince kombu and set aside.

In large pot over medium heat, sauté garlic and onion in oil 3 minutes. Add celery, carrots, cumin, cayenne and salt. Sauté 8 minutes or until carrots are tender.

Add beans to pot along with water or stock, kombu, tomatoes, mirin and tamari. Bring to simmer and cook 30 minutes to combine flavors. For a creamier texture, purée some of the soup with handheld blender. Garnish with cilantro and serve.

SERVES 8

Marinated Bitter Greens

THIS GREEN LEAFY SALAD MARINATES in its dressing just long enough to slightly wilt the greens, making them less bitter and easier to digest. The acidity of the apple cider vinegar helps this process and adds the perfect complement to fall's sweet squashes and fruits. For an extra-special touch, garnish with pomegranate seeds.

---

4 cups chopped fall salad greens (try watercress, endive, radicchio and romaine lettuce)

MARINADE

1 shallot, minced

2 tablespoons apple cider vinegar

2 tablespoons maple syrup

2 teaspoons maple or honey mustard

1 teaspoon Bragg Liquid Aminos

3 tablespoons toasted sesame oil

¼ cup walnut or grapeseed oil

Place mixed greens in large bowl. Whisk together marinade ingredients either by hand or with handheld blender. Pour marinade over greens, toss to coat and set aside 10 minutes. Toss again, transfer greens to salad bowl or individual plates and serve.

SERVES 4

Warm Greens with Citrus Dressing and Pomegranate

USING POMEGRANATE SEEDS IS A SPECIAL WAY to dress up a variety of dishes. Combining greens with this citrus dressing, you simply can't go wrong, and the addition of pomegranate seeds on top is like icing on the cake.

---

2 bunches greens (try bok choy, kale or collard greens)

1 bunch watercress

Seeds from ½ large pomegranate

DRESSING

Juice of 1 orange (about ¼ cup)

2 tablespoons extra virgin olive oil

½ teaspoon grated fresh ginger

1 tablespoon tamari

1 tablespoon apple cider vinegar

In small bowl, whisk together all dressing ingredients.

Prepare greens by trimming and discarding dried ends. Cut leaves into bite-size pieces. Keeping watercress aside, place all other greens in large sauté pan. Add citrus dressing and sauté 2 minutes or until bright green and tender. Fold in watercress and cook 1 more minute. Remove from heat and serve topped with pomegranate seeds.

SERVES 4–6

Julienned Beet, Broccoli Stem and Carrot Salad

THIS RAW SALAD IS FULL OF FLAVOR, COLOR AND TEXTURE and lends balance to a variety of menus, from light summer grilling to winter's heavier mixed grains and roasted tempeh.

---

1 raw golden beet, peeled and julienned

3 raw broccoli stems, peeled and julienned

2 carrots, julienned

1 cup cooked chickpeas

½ cup raisins

¼ cup chopped fresh parsley or cilantro

1 cup chopped toasted cashews

DRESSING

1 small shallot, minced

1 tablespoon lemon juice

2 tablespoons maple or honey mustard

1 tablespoon maple syrup

½ cup extra virgin olive oil

¼ teaspoon sea salt

Freshly ground black pepper

Water

Combine beet, broccoli stems, carrots, chickpeas, raisins, and parsley or cilantro in large bowl. In separate bowl, place all dressing ingredients except water and whisk to combine or emulsify with handheld blender. Add water 1 tablespoon at a time to thin to desired consistency. Pour desired amount of dressing over vegetables, toss to combine, top with toasted cashews and serve.

SERVES 6 (makes about 1 cup of dressing)

Quick Boiled Broccoli and Stems with Toasted Sesame Seeds

I CAN BE COMPLETELY SATISFIED with a bowl of quinoa topped with this simple broccoli dish. Even when I serve it to company, people exclaim that they've never tasted such delicious broccoli. Sometimes simple truly is better.

1	bunch broccoli
2	tablespoons flax seed oil or toasted sesame oil
1	teaspoon ume plum vinegar
2	tablespoons toasted sesame seeds

Cut broccoli florets from stems. Chop florets into pieces and place in pot. Trim and discard dry ends from broccoli stems. Peel, discard outer skins, chop stems and add to pot with florets. Add 2 inches of water, cover, bring to boil and cook 2–3 minutes or until bright green and just tender. Drain water and toss broccoli with flax seed or toasted sesame oil and vinegar. Sprinkle with sesame seeds and serve.

SERVES 4

Sautéed Garlic Greens

IF YOU'RE NEW TO EATING CLEAN, and don't know where to begin, start with something green. Green is one color of which we simply can't get enough. Dark leafy greens are full of chlorophyll, calcium and vitamins. Few other foods have their capacity to lift your mood, cleanse your liver and kidneys and balance blood pH.

---

2   bunches dark leafy greens (kale, collards, mustard greens, dandelion greens or chard)

2   tablespoons extra virgin olive oil

3   garlic cloves, minced

1   tablespoon mirin

Water as needed

Sea salt or ume plum vinegar

Remove dry stalk ends from greens and chop leaves into bite-size pieces. In Dutch oven or skillet over medium-low heat, sauté garlic in 1 tablespoon olive oil for 2–3 minutes until soft. Add greens and mirin and sauté 1 minute. Increase heat to medium, add water (one tablespoon at a time) as needed to prevent sticking, cover and cook until greens break down. Remove from heat and toss with remaining tablespoon olive oil. Season to taste with salt or a few dashes of vinegar and serve.

SERVES 6

Ginger Sesame Greens

WHAT'S IMPORTANT ABOUT DARK LEAFY GREENS is not how you *prepare* them, but simply that you *eat* them. This is one of the simplest ways to prepare greens. With choices like this one and Sautéed Garlic Greens *(page 179)*, you'll no longer need to skip over this section of the produce department.

---

2   bunches dark leafy greens (kale, collards, mustard greens, dandelion greens or chard)

1   tablespoon extra virgin olive oil

1   tablespoon grated fresh ginger

1   tablespoon mirin

1   tablespoon tamari

Water as needed

1   tablespoon toasted sesame oil

Toasted sesame seeds and sea salt or gomasio

Remove dry stalk ends from greens and chop leaves into bite-size pieces. In Dutch oven or skillet over medium heat, sauté ginger in olive oil, mirin and tamari for 1 minute. Add chopped greens, increase heat to medium-high, add water as needed to prevent sticking, cover and cook 3–5 minutes until greens are tender. Remove cover, toss greens to ensure even cooking and sauté 2–3 minutes longer. Turn off heat, drain excess cooking liquid and toss with toasted sesame oil. Sprinkle with toasted sesame seeds and salt or gomasio and serve.

SERVES 6

Kale with Caramelized Shallots

KALE COMES IN MANY VARIETIES. My favorite is lacinato (also known as dinosaur kale), but you can use all of the varieties interchangeably. This preparation makes it easy to benefit from kale's vitamins, minerals and chlorophyll. Submerging the whole leaves in boiling water not only saves you the effort of washing, but allows the kale to retain more of its nutrients.

2   tablespoons
    extra virgin olive oil
6   large shallots, thinly sliced
1   tablespoon lemon juice
2   bunches kale
⅛   teaspoon coarse sea salt
Freshly ground black pepper

In large skillet or Dutch oven over medium heat, sauté shallots in 1 tablespoon olive oil for 6–8 minutes or until very soft and caramelized. Add lemon juice and sauté another 2–3 minutes to brown. Remove from heat and set aside.

Bring large pot of water to boil. Cut and remove dried stem ends from kale and submerge whole leaves in boiling water for 2–3 minutes or until tender and bright green. Remove from heat, drain water and cut leaves into bite-size pieces. Add kale to pan with shallots and sauté 1 minute. Add remaining tablespoon oil, season to taste with salt and pepper and serve.

SERVES 6

Kale with Pine Nuts and Currants

KALE IS A NUTRITIONAL POWERHOUSE, but the addition of pine nuts in this recipe makes it more like an indulgence. For a complete meal, serve this dish with wild rice *(page 14)* and Seitan Bourguignon *(page 280)*.

⅓ cup currants

2 tablespoons extra virgin olive oil

2 garlic cloves, minced

½ red onion, diced

2 large bunches kale, chopped

Water as needed

4 dashes ume plum vinegar

¼ cup toasted pine nuts

Plump currants by placing in small pot with ¼ inch water. Bring to boil, then reduce heat and simmer uncovered 3–4 minutes. Remove from heat and set aside.

In large pan over medium heat, sauté garlic and onion in oil until soft (about 3 minutes). Add kale and sauté until tender (4–6 minutes). Add 1–2 tablespoons water as needed to prevent sticking. Drain currants and add to kale. Toss with vinegar, top with toasted pine nuts and serve.

SERVES 6

Tamari-Braised Mustard Greens

MUSTARD GREENS HAVE A BITE SIMILAR TO ARUGULA and can be eaten raw in salads or cooked as in this recipe. These bitter greens are particularly good cleansers and are a rich source of antioxidants. If their bitterness is too much for you, add some kale to your sauté or enjoy them raw and mixed with romaine lettuce in a salad.

2	bunches mustard greens
2	tablespoons grapeseed oil
2	garlic cloves, minced
2	tablespoons tamari
2	tablespoons mirin
1	tablespoon gomasio

Trim and discard tough ends of mustard greens. Cut leaves into bite-size pieces and set aside.

In large skillet over medium-low heat, sauté garlic in oil 2 minutes or until soft. Increase heat to medium and add greens, tamari and mirin. Stir to combine, cover and simmer 5 minutes or until greens are tender. Uncover, increase heat to medium-high and cook until liquid has been reduced. Remove from heat, sprinkle with gomasio and serve hot.

SERVES 6

Raw Kale Salad with Great Northern Beans and Kalamata Olives

THE BUMPER STICKER ON MY CAR SAYS IT ALL, "Eat More Kale!" This dark leafy green is so much a favorite of mine it's practically my mantra. While I love it sautéed and added to soups and stews, I like it even more served raw as it is here. Use this recipe as a template and add your favorite vegetables season by season throughout the year.

---

1   large bunch kale

3   tablespoons extra virgin olive oil

Zest and juice of 1 lemon

1½   avocados, pitted and chopped

¼   teaspoon sea salt

½   cup chopped red onion

1½   cups cooked great northern beans

1   cup kalamata olives, pitted and halved

¼   cup toasted pine nuts

Remove tough stems from kale and discard. Chop leaves into bite-size pieces, place in large mixing bowl and drizzle with olive oil. Remove zest from lemon and set aside. Add lemon juice, two thirds chopped avocado and sea salt to kale and massage all ingredients into leaves. Add remaining third of avocado, onion, beans and olives. Toss to distribute ingredients and serve topped with pine nuts.

SERVES 4

SERVING SUGGESTION
Surprisingly, this salad does not quickly wilt or brown and will last 2–3 days in the refrigerator, so feel free to make in advance.

Curried Parsnips

THESE PARSNIPS ARE DELICIOUS AS IS, or they can easily be turned into a smooth and silky soup. Just add 2 cups of vegetable stock after browning the parsnips, bring to a boil and purée.

2	pounds parsnips, peeled and thinly sliced
1	tablespoon extra virgin olive oil
1	large leek, quartered and thinly sliced
1	tablespoon grated fresh ginger
1	garlic clove, minced
1	tablespoon mirin
1	teaspoon curry powder

Water as needed

Sea salt

Chopped fresh parsley for garnish

Steam sliced parsnips until not quite tender (time will vary depending on how thick you've sliced your parsnips). Remove from heat and set aside.

In large pan over medium heat, sauté leek, ginger, garlic and mirin in oil until leeks are tender. Add curry powder and parsnips and sauté until parsnips start to brown. Deglaze pan with a little water, releasing any browned bits from the bottom of the pan. Season to taste with salt, top with chopped parsley and serve.

SERVES 4

Roasted Root Vegetables with Truffle Oil

I HAVE A TENDENCY TO EAT THE SAME VEGETABLES for weeks at a time, so every now and again I shop with the intention of buying only vegetables I haven't cooked recently, and that's how this recipe came to be. It usually disappears as soon as I make it, but on the rare occasion that I have some left over, I like to reheat it with cannellini beans or toss it with fresh watercress for a cooler, more cleansing combination.

12	Brussels sprouts
1	large rutabaga, peeled and diced
1	fennel bulb, halved and sliced into strips
1	daikon, peeled and diced
1	large onion, cut into wedges or 6 cipollini onions, peeled and halved
8	garlic cloves, peeled
2–3	tablespoons extra virgin olive oil
2	tablespoons balsamic vinegar
2	teaspoons coarse sea salt

White truffle oil

Chopped fresh tarragon

Preheat oven to 425°F.

Prepare Brussels sprouts by trimming off dry ends, peeling away any damaged leaves and cutting in half.

Place all vegetables in large bowl and toss with oil, vinegar and salt. Put into 2 glass roasting dishes and roast for 45 minutes or until caramelized. Toss vegetables every 10–15 minutes to prevent burning and encourage even browning. Remove from heat, drizzle with truffle oil, toss with fresh tarragon and serve.

SERVES 4

Spiced Sweet Potato Fries

ONE WAY TO WARD OFF CRAVINGS FOR non-nutritional sweets is to add more naturally sweet foods to your diet. Winter roots and squash offer that welcome addition to any meal, and cutting sweet potatoes into fries allows them to cook up in a snap. These fries are just as popular as leftovers as they are at mealtime.

3–4 sweet potatoes or yams

1 tablespoon extra virgin olive oil

1 tablespoon balsamic vinegar

1 tablespoon maple syrup

2 teaspoons cinnamon

Coarse sea salt

Juice of 1 lime, optional

Preheat oven to 400°F.

Wash potatoes and remove blemish spots and dried ends. Slice into sticks and place in large bowl. Drizzle on remaining ingredients except lime juice and toss to distribute evenly. Spread coated potatoes in single layer on cookie sheet and bake 10 minutes. Remove from oven, flip slices and bake another 10–20 minutes or until tender and browned. Cooking time will vary depending on thickness of potato slices. Toss with lime juice if desired and serve hot.

SERVES 6

VARIATION
Skip the vinegar, syrup and cinnamon for a simpler sweet and salty fry.

Sautéed Yams with Ginger and Lime

SOME RECIPES, LIKE BAKED SWEET POTATO FRIES, are so delicious and easy to make that we prepare them all the time. But after years of eating them no other way, I needed a change. I was looking for a new take on sweet potatoes, and a quicker way to get dinner on the table. Not only did it work, but the combination of flavors and texture of this dish were a hit from the start.

---

2   tablespoons
    extra virgin olive oil

2   tablespoons
    grated fresh ginger

1   red onion, minced

2   large yams or sweet
    potatoes, peeled and
    shredded

3   tablespoons lime juice

1   teaspoon ground nutmeg

Sea salt and freshly ground
    black pepper

In large sauté pan over medium heat, sauté ginger and onion in olive oil until soft (about 5 minutes). Add shredded yams and lime juice and increase heat to medium-high. Sauté 5–7 minutes or until yams start to soften. Season with nutmeg, and salt and pepper to taste. Cook 2–3 minutes longer. Remove from heat and serve.

SERVES 6

Root Veggie Fries

THESE ARE FAR FROM ORDINARY FRENCH FRIES. Use a variety of root vegetables for a colorful and sweet side dish that's rich in vitamins and nutrients. I like to double this recipe so I have leftovers to snack on the next day.

---

1   rutabaga, peeled

4   carrots

4   parsnips, peeled

3   tablespoons
     extra virgin olive oil

¼   cup yellow cornmeal

1   teaspoon coarse sea salt

½   teaspoon ground nutmeg

Cayenne pepper

Set oven to broil.

Cut vegetables into sticks and steam 3–4 minutes or until just tender. Remove from heat and place in large bowl. Coat with oil and toss with cornmeal, salt, nutmeg and cayenne. Lightly oil cookie sheet and spread out fries in single layer. Broil 3 minutes, then remove from oven, flip fries and broil another 3 minutes or until lightly browned. Serve hot.

SERVES 4

Three Sisters Deep-Dish Pie

THIS LIGHT AND EASY MEAL IN A POT requires just a little advance planning to roast the squash. The rest comes together quickly. Serve with Cranberry Chutney *(page 163)*, Apple Chutney *(page 164)* or Cranberry Applesauce *(page 241)* for a perfect finish.

---

2   medium delicata squash

2   tablespoons extra virgin olive oil, plus more for rubbing squash

1   large onion, diced

3   carrots, peeled and diced

3   stalks celery, diced

2   tablespoons mirin

½   pound green beans, trimmed

1½   cups corn, fresh or frozen

¾   cup water

2   tablespoons Bragg Liquid Aminos

2   tablespoons arrowroot

Freshly ground black pepper

1   frozen 9-inch pie crust, defrosted

Preheat oven to 400°F.

ROASTING SQUASH

Wash squash well, cut in half lengthwise, remove seeds and rub each section with some oil. Place cut side down on cookie sheet or in glass baking dish and roast 25 minutes or until soft throughout. Remove from heat and set aside.

PREPARING FILLING

In Dutch oven over medium heat, sauté onion in 2 tablespoons oil until soft (about 3 minutes). Add carrots, celery and mirin and sauté 3 minutes. Cut green beans into bite-size pieces, add to pot along with corn and sauté 5 minutes or until beans start to soften. Chop squash into bite-size pieces and fold into mixture.

In small bowl, whisk together water, liquid aminos and arrowroot until smooth. Pour into pot with vegetables and stir until liquid starts to thicken. Season to taste with pepper. Remove from heat and transfer to deep casserole.

FINISHING

Crumble pie crust over top of casserole and cover with foil. Bake 30 minutes. Remove foil and bake 8 minutes longer or until top is lightly browned. Remove from oven and serve.

SERVES 6

Sesame Brussels Sprout Sauté

I GREW UP DESPISING BRUSSELS SPROUTS but started cooking them on rare occasions after marrying a man who grew up loving them. I did not expect to fall for them myself, but once I learned the secret – to slice them thinly – I too became a believer. Using this recipe, I've since converted more non-lovers than I can count. A cast-iron skillet makes the difference in browning them to perfection.

---

16 Brussels sprouts

2   tablespoons extra virgin olive oil

4   garlic cloves, minced

1   tablespoon mirin

Water as needed

1   tablespoon toasted sesame oil

¼   cup toasted sesame seeds

Sea salt

Prepare Brussels sprouts by trimming off dry ends and peeling away any damaged outer leaves. With stems down, thinly slice and set aside (be sure to keep any leaves that fall off).

In large skillet over medium heat, sauté garlic in olive oil until soft. Add Brussels sprouts and mirin and sauté for 15 minutes. (Don't skimp on the time as extended cooking helps them caramelize and take on incredible flavor.) If they start to burn or stick to the bottom of the skillet, add water 1–2 tablespoons at a time to deglaze pan. Continue sautéing until sprouts start to brown. Remove from heat, toss with toasted sesame oil and sesame seeds. Season to taste with salt and serve.

SERVES 4

Rutabaga Purée with Orange and Ginger

THIS SWEET AND TANGY RUTABAGA purée makes a light, colorful and delicious change from potatoes or grains. The sweetness of this dish pairs nicely with bitter greens like Brussels sprouts or collard greens.

4–5 large rutabagas

1 tablespoon grated fresh ginger

1 cup orange juice

½ cup water, plus more as needed

Sea salt

Peel and chop rutabagas. Place in large pot with ginger, orange juice and ½ cup water. Bring to boil, reduce heat and simmer covered until soft throughout, adding water as needed to prevent burning. When soft, remove from heat and pour remaining liquid into separate bowl. Purée rutabagas with handheld blender, adding cooking liquid if needed to achieve desired texture. Season to taste with salt and serve.

SERVES 4

Roasted Squash with Fennel and Asparagus

ROASTING SQUASH BRINGS OUT ITS NATURAL SUGARS and blends the flavors of these vegetables beautifully. The slight bitterness of asparagus is a nice complement to these otherwise sweet vegetables and adds an always welcome splash of green. I like to serve this dish over pan-roasted millet.

1	large butternut squash, peeled, seeded and diced
1	large fennel bulb, halved, cored and thinly sliced
5	shallots, quartered
5	garlic cloves, peeled
2	tablespoons extra virgin olive oil
2	teaspoons balsamic vinegar
½	teaspoon coarse sea salt
2	pinches red pepper flakes
1	pound of asparagus, cut into 2-inch lengths
Chopped fresh parsley for garnish	

Preheat oven to 400°F.

In large bowl, combine squash, fennel, shallots and garlic. Add oil, vinegar, salt and pepper flakes and toss to coat evenly. Spread out vegetables on cookie sheet and roast 20 minutes. Remove from oven, fold in asparagus and return to oven for another 20 minutes or until all vegetables are tender. Garnish with parsley and serve.

SERVES 6

Savory Stuffed Pumpkins

TRY THIS RECIPE STUFFED in individual sweet pumpkins, delicata squash or acorn squash. For an even more dramatic presentation, clean out, roast and stuff a large hubbard squash.

1½ cups sweet brown rice

3 cups vegetable stock

1 thumb-size piece kombu

6 small sweet pumpkins (about 1½ pounds each)

1 8-ounce package tempeh

2 tablespoons grapeseed oil

2 tablespoons balsamic vinegar

2 tablespoons mirin

½ teaspoon cumin seeds

½ teaspoon coriander seeds

¼ teaspoon celery seeds

3 leeks, sliced

2 garlic cloves, minced

8 ounces cremini mushrooms

2 teaspoons fresh oregano or thyme leaves

Water

1 tablespoon prepared mustard

1 tablespoon tamari

Sea salt and freshly ground black pepper

1 cup chopped roasted cashews

PREPARING RICE

Soak rice for 1 hour in bowl with enough water to cover. Drain, rinse and place in pot with vegetable stock and kombu. Bring to boil, reduce heat and simmer covered 25 minutes or until liquid is absorbed. Remove from heat and discard kombu.

ROASTING PUMPKINS

Preheat oven to 400°F. Cut off tops of pumpkins and remove seeds. Replace tops, arrange on cookie sheet and roast 30 minutes or until just tender. Remove from the oven and set aside.

PREPARING STUFFING

While pumpkins are roasting, cut tempeh into 4 pieces and steam 10 minutes. Remove from heat and set aside to cool. Crumble tempeh into medium skillet and sauté over medium heat in 1 tablespoon oil until lightly browned. Stir in vinegar and mirin. Remove from heat and add mixture to rice.

Heat remaining tablespoon of oil in skillet over medium heat. Add cumin, coriander and celery seeds and stir. Add leeks, garlic, mushrooms and oregano and sauté 5 minutes. Deglaze as needed with 1 tablespoon of water at a time. Add to rice.

In small bowl, whisk together mustard and tamari. Season with salt and pepper and add to rice along with roasted cashews.

ASSEMBLING

Toss rice mixture to combine all ingredients, stuff into pumpkins and cover with tops. Place on cookie sheet, roast 40–45 minutes until pumpkins are cooked through and serve.

SERVES 6

Roasted Kabocha Squash and Creminis with Fresh Herbs

KABOCHA SQUASH HAS A SWEET AND THICK FLESH that requires very little fuss and cooks up surprisingly tender and delicious. When selecting kabocha, look for ones with smooth dark green outer skins. Irregularities on the skin are tough spots and should be cut away.

---

2   small or 1 large kabocha squash

2   leeks, sliced lengthwise and cut into ½-inch strips

3   tablespoons balsamic vinegar

3   tablespoons extra virgin olive oil

1   teaspoon coarse sea salt

1   pound cremini mushrooms, wiped clean

1   tablespoon minced fresh rosemary

1   tablespoon minced fresh sage

Preheat oven to 425°F.

Wash squash well, cut in half and remove seeds. Chop into bite-size pieces (leaving skin on) and toss in large bowl with leeks. Add vinegar, oil and salt. Spread out vegetables on a cookie sheet and roast 10 minutes. Remove from oven, add mushrooms and continue roasting another 10 minutes. Sprinkle with rosemary and sage and roast a final 10 minutes (a total of 30 minutes). Remove from oven and serve.

SERVES 6

Silky Sweet Potato Pie

CHICKPEA FLOUR IS RICH AND CREAMY and imparts wonderful texture and taste when used in baking. Combined with pecans, this crust becomes much more than a simple shell for a delicious filling. I serve this savory and sweet pie as a side dish but have also been known to sneak a piece for breakfast or make a pie just for snacking.

FILLING

3	medium sweet potatoes
¼	cup maple syrup
¼	cup rice milk
1	tablespoon vanilla extract
¼	teaspoon sea salt
½	teaspoon cinnamon
¼	teaspoon nutmeg
1	tablespoon arrowroot
1	teaspoon agar powder

CRUST

1½	cups pecans
¼	cup chickpea flour
2	tablespoons virgin coconut oil, melted, plus more to grease pie plate
2	tablespoons maple syrup

Pinch of sea salt

PREPARING SWEET POTATOES FOR FILLING

Preheat oven to 350°F. Wash sweet potatoes, place on cookie sheet and bake until soft (time will vary according to size of potatoes). Remove from oven and set aside.

PREPARING CRUST

Meanwhile, chop pecans in food processor until they resemble fine meal. Add chickpea flour and process briefly to combine. Add oil, syrup and salt and process to form dough. Lightly grease 9-inch pie plate, add dough and press to form even crust (about ¼-inch thick). Pierce several times with a fork and bake 12 minutes. Remove from oven and set on wire rack to cool.

PREPARING FILLING

When sweet potatoes are cool enough to handle, remove skins and cut into large pieces. Place in cleaned food processor bowl and add remaining filling ingredients. Process until smooth.

FINISHING

Pour filling into cooled pie crust, cover pie edges with foil and bake 50 minutes to 1 hour until lightly browned. Remove from oven and cool completely on wire rack. Serve at room temperature or cold.

SERVES 6–8

Stir-Fried Broccoli with Arame

IF YOU'RE NEW TO SEA VEGETABLES, arame is a great place to begin. Not only does it have a mild flavor and aroma, but it only needs to be soaked before using. This simple recipe is bursting with flavor, as well as alkalinizing calcium and minerals. Be sure to sauté the mushrooms for the full time to bring out their rich flavor.

½ cup dried arame

1 small bunch broccoli, cut into bite-size pieces

1 tablespoon extra virgin olive oil

½ red onion, diced

1 tablespoon tamari

10 shiitake mushroom caps, thinly sliced

Water as needed

Soak arame in 2 cups of water for 20 minutes. Drain and set aside. Steam broccoli until bright green and tender. Set aside.

In large skillet over medium heat, sauté onion in oil until soft and translucent (about 5 minutes). Add tamari and stir to deglaze the pan and caramelize the onions. Add mushrooms and sauté for 10 minutes. Deglaze pan with 1 tablespoon water at a time as needed. Add broccoli and arame, cook to heat through and serve.

SERVES 4

Arame with Caramelized Shiitakes

ARAME IS A RICH SOURCE of easily absorbable calcium and iron, is a powerful detoxifier, helps soften tissue masses, benefits the thyroid and supports hormone functions. Combined with shiitake mushrooms – known for their ability to lower blood cholesterol and regulate blood pressure – this recipe is definitely a nutritional heavy hitter.

---

1 cup dried arame

2 tablespoons grapeseed oil

12 shiitake mushroom caps, thinly sliced

2 tablespoons tamari

3–4 shallots, thinly sliced

2 carrots, shredded

1 3-inch piece daikon, peeled and cut into matchsticks

2 tablespoons mirin

2 tablespoons toasted sesame seeds

Toasted sesame oil

Sea salt

Place arame in bowl and fill with enough water to cover. Soak 20 minutes, rinse, drain and set aside.

In large skillet over medium heat, sauté shiitakes in grapeseed oil 10 minutes. If pan starts to stick, deglaze with 1 tablespoon tamari (or water) and continue stirring. (Even if mushrooms appear to be cooked, make sure to sauté the full time to bring out their richness, caramelized taste and texture.) Remove from heat and transfer mushrooms to a separate bowl. Return skillet to stovetop.

Heat remaining 1 tablespoon grapeseed oil in skillet and sauté shallots 3 minutes. Add carrots, daikon, mirin and remaining tablespoon tamari and sauté another 2–3 minutes. Add shiitakes and arame and heat through. Toss with toasted sesame seeds. Season to taste with sesame oil and sea salt and serve.

MAKES 6 servings

Wild Rice, Barley and Arame Salad

THIS SALAD COMBINES SOOTHING BARLEY (particularly healing to the stomach), with wild rice (high in protein) and arame (a sea vegetable high in absorbable calcium, iron and minerals). Talk about a powerhouse of a meal! Serve this salad as a side dish or enjoy its hearty flavors and textures as an energizing snack, a stand-alone salad or a light dinner.

½ cup hulled barley (not pearl) or gluten-free Job's tears

1 cup wild rice

3½ cups water

Pinch of sea salt

1 cup dried arame

1 cup roasted cashews, coarsely chopped

4 scallions, chopped

⅓ cup diced roasted red pepper

¼ cup toasted sesame seeds

3 tablespoons toasted sesame oil

1 tablespoon tamari

1½ teaspoons apple cider vinegar

Soak barley for 1 hour in bowl with enough water to cover. Drain, rinse and place in rice cooker or large pot. Add wild rice, water and salt. Cook 40 minutes or until liquid is absorbed. Set aside to cool before fluffing.

Meanwhile soak arame for 20 minutes in bowl with enough hot water to cover. Drain, rinse and set aside.

In large bowl, combine cooked grains, arame, cashews, scallions, roasted pepper and sesame seeds. In small bowl, whisk together sesame oil, tamari and vinegar. Pour over grains and toss to evenly coat. Serve at room temperature.

Note: If making this salad in advance, add cashews and scallions just before serving so they don't get soggy. Store salad in airtight container in refrigerator for up to 4 days.

SERVES 6

Millet, Aduki Beans and Corn with Lemon Dressing

THIS RECIPE COMBINES SAVORY, NUTTY MILLET with sweet corn and sour lemon for a dish that is as pleasing to the eye as it is to the palate. For a complete meal, serve this dish warm with greens or enjoy it chilled for a light lunch or snack.

---

1   cup millet

2   cups water

Pinch of sea salt

2   cups cooked aduki beans, rinsed well

¼   cup diced red onion

1   cup corn, fresh or frozen and thawed

½   cup chopped fresh parsley

DRESSING

2   tablespoons extra virgin olive oil

2   tablespoons lemon juice

¼   teaspoon ground cumin

Zest of 1 lemon

Sea salt and freshly ground black pepper

Place millet, water and pinch of salt in rice cooker or large pot over high heat. Cover and bring to boil. Reduce heat to low and cook covered until all water is absorbed (about 25 minutes). Remove from heat and cool 5 minutes (so that it does not turn to mush when fluffed).

Fluff millet and add aduki beans, onion, corn and parsley. In small bowl, whisk together dressing ingredients and pour over grain mixture. Fold to combine and serve. If serving chilled, fluff again gently with fork before serving.

SERVES 6

Refried Pinto Beans with Chiles

LEGUMES DON'T GET EASIER THAN THIS. Pinto beans are creamy and savory and require little fuss. I enjoy these beans as a side dish, stuffed into tacos and burritos, or served simply with brown rice, chopped tomato, lettuce and avocado.

2	tablespoons grapeseed oil
3	garlic cloves, minced
1	small onion, diced
4	cups cooked pinto beans
2	4-ounce cans chopped green chiles
1	teaspoon chile powder
1	teaspoon ground cumin
½	teaspoon sea salt
2	tablespoons lime juice
Chopped fresh cilantro for garnish	

In sauté pan or Dutch oven over medium heat, sauté garlic and onion in oil until soft (about 3 minutes). Add beans and remaining ingredients except cilantro and sauté another 3–4 minutes. With the back of a wooden spoon, gently mash the beans to your desired consistency. (I like my finished product to be fairly chunky so I mash only half the beans.) Remove from heat, top with cilantro and serve.

SERVES 6

White Beans and Escarole

I FIRST TASTED ESCAROLE WITH WHITE BEANS when my mother-in-law made it. I remember the aroma of the sautéed garlic luring me into her kitchen and the escarole melting in my mouth. From the very first bite, I was hooked. She makes hers with a bit of stock and *ancini ∂i pepe* (tiny pasta pearls). I like to serve mine with a crusty sourdough or Italian bread, which comes in handy for cleaning the plate when you're done.

---

2 tablespoons extra virgin olive oil

6 garlic cloves, minced

3½ cups cooked great northern or navy beans

2 large heads escarole, chopped

2 tablespoons flax seed oil or extra virgin olive oil

5 dashes ume plum vinegar

Gomasio

In Dutch oven over medium heat, sauté garlic in olive oil until soft (about 2 minutes). Add beans and escarole and stir until escarole starts to wilt. Continue cooking 3 minutes. Remove from heat, drizzle with flax oil and vinegar and toss to combine. Sprinkle with gomasio and serve.

SERVES 4 as a side dish

VARIATION
Turn this dish into a rich, nondairy cream soup by adding 3–4 cups vegetable stock, simmer 5 minutes, purée with handheld blender and serve.

Sweet Potato and Black Bean Burritos with Cashew Cheese

I LOVE MEXICAN FOOD, and while I do not usually crave spicy foods, I find many spicy Mexican dishes to be surprisingly cooling as well. Complete your menu by serving these burritos with Traditional Guacamole *(page 100)* and Tofu Sour Cream *(page 104),* topped with sautéed collard greens or chopped avocado and cilantro.

BURRITOS

3	sweet potatoes or yams
½	cup corn, fresh or frozen
3	tablespoons lime juice
1½	cups cooked black beans
½	red onion, diced
1	large tomato, diced
8–10	soft corn tortillas
1½	cups prepared salsa
¼	cup chopped scallions

CASHEW CHEESE

½	cup cashew pieces
¼	cup nutritional yeast
1	tablespoon extra virgin olive oil

Preheat oven to 400°F.

PREPARING SWEET POTATOES FOR BURRITOS

Place sweet potatoes on baking sheet or foil and bake 45 minutes or until soft. Remove from oven and cool.

PREPARING CASHEW CHEESE

In food processor, grind cashews to a fine meal. Add nutritional yeast and process briefly to combine. Add oil and process until you have a moist meal (do not overprocess or meal will become dough-like). Set aside.

ASSEMBLING BURRITOS

Set oven to broil. Place corn in strainer. Bring 1 cup water to boil and pour over corn to blanch or thaw.

Peel sweet potatoes and mash with lime juice. Fold in black beans, onion and tomato. Spoon filling into center of each tortilla, roll up and place, seam side down in shallow casserole. Spoon salsa over top and broil 3 minutes. Remove from broiler, top with cashew cheese and corn and broil 2 more minutes, watching closely to keep cheese from burning. Remove from broiler, top with chopped scallions and serve.

SERVES 8

Scrambled Tofu

THIS DISH MAKES A QUICK AND EASY PROTEIN-FILLED BREAKFAST.
For a colorful and complete meal, try it served with salsa and sautéed greens or wrap it all up in a corn tortilla for a meal on the go.

1	pound fresh firm or extra firm tofu
2	tablespoons extra virgin olive oil
1	onion, chopped
1	carrot, grated
1	cup cremini mushrooms, thinly sliced
1	tablespoon tamari

Wrap tofu in towels and press to remove excess water.

In large skillet over medium heat, sauté onion in olive oil until soft (about 3 minutes). Add carrot and mushrooms and sauté 3 minutes longer until mushrooms are soft. Mash tofu and add to the pan. Season with tamari and sauté 5 minutes. Remove from heat and serve.

SERVES 4

VARIATION
Add 1 tablespoon grated fresh turmeric root and 1 cup chopped kale or collard greens to your sauté to increase the nutritional value of this dish.

Marinated Tofu with Ginger Cashew Dipping Sauce

I LOVE TO KEEP BAKED TOFU IN THE HOUSE as a snack, but this rich and delicious dipping sauce makes it great for mealtime as well. Be sure to cook enough to compensate for the pieces that you'll sneak before it gets to the table. Serve on skewers satay-style for a fun presentation.

2	pounds firm tofu (not silken)
1	tablespoon grated fresh ginger
¼	cup Bragg Liquid Aminos
1	tablespoon chickpea or mellow white miso
1	garlic clove, minced
1	tablespoon toasted sesame oil
⅓	cup orange juice
2	tablespoons water

DIPPING SAUCE

1	tablespoon grapeseed oil
2	garlic cloves, minced
1	tablespoon grated fresh ginger
2	scallions, minced
3	tablespoons tamari
2	tablespoons maple syrup
⅓	cup coconut milk
1	cup finely ground cashews
¼	cup water
1	tablespoon toasted sesame oil
	Hot pepper sauce

PREPARING TOFU

Slice tofu lengthwise into ½-inch strips. In shallow baking dish, combine ginger, liquid aminos, miso, garlic, sesame oil, orange juice and 2 tablespoons water. Place tofu in dish and coat with marinade (flipping to coat both sides). Set aside to marinate 30 minutes.

Preheat oven to 400°F. Place tofu on ungreased baking sheet and save leftover marinade. Bake 15 minutes. Remove pan from oven, flip tofu, baste with remaining marinade and bake another 15 minutes.

PREPARING SAUCE

In small skillet over medium heat, gently sauté garlic and ginger in grapeseed oil for 2 minutes. Add scallions and sauté another 2 minutes. Add tamari, syrup, coconut milk, cashews and ¼ cup water and stir to combine. Increase heat briefly and then reduce heat and simmer 10 minutes, stirring occasionally, to combine flavors. Remove from heat and season to taste with toasted sesame oil and hot pepper sauce.

Serve tofu with sauce on side or drizzled on top.

SERVES 4

Baked Maple Mustard Tempeh

STEAMED TEMPEH PUFFS UP, allowing it to absorb more flavors and making it a nice complement to dark leafy greens. If I can keep myself from eating the tempeh straight out of the oven, I like to serve this dish with whole grains and vegetables or stuffed in a sandwich with watercress, grated carrots and avocado.

2	8-ounce packages tempeh
¼	cup extra virgin olive oil
2	garlic cloves, minced
2	tablespoons prepared mustard
2	tablespoons maple syrup or molasses
2	tablespoons lime juice
2	tablespoons tamari

Slice tempeh across into ½-inch strips and steam 10 minutes.

In shallow baking dish, whisk together remaining ingredients. Place steamed tempeh in marinade and flip to coat each side. Marinate for 30 minutes.

Preheat oven to 375°F.

Place tempeh with marinade in oven and roast 15 minutes. Remove from oven, flip tempeh and return to roast another 10 minutes. Remove from oven, serve hot or refrigerate for later use.

SERVES 4

Seitan Walnut Stuffed Collard Greens

AFTER THE FIRST FROST, collard greens in New England get heartier and sweeter. This dish is great for company because you can make it in advance, cover it with foil, refrigerate and then bake it just before your guests arrive. Ginger Pear Sauce *(page 161)* is a perfect accompaniment.

8	large collard green leaves
½	cup plus 2 tablespoons grated mochi

FILLING

1	pound seitan
1	tablespoon grapeseed oil
1	small onion, chopped
8–10	cremini mushrooms, diced
½	cup dried unsweetened cranberries
¼	cup mirin
1	cup toasted and chopped walnuts
1	tablespoon dried sage
Sea salt and freshly ground black pepper	

SAUCE

1½	cups chopped tomatoes
1	cup vegetable stock
3	tablespoons maple syrup
2	tablespoons lemon juice

PREPARING COLLARDS

Bring medium pot of water to boil. Cut stems at base of collard leaf and discard. Submerge whole leaves in boiling water for 1 minute. Drain, rinse with cold water and set aside.

PREPARING FILLING

Grind seitan in food processor using the pulse setting. In large pan over medium heat, sauté onion in oil until soft. Add mushrooms and cook 3 minutes. Add seitan, cranberries, mirin and walnuts and cook to heat through. Add sage, and salt and pepper to taste and remove from heat.

PREPARING SAUCE

In pot over medium heat, combine all sauce ingredients and cook for 4 minutes. Remove from heat and purée gently with handheld blender.

ASSEMBLING

Preheat oven to 350°F.

Lay collard leaf on cutting board. On the largest part of the leaf, sprinkle 1 tablespoon grated mochi plus enough filling to cover a third of the wide end of the leaf. Fold sides of leaf over filling, then roll up the leaf to enclose filling. Place stuffed leaf stem side down in baking dish. Repeat to fill casserole and use all filling. Sprinkle top with remaining 2 tablespoons mochi and pour sauce evenly over rolls in baking dish. Cover with foil and bake 30 minutes. Remove from oven and serve.

GLUTEN-FREE OPTION
Substitute 2 cups cooked wild rice for ground seitan.

SERVES 6

Tofu Kale Lasagna

THIS IS ONE OF MY MOST REQUESTED RECIPES, and not just because it's my daughter's favorite. Tofu can be used to achieve many different tastes and textures in lasagna. I've used fresh firm tofu in this version, but you can substitute silken tofu for a cheesier texture or freeze your tofu first for a meatier texture.

5–7	sun-dried tomatoes
12	lasagna noodles
6	tablespoons extra virgin olive oil
4	garlic cloves, minced
1	large onion, chopped
8–10	ounces cremini mushrooms, sliced
2	pounds fresh firm tofu
2	tablespoons mirin
2	teaspoons dried basil
2	teaspoons dried parsley
2	bunches kale, finely chopped
	Sea salt and freshly ground black pepper
4	cups tomato sauce
1½	cups grated soy or rice mozzarella

Preheat oven to 375°F. In small bowl, soak sun-dried tomatoes in enough hot water to cover. When soft, drain, chop and set aside. Cook lasagna noodles until just soft. Drain and set aside.

PREPARING FILLING

In large pot over medium heat, sauté garlic and onions in oil until soft. Add mushrooms and sauté 3 minutes. Drain tofu, wrap in towels, press to remove excess water and crumble into pot. Add mirin, sun-dried tomatoes, basil and parsley and sauté 5 minutes. Fold in kale, cover and cook 3 minutes. Season to taste with salt and pepper and remove from heat.

ASSEMBLING

Spread ½ cup tomato sauce over bottom of 9 x 12-inch lasagna pan. Place single layer of noodles over sauce and cover with half the kale mixture. Cover with 1½ cups tomato sauce. Sprinkle with ½ cup soy mozzarella. Cover with another layer of noodles and remaining kale mixture. Add 1½ cups sauce, ½ cup soy mozzarella, and final layer of noodles, ½ cup sauce and remaining soy mozzarella. Cover tightly with foil and bake 35 minutes. Remove foil and bake 10 more minutes. Remove from oven and set aside for 10 minutes before serving.

SERVES 8

VARIATION

For a meatier texture, freeze tofu first, then defrost, press out excess liquid, place in food processor and process to crumble. Add to filling as described above. Add extra liquid before adding kale – I use ½ cup tomato sauce thinned with ½ cup water. Add an additional cup of sauce to the tofu mixture to season. Add kale and proceed as above.

Skillet Cornbread

CORNBREAD IS A MUST WITH EVERYTHING from Savory "Unbaked" Beans *(page 272)* to Sweet Potato and Black Bean Burritos *(page 206)*. The addition of whole corn kernels, red pepper and jalapeño pepper make this cornbread burst with flavor and color. For a richer taste, add one cup of shredded Cheddar-style rice or soy cheese. I bake it the traditional southern way, in a seasoned cast-iron skillet, to produce a crisp outside. Serve it straight from the skillet for an authentic and easy presentation.

½   cup corn flour

½   cup yellow cornmeal

1   cup millet flour

2   teaspoons powdered egg replacer

1   teaspoon baking powder

½   teaspoon baking soda

½   teaspoon salt

1   cup rice milk

3   tablespoons maple syrup

3   tablespoons extra virgin olive oil, plus more for skillet

1   jalapeño, seeded and minced

½   red bell pepper, minced

1   cup corn, fresh or frozen

Preheat oven to 375°F.

In large bowl, combine all dry ingredients. In separate bowl, combine all wet ingredients including the jalapeño, red pepper and corn. Pour wet ingredients into dry and mix to combine.

Heat a well-seasoned 10-inch cast-iron skillet over medium-high heat until hot. Pour in enough olive oil to coat the bottom and sides. Pour batter into skillet and spread it out evenly. Remove from burner, place in oven and bake 20 minutes or until a toothpick inserted in center comes out clean. Remove from oven and place on wire rack to cool and set before serving.

SERVES 8

Quinoa with Sweet Corn

I NEVER GET TIRED OF NATIVE SWEET CORN, and I especially like using leftover grilled corn for this recipe. By combining corn with quinoa, which takes only 15 minutes to cook, and some sautéed greens, you'll have a complete meal that your whole family will love.

---

1   cup quinoa

1½ cups water

Sea salt

1   tablespoon
    extra virgin olive oil

1   small onion, chopped

1½ cups corn, fresh or frozen

2   tablespoons
    chopped fresh parsley

Extra virgin olive oil or
    toasted sesame oil

Rinse and drain quinoa and place in pot with water and salt. Bring to boil, cover, reduce heat to low and simmer 15 minutes or until water is absorbed. Remove quinoa from heat and set aside to cool slightly before fluffing.

In large skillet or Dutch oven over medium heat, sauté chopped onion in olive oil until soft. Add corn and heat through. Fold in quinoa and parsley and drizzle with olive oil or toasted sesame oil. Season to taste with salt and serve.

SERVES 6

Multigrain Pilaf with Toasted Sunflower Seeds

SUNFLOWER SEEDS IN THIS RECIPE BRING OUT the nutty flavors of the grains and turn this simple dish into something special. Experiment with different grain and seed combinations for a variety of tastes and textures.

½ cup hulled barley (not pearl)

½ cup sweet brown rice

⅔ cup sunflower seeds

½ cup millet

3 cups water

1 thumb-size piece kombu

1 tablespoon extra virgin olive oil

1 large onion, diced

Chopped fresh parsley

Soak barley and sweet brown rice for 1 hour in bowl with enough water to cover. Drain, rinse and drain again.

Meanwhile, preheat oven to 250°F.

Spread sunflower seeds on cookie sheet and roast 8–10 minutes until golden brown. Remove from oven and set aside to cool.

Rinse millet, place in large Dutch oven over medium heat and dry-roast until fragrant. Add barley, sweet brown rice, 3 cups water and kombu and bring to boil. Cover, reduce heat and simmer until water is absorbed (about 35 minutes). Remove from heat, discard kombu and let set 5 minutes before fluffing.

In large skillet over medium heat, sauté onion in olive oil until soft. Add to grains and stir to combine. Top with sunflower seeds, garnish with chopped parsley and serve.

GLUTEN-FREE OPTION
Substitute Job's tears for barley.

SERVES 8

Pan-Roasted Millet with Pumpkin Seeds

THE FIRST TIME I MADE MILLET FOR MY CHILDREN it was not a hit. The next time I made it I used four times the amount of water and called it porridge. They devoured it. After a year of porridge, I made the millet with the regular amount of water and served it with dinner. They didn't even flinch. Both said, "Yeah, porridge!" and continued to eat it as if I hadn't changed a thing.

---

1   cup millet
1   cup water
1   cup vegetable stock
    Pinch of sea salt
2   tablespoons flax seed oil
    or extra virgin olive oil
½   teaspoon
    ume plum vinegar
¼   cup plain or tamari-
    roasted pumpkin seeds

Rinse and drain millet. Place in Dutch oven over medium heat and dry-roast until water is absorbed and millet starts to give off a nutty aroma. Add water, stock and salt, cover, reduce heat and simmer until all liquid is absorbed (about 25 minutes). Set aside to cool slightly then fluff with fork, drizzle with flax seed oil and vinegar and toss. Top with toasted pumpkin seeds and serve.

SERVES 4

VARIATION
Fold ¼ cup reconstituted goji berries into the millet after fluffing to add sweetness and a burst of color and antioxidants.

Quinoa with Almonds and Currants

QUINOA IS MUCH LIGHTER THAN OTHER GRAINS and every bit as satisfying. Cooking quinoa with currants as I do here imparts a sweetness that is then balanced with savory and pungent spices. Serve it as a side dish, or press the quinoa into small ramekins, then release the molded quinoa onto plates composed for individual servings.

1½	cups quinoa
2¼	cups water
¼	cup currants
	Pinch of sea salt
1	tablespoon extra virgin olive oil
1	red onion, diced
¼	teaspoon ground cinnamon
¼	teaspoon ground ginger
¼	teaspoon ground coriander
⅛	teaspoon ground turmeric
¾	teaspoon ground cumin
3	tablespoons toasted sliced almonds
¼	cup chopped fresh parsley
Sea salt and freshly ground black pepper	

Rinse quinoa and place in large pot or rice cooker with water, currants and salt. Bring to boil, then reduce heat and simmer 15 minutes or until all water is absorbed. Let cool slightly before fluffing with fork.

In large skillet over medium heat, sauté onion and spices in oil until soft (about 5 minutes). Fold into cooked quinoa along with almonds and parsley. Season to taste with salt and pepper and serve.

Note: To make this dish less sweet, cook quinoa without currants and add them at the end with the almonds and parsley.

SERVES 6

Stovetop Barley with Sweet Vegetables

THIS IS THE QUINTESSENTIAL "MEAL IN A POT." When I first taught this recipe in one of my classes, I purposely neglected to mention that Brussels sprouts were a significant ingredient. Once there, all felt obliged to at least try a taste, and every Brussels sprout hater loved this dish.

---

1   cup hulled barley
    (not pearl) or
    gluten-free Job's tears

½   cup brown rice

1   thumb-size piece kombu

2   tablespoons tamari

4½ cups water or vegetable
    stock, plus more as
    needed

1   onion, chopped

3   carrots, chopped

1   rutabaga, peeled
    and cubed

12 Brussels sprouts, halved

1   small fennel bulb, halved,
    cored and sliced

Extra virgin olive oil

Ume plum vinegar

Chopped fresh parsley
    for garnish

Soak barley and brown rice together for 1 hour in bowl with enough water to cover. Rinse and drain grains and place in large pot or Dutch oven. Add kombu, tamari and water or stock. Cover and bring to boil.

When grains start to boil, add vegetables in order listed. Cover, reduce heat and simmer 2–2½ hours. Add more water or stock as needed to achieve desired consistency. Remove from heat and drizzle with olive oil and several dashes of vinegar. Garnish with parsley and serve directly from the pot.

SERVES 6

Kabocha Squash Stuffed with Brown Rice and Chickpea Pilaf

HEARTY KABOCHA MAKES A GREAT EDIBLE SERVING DISH for a variety of stuffings, including sweet brown rice, wild rice and quinoa.

---

1   kabocha squash

Extra virgin olive oil

½   cup chopped
      toasted pecans

BROWN RICE STUFFING

1   cup medium grain
      brown rice

2   cups water

1   thumb-size piece kombu

⅓   cup currants

1   teaspoon ground allspice

1   tablespoon dried dill

2   tablespoons grapeseed oil

1   onion, chopped

1½   cups cooked chickpeas

½   cup toasted pine nuts

¼   cup chopped fresh parsley

Juice of 1 lemon

Sea salt and freshly ground
      black pepper

PREPARING RICE FOR STUFFING

Soak rice for 1 hour in bowl with enough water to cover. Drain, place rice in pot with 2 cups fresh water, kombu, currants, allspice and dill. Bring to boil, then reduce heat, cover and simmer 30 minutes or until water is absorbed. Set aside to cool.

ROASTING SQUASH

Preheat oven to 400°F. Wash squash well and cut in half from top to bottom. Remove seeds and rub skin and flesh with olive oil. Place cut side down on cookie sheet and roast 25 minutes or until soft (time will vary according to size of squash).

PREPARING STUFFING

In large skillet over medium heat, sauté onion in grapeseed oil until soft (about 3 minutes). Remove kombu from rice and discard. Add rice and chickpeas to onion in skillet and sauté 3 minutes. Remove from heat and toss with pine nuts, parsley and lemon juice. Season to taste with salt and pepper.

FINISHING

Slice cooked squash into boats, place on individual plates or group on a platter. Spoon brown rice stuffing over the center so that it spills down on each side, sprinkle with toasted pecans and serve.

SERVES 4

Sweet Dumpling Squash with Orange-Scented Quinoa Stuffing

DUMPLING SQUASH IS NOT ONLY SWEET AND DELICIOUS, it also makes a very pretty presentation. Serve it sliced into boat shapes, cut into rings or stuffed with grains, as I've done here.

6	small dumpling squash (one per person)
2	tablespoons extra virgin olive oil, plus more for rubbing squash
2	cups quinoa
3½	cups water
Pinch of sea salt	
6	shallots, diced
1	pound cremini mushrooms, thinly sliced
2	tablespoons mirin
3	stalks celery, diced
1	cup dried cranberries
½	teaspoon ground nutmeg
1	cup toasted pine nuts
2	tablespoons walnut oil
2	tablespoons fresh orange peel
½	cup chopped fresh parsley, plus more for garnish
Sea salt and freshly ground black pepper	

ROASTING SQUASH

Preheat oven to 450°F. Wash squash well. Rub each squash with some oil and place whole on parchment-lined cookie sheet. Bake 45 minutes or until just soft (time will vary depending on size of squash). Remove from oven and set aside.

PREPARING QUINOA

Rinse and drain quinoa. Place in large pot with water and salt and bring to boil. Cover, reduce heat and simmer 15 minutes or until all liquid is absorbed. Set aside to cool slightly.

PREPARING STUFFING

In large skillet over medium heat, sauté shallots and mushrooms in 2 tablespoons olive oil until soft. Add mirin, celery, cranberries and nutmeg and sauté 3 minutes longer. Fluff quinoa with fork and add to the skillet. Remove from heat, fold in pine nuts, walnut oil, orange peel and parsley. Season to taste with salt and pepper.

ASSEMBLING

Carefully cut a circle around the stem of each squash to remove the "lid." Scoop out seeds and fill with stuffing. Top with a sprinkle of fresh parsley, set lid on side and serve.

SERVES 6

Mediterranean Pasta with Greens

I'VE BEEN MAKING THIS DISH FOR YEARS. It wasn't as much a recipe as it was a quick and easy meal that everyone liked. It could be because the ingredients were always available in my kitchen, or simply because it was so yummy and satisfying.

---

1 pound penne or fusilli

3 tablespoons extra virgin olive oil

3 garlic cloves, minced

1 small onion, chopped

1 tablespoon dried basil

2 teaspoons dried oregano

1½ cups cooked chickpeas

2 cups canned diced tomatoes with their liquid

2 tablespoons tomato paste

¼ cup mirin

1 small bunch kale, chopped into bite-size pieces

Sea salt and freshly ground black pepper

Chopped fresh parsley for garnish

Cook pasta according to directions on package. Rinse, drain and return to pot. Drizzle with 1 tablespoon olive oil and set aside.

In large Dutch oven over medium heat, sauté garlic and onion in remaining 2 tablespoons olive oil until soft (about 3 minutes). Add basil, oregano, chickpeas, tomatoes, tomato paste and mirin. Sauté 5 minutes more. Add kale, then cover and cook 3 minutes or until soft. Uncover and stir to combine all ingredients. Season with salt and lots of pepper and toss with pasta. Cook to heat through, garnish with parsley and serve.

SERVES 6

Apple Crisp

A GUILT-FREE VERSION OF AN ALL-TIME FAVORITE. To make the topping gluten-free, use brown rice flour instead of whole wheat and substitute chopped nuts for the oats.

FILLING

12 apples (peeled, unpeeled or both), cored and sliced

¼ cup maple syrup

2 teaspoons ground cinnamon

⅓ cup dried currants

1 tablespoon brown rice flour

TOPPING

2 cups rolled oats

1 cup brown rice flour or almond meal

½ cup chopped walnuts

1 tablespoon ground cinnamon

½ cup maple syrup

½ cup virgin coconut oil, melted

Preheat oven to 375°F.

To prepare filling, place apples in large bowl. Fold in syrup, cinnamon and currants. Sprinkle on flour and gently fold until combined. Spread mixture into 9 x 12-inch baking casserole.

To make topping, use the same mixing bowl and combine oats, flour, nuts and cinnamon. In separate bowl, whisk together syrup and oil, add to dry ingredients and mix until crumbly. Spread topping evenly over apples, cover with foil and bake 30 minutes. Remove foil and bake an additional 20 minutes or until apples are cooked through. Remove from oven and serve.

SERVES 8–10

Ginger Pear Crisp

CRISPS ARE SO EASY TO MAKE, and in my family they're served not only for dessert but for breakfast or a midday snack, too. This one tastes great with a scoop of vanilla bean ice (or rice) cream. As with my Apple Crisp recipe *(page 224),* this is easily made gluten-free by substituting brown rice flour for wheat and using chopped nuts in place of oats for the topping.

FILLING

8	large pears (Bosc or D'Anjou work well)
¼	cup maple syrup
1	teaspoon almond extract
2	teaspoons grated fresh ginger

Zest and juice of 1 lemon

Zest of 1 orange

½	cup apple juice or cider
1	tablespoon arrowroot

TOPPING

2	cups rolled oats
1	cup brown rice flour or almond meal
1	cup toasted sliced almonds

Pinch of sea salt

½	cup maple syrup
⅓	cup virgin coconut oil, melted
1	teaspoon almond extract

Preheat oven to 350°F.

Peel, core and slice pears and place in large casserole.

In medium bowl, combine syrup, almond extract, ginger, lemon zest, lemon juice, orange zest and apple juice. Whisk in arrowroot until dissolved, pour mixture evenly over pears and set aside.

Prepare topping in separate bowl by combining oats, flour, almonds and sea salt. In separate bowl, whisk together syrup, oil and almond extract. Add wet ingredients to dry, fold to combine, then sprinkle over pears. Cover with foil and bake 35 minutes. Remove foil and bake another 15 minutes or until crumb topping is crisp and lightly browned. Remove from oven and serve warm.

SERVES 8–10

Chocolate Lover's Tart

LET'S FACE IT – WE ALL HAVE CRAVINGS we simply can't deny! You might as well make peace with them and enjoy. This recipe comes together so easily, you may find yourself making it far too often. But, seeing as it doesn't call for eggs, brown sugar, butter or even white flour, you can go ahead and enjoy it without nearly as much guilt.

CRUST

2	cups pecans
1	cup brown rice flour
¼	cup cacao powder
¼	teaspoon sea salt
⅓	cup virgin coconut oil, melted
⅓	cup maple syrup

FILLING

12½	ounces firm silken tofu
½	cup cashew butter
¼	cup maple syrup
1	teaspoon vanilla extract
Pinch of sea salt	
1	cup semisweet or dark chocolate chips
1	6-ounce block dark chocolate for shaving (I like 70%)

Preheat oven to 350°F. Lightly oil an 11-inch tart pan.

PREPARING CRUST

Combine pecans, rice flour, cacao and salt in food processor to make a crumb-like mixture. Add oil and syrup and process to form a moist ball. Place ball in tart pan and press to form crust. Pierce several times with a fork and bake 15 minutes or until lightly browned. Remove from oven and set on wire rack to cool completely.

MAKING FILLING

Whip tofu in food processor until smooth. Add cashew butter, syrup, vanilla and salt and process until well combined. In small pan over low heat, melt chocolate chips, then add to food processor and blend until combined.

FINISHING

Pour chocolate mixture into tart shell, smooth top with spatula and refrigerate at least 30 minutes. With a sturdy chef's knife, shave chocolate from block, spread evenly over tart and serve.

SERVES 8–10

Maple Poached Pears

POACHED PEARS ARE SIMPLE AND SATISFYING and will fill your house with the most wonderful aroma. Serve them on their own, with ice cream or in a small pool of syrup and topped with chopped nuts. Save the syrup to serve over ice cream, pancakes or French toast or mixed with hot tea for a special warming after-dinner drink.

4–6 ripe, but firm, pears
1 cup water
1 cup maple syrup
Zest of 1 lemon or orange
1 teaspoon vanilla extract
4–5 whole cloves
1 cinnamon stick
1 1-inch piece gingerroot, peeled and thinly sliced

In large pot over medium heat, combine all ingredients except pears and bring to simmer. Cut pears in half, remove cores and place in simmering syrup. Cook 20 minutes then remove from heat, let cool slightly and serve.

SERVES 4

Green Tea Poached Pears with Pomegranate Glaze and Pistachios

THIS DESSERT HAS A LITTLE SOMETHING FOR EVERYONE. Cool and refreshing pears, bitter green tea, salty pistachios and plenty of color for a beautiful presentation.

---

6 cups water

3 green tea teabags

½ cup maple syrup

6 pears, peeled, halved and cored

½ cup roasted pistachios, finely chopped

Mint leaves for garnish

GLAZE

1½ cups pomegranate juice

1 cup water

½ cup maple syrup

1½ tablespoons arrowroot dissolved in 3 tablespoons water

PREPARING PEARS

In large pot, bring water to boil. Add teabags and maple syrup, turn off heat, cover and steep 5 minutes (longer steeping will make tea bitter). Remove teabags, add pears and bring to simmer. Poach pears until tender but still held together (6–10 minutes depending on ripeness). Remove poached pears with slotted spoon and let cool.

Make glaze in medium pot by stirring juice, water and syrup together over medium-high heat until liquid is reduced by half. Remove from heat and immediately stir in dissolved arrowroot. Refrigerate until ready to use.

To serve, place pear halves decoratively on each plate, drizzle with pomegranate glaze and top with chopped pistachios. Garnish with mint leaves and serve.

SERVES 6

Tofu Pumpkin Pie with Gingersnap Crust

EVERY THANKSGIVING I MAKE TWO OF THESE PIES —one for the company and one to enjoy with our leftovers. An easy way to make a terrific crust is with store-bought gingersnaps. If possible, make this pie a day ahead to allow pie to set and flavors to blend.

CRUST

2   heaping cups gluten-free gingersnaps

3   tablespoons virgin coconut oil, melted

3   tablespoons maple syrup

FILLING

12   ounces silken extra firm or firm tofu

2   cups cooked pumpkin purée

½   cup maple syrup

1   teaspoon vanilla extract

1   generous tablespoon pumpkin pie spice

Preheat oven to 350°F.

Place ginger snaps in food processor and process until they resemble coarse flour. In separate bowl, whisk together melted coconut oil and 3 tablespoons maple syrup. Add to food processor and process to combine. Transfer to a lightly greased 9-inch pie plate and press down to form crust.

Meanwhile, wrap tofu in towels and press to remove excess water. In clean food processor bowl, process tofu until smooth. Scrape down sides of bowl and process again to incorporate all the tofu. Add all remaining filling ingredients and process until smooth and well combined. Pour into pie crust, cover edges with foil to prevent burning and bake 50 minutes or until lightly browned. Remove from oven and set aside for 1 hour to cool and set. Serve at room temperature.

SERVES 8

Glazed Oranges with Pomegranate Seeds

POMEGRANATES ARE IN SEASON for such a short time that I like to use them as much as possible to satisfy me until the next year. This is a very simple yet decadent, refreshing and festive-looking dessert.

4	oranges
1	pomegranate
½	cup water
¼	cup maple syrup
1	cinnamon stick
5	cloves
Zest of 1 orange	
Zest and juice of 1 lemon	

Remove and discard peel and outside skin from oranges and slice oranges across into rounds. Place in serving dish and set aside. Cut pomegranate in half. Remove seeds from one half and add to bowl with oranges. Set the other half aside.

In small pot over medium heat, combine water with syrup, cinnamon stick, cloves, zests and lemon juice. Bring to boil, reduce heat and simmer 7 minutes to reduce to a glaze. Remove from heat. Squeeze remaining pomegranate through a sieve to get juice and stir into glaze. Pour over oranges and serve warm or chilled.

SERVES 4

Winter is the time of promise
because there is so little to do –
or because you can now and then permit
yourself the luxury of thinking so.

STANLEY CRAWFORD

Winter

The early weeks of winter feel like one long celebration of food as I taste my way through a never-ending series of holiday parties. Aromatic roasted nuts, sugary winter squashes, savory wild rices, exotic mushrooms and decadent sweets tempt me at every turn and prove that all food tastes best when shared with friends and family. By mid-January, I am completely content with winter's simple menu of warming soups and stews, casseroles, roasted roots and sautéed greens. Soups and sauces simmer all day in my kitchen and fill my home with wonderful aromas. The freezer and pantry overflow with freshly frozen and canned foods – the summer's pesto, berries from the picking patch and freshly pickled beets and beans – all ready to add just enough spice to winter's comforting menu. Everything about winter, from its short, cold days to its simple and sweet tastes, allows my mind and body to rest.

WINTER

DIPS, DRESSINGS AND MORE

Maple Apple Vinaigrette 236
Pomegranate Vinaigrette. 237
Olive Tapenade 239
Garlic Crostini 240
Cranberry Applesauce 241
Mexican Layer Dip 242

SOUPS AND STEWS

Goodness Soup. 243
Lentil Soup. 244
Golden Split Pea Soup. 245
Sweet and Savory Root Vegetable Stew 246
Super-Strengthening Stew. 248
Three Bean Chili 249
Tuscan Bean Soup 251
Winter Squash and Aduki Bean Soup. 252
Spicy Coconut Pumpkin Soup 253
Winter Vegetable Soup. 254

VEGETABLES

Bok Choy and Mung Bean Sprout Sauté
  with Peanuts and Scallions 255
Winter Green Salad with Sugared Walnuts,
  Crispy Pears and Pomegranate 256
Collard Greens and Black-Eyed Peas 258
Shiitake Mushrooms and Bitter Greens in Filo 259
Roasted Brussels Sprouts
  with Fennel and Shiitake Mushrooms. 260
Not Mashed Potatoes. 261
Sweet Potato and Parsnip Pancakes 263
Tree of Life Stir-Fry. 264
Simply Delicious Spaghetti Squash 265
Butternut Squash Casserole 266
Winter Squash and Chestnut Casserole 267
Roasted Kabocha Squash with Kale 268
Chestnut Stuffing. 269

LEGUMES

Thai Black Beans with Mangoes and Cilantro 270
Lentil Apple Walnut Loaf 271
Savory "Unbaked" Beans 272

TOFU, TEMPEH AND SEITAN

Orange Ginger Tofu 274
Roasted Tofu with Green Beans. 275
Pad Thai with Tofu 276
Spicy Thai Tempeh with Cashews 277
Sautéed Tempeh with Coconut Milk and Snow Peas. . . . 278
Seitan Shepherd's Pie 279
Seitan Bourguignon 280

GRAINS AND PASTA

Wholegrain Pancakes 281
Zesty Basmati Rice with Cinnamon and Cumin. 282
Sweet Brown Rice and Mung Beans
  with Indian Spices 283
Jasmine Rice with Sweet Peas. 284
Millet with Cranberries and Pistachios 285
Polenta au Gratin. 286
Baked Stuffed Shells 287

DESSERTS

Sinful Stuffed Dates. 289
Coconut Cranberry Pecan Balls 290
Maple Spiced Almonds 291
Sesame Almond Balls 292
Poached Winter Fruit Medley. 293
Apple Tart 294
Pear and Fig Tart in Pecan Crust. 296
Chocolate Pecan Pie 297
Chestnut Cream Pie 298
Tiramisu. 299

Maple Apple Vinaigrette

I LEARNED EARLY ON THAT MY CHILDREN will eat anything they get to make with the handheld blender. I let them make salad dressings all of the time. The result? They love when I serve salad and eat every last bite without fail. Some of their combinations are suspect, but this one is a winner.

1	garlic clove, minced
1	shallot, minced
1	tablespoon apple butter
2	tablespoons prepared mustard
2	tablespoons maple syrup
2	teaspoons dried dill
1	teaspoon dried parsley
1	tablespoon lemon juice or apple cider vinegar
1	tablespoon toasted sesame oil
¼	cup red wine vinegar
½	cup extra virgin olive oil

Sea salt and freshly ground black pepper

Water as needed

Place all ingredients except water in bowl and whisk together. A handheld blender will emulsify vinaigrette but is not necessary. Thin vinaigrette by adding water 1 tablespoon at a time until you reach the desired consistency. Store refrigerated for up to one week.

MAKES 1½ cups

Pomegranate Vinaigrette

THIS SIMPLE SALAD DRESSING takes people by surprise every time.
Perhaps it is pomegranate's reputation as the fruit of the gods, or its rich
supply of vitamin C, folic acid and antioxidants all packaged together
in this sweet and exotic juice – whichever the case, this vinaigrette can
turn even the most simple salad into something special.

---

1   garlic clove, minced

1   shallot, minced

⅓ cup pomegranate juice

½ cup extra virgin olive oil

2   tablespoons
    balsamic vinegar

1   tablespoon
    zesty honey mustard
    (I like Honeycup brand)

Sea salt

In medium bowl, whisk together all ingredients except salt by hand or
with handheld blender. Season to taste with salt. Vinaigrette will keep
refrigerated for one week.

MAKES 1 cup

Olive Tapenade

I OFTEN PREPARE THIS TAPENADE FOR COMPANY and serve it with Garlic Crostini *(page 240)* as an appetizer or as an accompaniment to a pasta dinner. But I enjoy it even more the next day spread on toasted sourdough bread in a roasted vegetable or portobello mushroom sandwich.

---

2   garlic cloves, peeled

1½   cups kalamata olives, pitted

1   cup oil-cured black Greek olives, pitted

2   generous tablespoons capers

¼   teaspoon dried thyme

¼   cup fresh parsley

1   tablespoon lemon juice, plus more if desired

Freshly ground black pepper

Extra virgin olive oil, as needed

With food processor running, drop in garlic and mince. Turn processor off, add olives, capers, thyme, parsley, lemon juice and pepper to taste. Process until smooth, scraping down sides as needed. Add olive oil a little at a time to achieve the desired consistency. Adjust flavor with more lemon juice and transfer to bowl. Store in airtight container in refrigerator or freezer.

MAKES 1¼ cups

Garlic Crostini

I TEACH MY CHILDREN that white foods are generally filler foods and not nutritionally packed. Unfortunately, I don't always follow my own teaching. While the garlic and olive oil in this dish are heart-healthy, the real reason that I make crostini is that it's simply delicious whether served with Olive Tapenade *(page 239)* or whatever your pleasure. Cut leftover crostini into cubes and freeze to use later as croutons.

1   long, thin baguette
Extra virgin olive oil
2–3 garlic cloves, peeled
2–3 tablespoons dried herbs of
    choice (rosemary, thyme,
    basil or oregano)
Pinch of sea salt

Preheat oven to 450°F.

Cut baguette on the diagonal into thin slices and place side by side on cookie sheet. Brush top of each piece of bread with olive oil. Slice garlic cloves in half and rub them over each piece of bread. Place bread slices in oven and bake 3 minutes. Remove from oven. Flip bread slices, brush the other side with oil and rub with garlic. Sprinkle with dried herbs and salt, return to oven and bake until lightly browned and crisp. Remove from oven and serve.

GLUTEN-FREE OPTION
If using frozen or refrigerated gluten-free bread, bring slices to room temperature then prepare whole slices as described above and slice diagonally into triangles before serving.

VARIATION
Brush bread slices with pesto, then toast as described above.

Cranberry Applesauce

EVERY FALL WE GO APPLE PICKING and return home with more apples than we can possibly consume. When we simply cannot eat any more apple crisp, I steam the rest to make applesauce. This simple version makes a sweet accompaniment to a savory winter meal.

---

6   apples of choice, peeled and cored

1   cup water or apple cider

½   cup unsweetened cranberry juice

2   tablespoons maple syrup

Place apples in pot with water or cider and cranberry juice. Cover, bring to boil, reduce heat and simmer until apples are soft. Remove from heat, add syrup and purée with handheld blender. Serve warm or chilled. Store in airtight container in refrigerator or freezer.

SERVES 4

VARIATION
For a more traditional applesauce, use 1½ cups apple cider and a dash of cinnamon and omit the cranberry juice.

Mexican Layer Dip

MY MOTHER USED TO MAKE THIS DIP for parties when we were children. When we eliminated dairy from our diets, this dip, sadly, went by the wayside. Years later, after discovering the wonders of tofu, my mother reintroduced this nondairy version and it was even better than I remembered.

TOFU SOUR CREAM

- 12 ounces silken extra firm tofu
- 3 tablespoons lemon juice
- 2 tablespoons extra virgin olive oil
- 1 tablespoon apple cider vinegar
- ½ teaspoon sea salt
- 1 tablespoon taco seasoning

LAYER DIP

- 16 ounces prepared bean dip of choice
- 2 4-ounce cans chopped green chiles
- 4 avocados
- 2 tablespoons lime juice
- 1 teaspoon sea salt
- ¼ teaspoon garlic powder
- 2 cups shredded soy or rice cheese
- 2 cups sliced scallions
- 2 cups chopped tomatoes
- 1½ cups pitted and chopped black olives

Tortilla chips

PREPARING SOUR CREAM

In food processor, combine all tofu sour cream ingredients except taco seasoning and process until smooth. Add taco seasoning and pulse to combine.

ASSEMBLING

Spread bean dip evenly in a 10 x 15-inch casserole. Top with tofu sour cream. Spread chiles evenly over tofu sour cream. Slice avocados in half, remove pits, scoop out flesh and place in large bowl. Add lime juice, salt and garlic powder, mash to combine and spread on chiles. Sprinkle with soy or rice cheese, scallions, tomatoes and olives. Refrigerate and serve chilled with a basket of tortilla chips.

Goodness Soup

MY MOTHER COINED THE NAME FOR THIS SOUP when I was a child. We never knew what was in it – we just knew it would be thick and delicious. Now that I'm a parent, I appreciate this soup even more. Not only does it allow me to make soup out of whatever I have on hand, but it helps me hide a host of nutritious foods that are otherwise a challenge to get my children to eat. Use this recipe as a template and add or substitute freely with whatever vegetables happen to be in your refrigerator.

2	thumb-size pieces kombu
2	tablespoons extra virgin olive oil
1	onion, chopped
1	pound mushrooms (any variety), chopped
5	carrots, chopped
3	stalks celery, chopped
1½	cups cooked navy or great northern beans
1	cup hulled barley, rinsed
1	cup lentils, rinsed
1	tablespoon dried parsley
1	tablespoon dried basil
1	bay leaf
¼	cup mirin or white wine
2	tablespoons tamari
12	cups water, plus more as needed
	Sea salt and freshly ground black pepper

Place kombu in bowl with enough water to cover, soak 10 minutes or until soft. Drain, mince and set aside.

In large pot over medium heat, sauté onion and mushrooms in olive oil for 5 minutes. Lower heat and add carrots, celery, beans, barley, lentils, parsley, basil, bay leaf, mirin and tamari. Stir to combine, add water and bring to boil.

Reduce heat to low, add kombu and continue cooking covered for a minimum of 3 hours – the longer it cooks, the thicker it will get. Add water as desired to thin. Remove bay leaf, season with salt and pepper to taste and serve. Soup will keep in refrigerator for up to one week or can be frozen in airtight containers.

GLUTEN-FREE OPTION
Substitute split peas, quinoa, amaranth or even cubed butternut squash for barley.

MAKES 8 hearty servings

VARIATION
Stir 1 teaspoon miso dissolved in 3 tablespoons water into each serving.

Lentil Soup

THERE'S NOTHING LIKE A POT OF LENTIL SOUP that's been simmering all day. If you have a hearty appetite, serve this over basmati rice – a great combination – or add some steamed kale or collards for a well-balanced and satisfying meal.

---

1   thumb-size piece kombu

2   tablespoons extra virgin olive oil

1   large onion, chopped

3   garlic cloves, minced

3   stalks celery, diced

3   carrots, diced

2   cups chopped tomatoes

¼   cup red wine

4   cups dried lentils

10   cups water or vegetable stock

1   tablespoon brown rice vinegar

2   tablespoons maple syrup

1   tablespoon molasses

1   tablespoon tamari

Sea salt and freshly ground black pepper

Place kombu in bowl with enough water to cover and soak 10 minutes or until soft. Drain, mince and set aside. In large soup pot over medium heat, sauté onion and garlic in olive oil until soft (about 3 minutes). Add celery, carrots, tomatoes and red wine. Rinse lentils and add to pot along with water or stock. Add vinegar, syrup, molasses, tamari, kombu, and salt and pepper to taste. Stir, bring to boil, then reduce heat. Cover and simmer 2 hours. Adjust seasonings and serve.

SERVES 8

VARIATION
For a richer, more decadent soup, add 2 tablespoons cacao powder along with molasses.

Golden Split Pea Soup

THIS BEAUTIFUL, GOLDEN, HIGH-PROTEIN SOUP gets better and better the longer it simmers on your stove. Serve it alone, over basmati rice or with a side of leafy greens for a satisfying and simple meal.

2	tablespoons extra virgin olive oil
1	large yellow onion, diced
4	garlic cloves, minced
4	stalks celery, diced
4	carrots, diced
2	cups chopped tomatoes
1	potato, peeled and diced
¼	cup mirin
2	tablespoons red wine vinegar
½	teaspoon ground mustard
4	cups golden split peas
10	cups water, plus more as needed
½	teaspoon sea salt
Freshly ground black pepper	
1	bay leaf

In large soup pot over medium heat, sauté onion and garlic in olive oil until soft. Add celery and carrots and sauté another 3 minutes. Add tomatoes, potato, mirin, vinegar and mustard and stir to combine. Rinse and drain split peas and add to pot along with 10 cups water and remaining ingredients. Bring soup to boil, cover, reduce heat and simmer at least 4 hours, adding more water as needed to thin. Remove bay leaf and serve.

Note: For a smoother texture, lightly purée soup with handheld blender before serving.

SERVES 8

Sweet and Savory Root Vegetable Stew

I TAKE THE SAME APPROACH WITH THIS STEW as I do with my Goodness Soup *(page 243)* – I make it with whatever root vegetables I have on hand. Root vegetables are particularly strengthening, grounding and easy to digest, and they are abundant during the winter months. If you've shied away from them in the past because you didn't know how to cook them, this is a good place to start.

1	tablespoon extra virgin olive oil
6	shallots, diced
2	tablespoons grated fresh ginger
2	parsnips, peeled and diced
2	medium rutabagas, peeled and diced
2	turnips, peeled and diced
2	sweet potatoes, peeled and diced
1	celeriac (celery root), peeled and diced
1	fennel bulb, halved, cored and diced (save fronds for garnish)
1	cinnamon stick
	Vegetable stock
	Ume plum vinegar

In large pot over medium heat, sauté shallots and ginger in oil 5 minutes or until soft. Add parsnips, rutabagas, turnips, sweet potatoes, celery root, fennel and cinnamon stick. Add enough stock to barely cover vegetables, bring to boil, cover, reduce heat and simmer 25 minutes.

Remove from heat, discard cinnamon stick and gently purée soup 3 seconds using handheld blender to slightly thicken liquid and blend flavors. Season to taste with a few dashes of vinegar, garnish with fennel fronds and serve.

SERVES 6–8

Super-Strengthening Stew

MANY PEOPLE ASSOCIATE STRENGTH WITH PROTEIN, but too much protein can be dangerous. Root vegetables are particularly strengthening and can provide some of the sweetness that you may be craving – particularly if you've recently cut down on carbohydrates. From the purifying effects of burdock and rutabaga to the fat-dissolving ability of daikon and onion, this dish is packed with nutritional heavy hitters. Finishing the stew with a bit of soothing kudzu, you have a perfect winter meal.

1	strip kombu
1	tablespoon grapeseed oil
½	onion, diced
1	small yam
1	carrot
1	rutabaga
2	burdock roots
1	8-inch piece daikon
1	stalk celery, diced
2½	cups vegetable stock
⅛	teaspoon sea salt
1	head escarole, chopped
Water as needed	
2	tablespoons kudzu, dissolved in 2 tablespoons water
1	teaspoon toasted sesame oil
Gomasio for garnish	

Place kombu in bowl with enough water to cover and soak 10 minutes or until soft. Drain, mince and set aside.

In Dutch oven over medium heat, sauté onion in grapeseed oil 3 minutes or until soft.

Peel and dice yam, carrot, rutabaga, burdock and daikon and add to pot along with celery and kombu. Add stock and salt, bring to boil, then reduce heat and simmer 10–15 minutes or until vegetables are soft. Fold in escarole, add water if needed to thin and simmer until esarole is soft.

Add kudzu mixture to stew and stir 3–4 minutes or until liquid thickens. Remove from heat, drizzle with toasted sesame oil, garnish each serving with gomasio and serve.

SERVES 4

Three Bean Chili

MANY PEOPLE AVOID LEGUMES because of their unpleasant side effects. This chili, however, features smaller beans that are less gaseous and kombu, a sea vegetable that tenderizes and further reduces beans' gaseous properties. Black beans and aduki beans are particularly great for stabilizing blood sugar levels, so you can enjoy chili once again with nothing but benefits to your health.

1	thumb-size piece kombu
2	tablespoons extra virgin olive oil
3	garlic cloves, minced
2	onions, chopped
2	green bell peppers, diced
4	cups chopped tomatoes
½	cup tomato paste
¼	cup red wine
½	teaspoon dried oregano
1	teaspoon cumin
2	tablespoons chile powder
6–8	drops hot sauce
¼	teaspoon cayenne (or to taste)
¼	teaspoon sea salt
1½	cups cooked black beans
1½	cups cooked aduki beans
1½	cups cooked pinto beans
	Vegetable stock as needed
	Garnishes: chopped scallion, shredded soy or rice cheese, Tofu Sour Cream (page 104)

Place kombu in bowl with enough water to cover and soak 10 minutes or until soft. Drain, mince and set aside.

In large pot over medium heat, sauté garlic and onion in olive oil 3 minutes or until soft. Add green peppers and sauté 2 minutes more. Add chopped tomatoes and tomato paste, wine, oregano, cumin, chile powder, hot sauce, cayenne and salt. Add cooked beans and kombu, stir to combine and simmer at least 45 minutes. Add vegetable stock as needed to thin. Garnish as desired and serve.

SERVES 6

Tuscan Bean Soup

THIS SOUP HAS IT ALL – protein, calcium, minerals, and more! If you're short on time, use canned beans. For a heartier meal, serve over pasta or grilled polenta. Add some garlic bread and you have a delicious feast.

1	thumb-size piece kombu
2	tablespoons extra virgin olive oil
4	garlic cloves, minced
1	cup chopped onion
1	tablespoon dried basil
2	teaspoons dried oregano
¼	teaspoon dried rosemary
1½	cups cooked chickpeas
1½	cups cooked white beans
1½	cups cooked aduki beans
4	cups canned chopped tomatoes with their juices
1	bunch kale or collards, chopped into bite-size pieces
2	cups vegetable stock
1	tablespoon apple cider vinegar
1	cup red wine
	Sea salt and freshly ground black pepper
¼	cup chopped fresh parsley

Place kombu in bowl with enough water to cover and soak 10 minutes or until soft. Drain, mince and set aside.

In Dutch oven over medium heat, sauté garlic and onion in olive oil 3 minutes or until soft. Add basil, oregano and rosemary and stir. Add chickpeas, white beans, aduki beans, tomatoes, greens, kombu and stock. Bring to boil, then reduce heat and simmer. Stir in vinegar and wine, season with salt and pepper to taste, cover and cook for 45 minutes. Remove from heat, garnish with parsley and serve.

SERVES 6

Winter Squash and Aduki Bean Soup

ADUKI BEANS ADD A DELICIOUS TANG AND BALANCE to this otherwise sweet soup. They are one of the easiest legumes to digest and are particularly healing to the kidneys. Serve this soup with pan-roasted millet *(page 14)* and sautéed collard greens for color and balance.

---

1 thumb-size piece kombu

2 tablespoons extra virgin olive oil

1 large onion, chopped

2 stalks celery, diced

¼ teaspoon ground cumin

½ teaspoon ground cardamom

¼ teaspoon ground nutmeg

1 large butternut squash

1 cup apple cider

¼ cup mirin

Water or vegetable stock

3 cups cooked aduki beans

1 tablespoon apple cider vinegar

Sea salt and white pepper

Chopped scallions and/or fresh mint leaves for garnish

Place kombu in bowl with enough water to cover and soak 10 minutes or until soft. Drain, mince and set aside.

In large pot over medium heat, sauté onion and celery in olive oil 3 minutes or until soft. Add cumin, cardamom and nutmeg and stir. Peel and halve squash, remove seeds, cut into 1-inch chunks and add to pot along with cider, mirin and minced kombu. Add enough water or stock to cover squash. Cover pot and bring to boil. Reduce heat and simmer 45 minutes or until squash is tender.

Remove soup from heat and purée until smooth using handheld blender. Add cooked beans and vinegar and season to taste with salt and white pepper. Return to low heat and simmer 10 minutes to blend flavors. Remove from heat, garnish as desired and serve.

SERVES 6

Spicy Coconut Pumpkin Soup

I LOVE TAKING THE FIRST SPOONFUL OF THIS SOUP and tasting the unexpected. You may need to make a trip to your local Asian grocery store to find some of these unusual ingredients, but it will be worth the effort. I often use butternut squash instead of pumpkin, as it has more flesh. Sugar pumpkins and red kuri squash are other tasty options. If using canned pumpkin, reduce your water or stock by 1 to 2 cups.

1	large pumpkin or butternut squash (3½–4 pounds)
2	tablespoons grapeseed oil
3	garlic cloves, minced
1	large onion, chopped
1	tablespoon grated fresh ginger
2	cups coconut milk
5	cups water or vegetable stock
6	lemongrass stalks (bottom 5 inches only), chopped
1	1-inch piece of galangal (or ginger root), peeled and chopped
4–5	dried Thai chiles, quartered
4	kaffir lime leaves, chopped
¼	cup chopped scallions

Preheat to 400°F.

Cut pumpkin or squash in half, remove seeds and place squash flesh side down on baking sheet. Roast in oven until just soft throughout (about 30–40 minutes). Remove from oven. Peel away and discard skin, dice and set aside.

In soup pot or Dutch oven over medium heat, sauté garlic, onion and ginger in 1 tablespoon grapeseed oil until soft. Add pumpkin, coconut milk, and water or stock. Bring to boil, reduce heat and simmer covered 15–20 minutes.

Meanwhile, in small skillet over medium heat, sauté chopped lemongrass, galangal and chiles in remaining tablespoon of grapeseed oil until lightly browned. Remove from heat and set aside.

Using handheld blender, purée soup until smooth. Stir in lemongrass mixture and kaffir leaves. Simmer 15 minutes to infuse soup with spices. Pour through a mesh strainer and serve topped with chopped scallions.

SERVES 8

Winter Vegetable Soup

THIS EASY-TO-MAKE CABBAGE SOUP COOKS UP QUICKLY, but tastes like you spent hours fussing over it. It is a sweet and nutritious addition to any meal and makes a great midday snack.

---

1   tablespoon
    extra virgin olive oil

2   leeks (white and light
    green parts only), diced

3   tablespoons tamari

2   tablespoons mirin

1   large potato,
    peeled and diced

3   large carrots, diced

½   green cabbage, diced

2   stalks celery, diced

1   teaspoon sea salt

Freshly ground black pepper

Water or vegetable stock

2   cups corn, fresh or frozen

In large Dutch oven over medium heat, sauté leeks in olive oil, tamari and mirin until tender (about 5 minutes). Add potato, carrots, cabbage, celery, salt, and pepper to taste. Stir to combine and add enough water or stock to come ½-inch below top of vegetables. Bring to boil, reduce heat and simmer covered 20 minutes or until vegetables are soft. Remove from heat and purée using handheld blender. Add corn, adjust seasoning with salt and pepper and serve.

SERVES 6

Bok Choy and Mung Bean Sprout Sauté with Peanuts and Scallions

MUNG BEANS ARE PARTICULARLY COOLING, cleansing and beneficial to the heart. When buying them, be sure to check the freshness date on the bag and look for firm white sprouts that don't have brown, dried ends. Buy sprouts just before you're ready to use them, as they will not last long, and wash them well before adding them to your recipe.

2	tablespoons extra virgin olive oil
3	garlic cloves, minced
1	tablespoon grated fresh ginger
1	large leek, thinly sliced
½	pound shiitake mushroom caps, thinly sliced
3	tablespoons tamari
2	tablespoons mirin
Water as needed	
8	cups chopped bok choy (4 medium heads)
1	cup chopped scallions
2	cups mung bean sprouts, rinsed well
1½	cups dry-roasted peanuts

In large Dutch oven over medium heat, sauté garlic, ginger and leek in olive oil 5 minutes or until tender. Add shiitake mushrooms, half the tamari and half the mirin and sauté 5 minutes or until mushrooms start to caramelize. Add water 1 tablespoon at a time to deglaze pan as needed and continue sautéing mushrooms. Add remaining tamari and mirin and sauté another 3–4 minutes until mushrooms are glazed deep brown, but not burnt.

Stir in bok choy 2 cups at a time until it wilts and all fits in pot. Add water as needed to prevent sticking, cover and steam 1 minute. Remove cover, fold in scallions and cook 1 more minute. Remove from heat, fold in bean sprouts, top with peanuts and serve.

SERVES 6

Winter Green Salad with Sugared Walnuts, Crispy Pears and Pomegranate

THIS RECIPE COMBINES CRISP AND REFRESHING greens and pears with sweet and savory walnuts for a salad that is beautiful whether you serve it tossed in a large bowl or composed in individual servings. Substitute toasted and salted pumpkin seeds for the sugared walnuts for an equally satisfying variation.

POMEGRANATE VINAIGRETTE

Prepare recipe as on page 237

SUGARED WALNUTS

1	tablespoon maple syrup
1	tablespoon walnut oil
1	tablespoon maple sugar
1	teaspoon ground cinnamon
2	dashes ground cayenne
2	cups walnuts

SALAD

6	cups chopped or torn greens (arugula, romaine lettuce, frisée, dandelion greens or watercress)
2	D'Anjou pears (red or green), thinly sliced

Seeds from ½ pomegranate

Prepare vinaigrette, cover and refrigerate until ready to use.

PREPARING WALNUTS

Preheat oven to 350°F. In medium bowl, combine syrup, walnut oil, maple sugar, cinnamon and cayenne to taste. Add walnuts, toss to coat and spread out on parchment-lined cookie sheet. Bake until lightly browned (about 20 minutes). Remove from oven and set aside.

ASSEMBLING SALAD

Place greens in salad bowl, combine with most (but not all) of the sliced pears, drizzle with desired amount of pomegranate vinaigrette and toss to coat. Arrange remaining pears and sugared walnuts over salad greens, top with pomegranate seeds and serve.

SERVES 6

Collard Greens and Black-Eyed Peas

THIS SOUTHERN DISH IS TRADITIONALLY EATEN on New Year's to ensure good luck and prosperity in the year ahead. I could give you more reasons to include this recipe in your diet, but I think this tradition speaks volumes. So don't question, just do it. What have you got to lose?

1   large bunch collard greens

2   tablespoons extra virgin olive oil

2   garlic cloves, minced

½   onion, diced

Water as needed

1½ cups cooked black-eyed peas

Dash of apple cider vinegar

Sea salt and freshly ground black pepper

Remove dry ends from collard green stems and chop leaves into bite-size pieces.

In large Dutch oven over medium heat, sauté garlic and onion in olive oil until soft. Add collard greens and stir until they turn bright green and wilt. Add water 1 tablespoon at a time as needed to keep greens from burning.

Add black-eyed peas and vinegar and continue cooking for 3–4 minutes to heat through. Season to taste with salt and pepper and serve.

SERVES 6

Shiitake Mushrooms and Bitter Greens in Filo

FILO HAS THE MAGICAL POWER of turning a simple dish into a sensation. Make small triangles to serve as an appetizer or side dish, or larger pockets to make into a main dish. I've yet to find or make gluten-free filo, but this recipe is equally as delicious stuffed in puffed mochi or served over sweet brown rice.

2	tablespoons grapeseed oil
4	garlic cloves, minced
1	large red onion, diced
20	shiitake mushroom caps, thinly sliced
2	tablespoons mirin
4	cups chopped bitter leafy greens (collards, kale, mustard greens or dandelion greens)

Sea salt and freshly ground black pepper

1	package filo dough (at least 9 sheets)

Extra virgin olive oil

PREPARING FILLING

In large sauté pan over medium heat, sauté garlic and onion in grapeseed oil until soft. Add mushrooms and sauté 5 minutes. Stir in mirin and greens, cover and cook 5 minutes or until greens wilt and turn bright green. Season with salt and pepper to taste and set aside to cool.

ASSEMBLING FILO POCKETS

Preheat oven to 350°F.

Defrost filo according to directions on package. On dry surface, lay out 2 sheets of filo – one on top of the other. Brush or spray lightly with olive oil, top with one more sheet of filo and again brush or spray with oil. Cut sheets from top to bottom into 4 strips.

Gently scoop out filling, draining excess liquid from each scoop, and place along edge of filo closest to you at the bottom of each strip. Fold bottom corner up and over greens to opposite edge and continue folding, as you would fold up a flag, until you reach the top of each strip. Continue making pockets until all greens are used up. Gently place pockets on parchment-lined cookie sheet, brush or spray lightly with olive oil and bake 25 minutes or until filo is golden brown.

SERVES 6

VARIATION

Layer 3 sheets of filo and place filling along the bottom edge, leaving 3 inches on either side. Fold in sides and then roll filo into the shape of a log. Brush or spray with olive oil and bake as above.

Roasted Brussels Sprouts with Fennel and Shiitake Mushrooms

ROASTING BRUSSELS SPROUTS CHANGES their dense texture and makes them soft and delicious, particularly when combined with these other caramelized vegetables. Brussels sprouts are a rich source of antioxidants and are desirable for their antibiotic and antiviral properties.

1½ pounds Brussels sprouts

4 shallots, quartered

10 garlic cloves, peeled

½ pound shiitake mushroom caps

1 large fennel bulb

¼ cup extra virgin olive oil

3 tablespoons balsamic vinegar

2 tablespoons fresh tarragon or rosemary

Coarse sea salt and freshly ground black pepper

Preheat to 425°F.

Prepare Brussels sprouts by cutting away tough root ends and removing any blemished outer leaves. Slice in half through the base and place in large bowl. Add shallots, garlic and mushroom caps.

Prepare fennel by trimming off dried root end and slicing bulb thinly crosswise. Add to vegetables and toss with remaining ingredients. Place in 9 x 12-inch glass or ceramic baking dish and roast uncovered 25 minutes. Stir vegetables and roast 25 minutes more. Remove from oven and serve.

SERVES 6

Not Mashed Potatoes

GETTING HEALTHY FOODS INTO OUR CHILDREN can be a challenge, and healthy additions like this one can be a mother's best friend. For years, my children had no idea that their mashed potatoes were half parsnips. They were happy because they were sweet and delicious, and I was happy because they were full of nutritional value. Whether adding powdered kelp to a smoothie or parsnips to your mashed potatoes, adults and children alike benefit from improving the nutrition of everyday foods.

---

2 medium baking potatoes
5 parsnips
¼ cup rice milk
2 tablespoons extra virgin olive oil
Sea salt

Peel potatoes and parsnips. Cut into chunks and place in pot with 1–2 inches water. Cover and bring to boil. Cook until vegetables are soft, adding more water as needed. Drain vegetables in a collander set over a large bowl and reserve cooking water. Return vegetables to pot, add rice milk and olive oil and process with handheld blender until smooth. If too thick, add reserved cooking water to thin. Season to taste with salt and process to the desired consistency. Serve hot.

SERVES 4

Sweet Potato and Parsnip Pancakes

THESE SWEET LITTLE PANCAKES ARE PERFECT with applesauce, maple syrup or even just a touch of sea salt. This is a great time to learn how to use the grating attachment on your food processor.

---

2   tablespoons ground golden flax seeds

1   large onion

3   parsnips, peeled

2   sweet potatoes, peeled

2   tablespoons mirin

½   cup cornmeal

Sea salt and freshly ground black pepper

Grapeseed oil for frying

Soak ground flax seeds for 10 minutes in bowl with ½ cup water.

Using the grating disc on your food processor or a box grater, grate onion, parsnips and sweet potatoes. Place grated vegetables in large bowl. Add mirin and soaked flax. Sprinkle with cornmeal, salt and pepper to taste and combine.

Preheat oven to 250°F.

Heat skillet or griddle over medium-high heat and add enough grapeseed oil to coat the bottom of the pan. Using your hands, scoop out potato mixture, form into small balls, place in skillet and press flat with spatula to form pancakes. Fry pancakes 2–3 minutes on each side until golden brown and crisp. Remove from skillet and keep in warm oven while frying remaining batches, adding oil to skillet as needed. Serve hot.

MAKES 20 pancakes

Tree of Life Stir-Fry

THIS STIR-FRY GETS ITS NAME from the combination of broccoli and cauliflower, as well as the addition of strengthening and toning vegetables such as carrots, onions and arame. Ginger provides heat and energy to your core for healing. All together, this dish overflows with calcium, vitamins, antioxidants and beta-carotene.

1	cup dried arame
1	tablespoon grapeseed oil
1	small onion, cut into wedges
3	carrots, cut into matchsticks
1	small head broccoli, cut into bite-size pieces
½	head cauliflower, cut into bite-size pieces
1	tablespoon mirin

Water as needed

2	teaspoons kudzu, dissolved in ¼ cup water
1	tablespoon mellow white or chickpea miso
1	tablespoon maple syrup
1	tablespoon grated fresh ginger
¼	cup toasted sesame seeds

Place arame in bowl with enough water to cover. Soak 10 minutes, drain and set aside.

In large skillet over medium heat, sauté onion in grapeseed oil 3 minutes until soft. Add carrots, broccoli, cauliflower and mirin and continue to stir-fry until vegetables become brighter in color. Drain arame and add to stir-fry, adding water as needed to prevent sticking.

In small bowl, combine dissolved kudzu with miso, syrup and ginger. Add to stir-fry and cook 3–4 minutes to thicken sauce. Remove from heat, top with sesame seeds and serve.

SERVES 4

VARIATION
Use this recipe as a template and add your favorite vegetables. Cabbage, shiitake mushrooms and snow peas are among my favorites.

Simply Delicious Spaghetti Squash

SPAGHETTI SQUASH IS LESS SWEET than other winter squash varieties. It has a beautiful golden color and slightly crisp texture. Try it by itself or topped with your favorite pasta sauce. This recipe is a perfect complement to Sautéed Garlic Greens *(page 179)*.

---

1 spaghetti squash

¼ cup extra virgin olive oil

3 garlic cloves, minced

2 tablespoons chopped fresh parsley

Coarse sea salt and freshly black ground pepper

Preheat oven to 400°F.

Place squash on cookie sheet, pierce a few times with a knife and bake 1 hour or until soft. Remove from oven and set aside.

In small skillet over low heat, sauté garlic in olive oil until soft (about 2 minutes). Cut squash in half lengthwise and remove and discard seeds. Hold half of the squash over a serving bowl and using a fork, scrape out flesh from top to bottom to separate the strands of squash. Repeat with other half, toss with garlic oil, parsley, and salt and pepper to taste. Serve hot.

SERVES 4

Butternut Squash Casserole

ONE WAY TO WARD OFF SWEET CRAVINGS is to add more nutritional sweetness to your diet. Winter squash is a delicious "sweet" and I particularly like this recipe, as it's easy to prepare and can be made in advance. Your guests will be overtaken by the wonderful aroma when they enter your home and will be even more impressed when you serve this sweet and satisfying dish.

---

1   small butternut squash, peeled, halved, seeded and thinly sliced

1   small red onion, thinly sliced

⅓   cup apple cider or juice

2   tablespoons grapeseed oil

2   tablespoons maple syrup

¼   cup toasted slivered almonds

Preheat oven to 350°F.

Combine squash and onion in 9 x 12-inch casserole. In small bowl, whisk together apple cider, oil and syrup and pour over squash. Top with almonds, cover with foil and bake 45 minutes or until tender.

SERVES 6

Winter Squash and Chestnut Casserole

FOR A WARMING AND SATISFYING DISH, try this combination of winter squash, rich and creamy chestnuts and crunchy nut topping. Bottled prepared chestnuts are sold around the holidays and often go on sale in January. I stock up then so that we can enjoy this recipe throughout the winter.

1   small butternut squash, peeled, halved, seeded and cubed

2   cups cooked chestnuts

3   cups apple cider or juice

1   teaspoon ground cinnamon

½   teaspoon ground nutmeg

Pinch of ground cloves

½   cup toasted almonds, coarsely chopped

3   tablespoons maple syrup

½   teaspoon vanilla extract

Place squash, chestnuts, apple cider and spices in large pot. Bring to boil, cover, reduce heat and simmer 20–25 minutes until squash is soft. Remove from heat and purée with handheld blender until smooth. Spoon into an 8 x 8-inch baking dish.

Set oven to broil.

In small mixing bowl, combine almonds, syrup and vanilla. Sprinkle as evenly as possible over squash. Place baking dish under broiler for 2 minutes or until nuts are browned but not burnt. Remove from oven and serve.

SERVES 6

Roasted Kabocha Squash with Kale

THESE TWO WINTER STAPLES COMBINE to make an alkalinizing dish that's big in color, texture and taste.

---

1   small kabocha squash

4   shallots, quartered

3   tablespoons balsamic vinegar

3   tablespoons extra virgin olive oil

1   teaspoon coarse sea salt

2   garlic cloves, minced

2   bunches kale, chopped

Water as needed

¼   cup pumpkin seeds

Preheat oven to 425°F.

Leaving the skin on, cut squash in half, remove seeds and chop into bite-size pieces. In large bowl, combine squash with shallots, vinegar, 2 tablespoons olive oil and salt. Spread out onto cookie sheet and roast 30 minutes or until soft. Remove from oven and set aside.

Heat remaining tablespoon of oil in Dutch oven over medium heat and sauté garlic until fragrant (about 2 minutes). Fold in kale a little at a time until it all fits in pot and cook until tender, adding water as needed to prevent burning. Remove from heat, add roasted squash and toss to evenly distribute. Top with pumpkin seeds and serve.

SERVES 6

Chestnut Stuffing

THIS STUFFING FEATURES RICE BREAD, which is slightly heavier than other breads and has a sourness similar to sourdough. Rice bread also has no gluten, making it perfect for the wheat-sensitive members of my family. Look for rice bread in the freezer section of your natural foods store. For an extra-special presentation, roast a hubbard squash, fill it with the stuffing and bake. To serve, scoop out the stuffing along with some squash.

3	tablespoons extra virgin olive oil
1	large yellow onion, diced
5	stalks celery, diced
½	pound cremini mushrooms, diced
½	cup diced dried apples
2	tablespoons chopped fresh rosemary
2	tablespoons dried parsley
2½	cups cooked chestnuts, diced
6	slices brown rice bread, cut into ½-inch cubes and toasted
½	cup vegetable stock
¼	cup tamari
2	tablespoons mirin

Freshly ground black pepper

1	roasted butternut squash, optional
½	cup toasted slivered almonds

Chopped fresh parsley for garnish

Preheat oven to 400°F.

In large Dutch oven over medium heat, sauté onion in olive oil until soft. Add celery, mushrooms, apples, rosemary and dried parsley and sauté 4 minutes. Fold in chestnuts and toasted bread cubes and remove from heat.

In small bowl, whisk together stock, tamari and mirin. Drizzle over stuffing mixture to evenly soak. Season with pepper to taste and gently fold to combine all ingredients. Place in large casserole or stuff into roasted winter squash and bake 25 minutes until top is lightly toasted.

Remove from oven, top with almonds and fresh parsley and serve.

SERVES 6

Thai Black Beans with Mangoes and Cilantro

USED TRADITIONALLY IN THAI FOOD, fermented black beans taste like dried and salted black beans. They give this dish a strong savory flavor that complements the sweet mango and fresh cilantro, and provides welcome warmth during the cold months of winter.

¼ cup fermented black beans

2 garlic cloves, peeled

1 tablespoon grated fresh ginger

1 teaspoon roasted red chili paste

2 teaspoons toasted sesame oil

1 tablespoon sucanat

1 tablespoon lime juice

4 cups cooked black beans

2 mangoes, peeled, pitted and diced

½ cup coarsely chopped cilantro

Soak fermented black beans for 2 minutes in bowl with enough hot water to cover. Drain, rinse and drain again. Add garlic, ginger, chili paste, sesame oil, sucanat and lime juice. With handheld blender, mix to combine and set aside.

Heat cooked black beans in pot over medium heat for 4 minutes. Add fermented black bean sauce and stir continuously to combine and heat through. Using a rounded glass or stainless steel serving bowl as a mold, press in bean mixture, invert over the center of your serving dish, then remove mold. In separate bowl, combine mangoes and cilantro. Spoon mixture around black beans and serve.

SERVES 6

Lentil Apple Walnut Loaf

THIS HIGH-PROTEIN LOAF MAKES a nice main course for a vegetarian meal and a great sandwich stuffer as leftovers. Serve with Cranberry Applesauce *(page 241)* and sautéed greens *(pages 179–180)* for a complete meal.

1	cup dried lentils
3	cups vegetable stock
1	thumb-size piece kombu
3	tablespoons ground golden flax seed
2	tablespoons extra virgin olive oil
1	yellow onion, diced
1	carrot, grated
1	stalk celery, minced
2	tablespoons mirin
1	apple, peeled, grated and mixed with 1 tablespoon lemon juice
¼	cup raisins
¾	cup toasted walnuts, chopped
1	teaspoon dried thyme
6–7	dashes ume plum vinegar
	Freshly ground black pepper
	Water
½	cup plus 1 tablespoon gluten-free bread or rice crumbs

GLAZE

2	tablespoons ketchup
1	tablespoon balsamic vinegar
1	tablespoon maple syrup
1	tablespoon apple butter
1	teaspoon arrowroot

PREPARING LENTILS

Rinse lentils, place in rice cooker or pot and add stock and kombu. Bring to boil then reduce heat and simmer covered until liquid is absorbed and lentils are tender. Remove from heat, discard kombu and set aside.

PREPARING LOAF

Preheat oven to 350°F. Line loaf pan and baking sheet with parchment paper and set aside. Soak flax seed in ½ cup water and set aside.

In large skillet over medium heat, sauté onion, carrot and celery in olive oil for 2 minutes. Add mirin and sauté 3 minutes more or until soft. Add apple, raisins and walnuts and sauté another minute. Add thyme, vinegar and pepper to taste.

Add half the cooked lentils to vegetable mixture. Process remaining lentils with handheld blender or food processor until smooth, adding water 1 tablespoon at a time as needed (not to exceed ¼ cup extra water). Fold into lentil apple mixture, then add bread crumbs and another ¼ cup water and mush all ingredients together so evenly distributed. Transfer to prepared loaf pan and press firmly to form. Flip onto prepared baking sheet, lift off loaf pan and press loaf with your hands to round edges and make sure loaf is pressed firmly together. Remove and discard parchment paper and set aside loaf.

PREPARING GLAZE

In small saucepan over no heat, combine all glaze ingredients. Place over medium heat and stir continuously until thick (about 2–3 minutes). Spread evenly over loaf and bake, uncovered, 35 minutes. Remove from oven and let stand 5 minutes before serving.

SERVES 6

Savory "Unbaked" Beans

FOR A QUICK MEAL, there's nothing like canned beans. Eden makes theirs with kombu, so I always keep a few cans in my pantry. I make this meal when I have leftover brown rice. Simply reheat the rice in a pan with a bit of water, sauté some greens and heat the canned beans with your favorite seasonings. For a change, serve the beans and rice in soft tortillas with chopped lettuce and tomatoes. Either way, this is a 10-minute meal that my family loves.

1½ cups cooked black beans

1½ cups cooked aduki beans

1 tablespoon tahini

1 tablespoon molasses

1 tablespoon apple butter

1 tablespoon prepared mustard

2 tablespoons maple syrup

½ teaspoon ground cinnamon

½ teaspoon ground cumin

Hot pepper sauce

Drain and rinse canned beans and place in medium pot over medium heat. Add all other ingredients, stir to combine, cook to heat through and serve.

SERVES 4

VARIATION
Prepare recipe as above; while bean mixture is cooking, sauté ¼ cup chopped onion, 1 tablespoon grated fresh ginger and 1 tablespoon grated fresh turmeric in 1 tablespoon extra virgin olive oil. When soft, add to beans and serve.

Orange Ginger Tofu

I FIRST DISCOVERED TOFU ON A SALAD BAR. I took one bite into the mysterious, cold, bland cube and vowed never to eat it again. When I realized that tofu would take on the flavor of whatever I cooked it with, I changed my mind. I started adding it to recipes like my Tofu Kale Lasagna *(page 213)*, and roasting it with herbs, spices and marinades as I do here. If you've ever wondered what to do with tofu, this recipe is a great place to start. It's quick and easy and yields a sweet and savory tofu that complements everything from greens and winter squash to stir-fries and salads.

---

16 ounces firm tofu

MARINADE

2 tablespoons grated fresh ginger

3 garlic cloves, minced

3 tablespoons minced red onion

1 cup orange juice

¼ cup brown rice vinegar

¼ cup tamari

2 tablespoons toasted sesame oil

2 tablespoons maple syrup

Wrap tofu in towels and press to remove excess liquid. Cut lengthwise into 4 rectangular slices and then into cubes. In shallow baking dish, combine all marinade ingredients. Add tofu in a single layer and turn pieces to completely coat. Cover and refrigerate for 30 minutes.

Preheat oven to 350°F.

Uncover tofu and bake in marinade 15 minutes. Turn pieces and bake another 15–20 minutes or until golden brown. Serve hot or chilled.

SERVES 4

Roasted Tofu with Green Beans

MY FRIEND JERILYN MADE THIS RECIPE FOR ME years ago, and it instantly became a winter favorite. Roasting is a great way to dress up basic tofu, and this recipe lends itself to improvisation. Make it your own by experimenting with asparagus, onion, fennel or Brussels sprouts. For a heartier meal, serve this dish over brown rice.

---

2 pounds fresh firm tofu (not silken), cut into cubes

10 garlic cloves, peeled

2 pounds green beans, dried ends removed

½ pound cremini mushrooms, stems removed

2 leeks

3 tablespoons extra virgin olive oil

¼ cup Bragg Liquid Aminos

All-purpose seasoning blend

Preheat oven to 375°F.

Place tofu, garlic, green beans and mushrooms in 9 x 12-inch baking pan. Cut leeks in half lengthwise, rinse, cut into ¼-inch slices and add to pan. Drizzle olive oil and liquid aminos over tofu mixture, sprinkle generously with seasoning blend and toss to combine. Roast uncovered 1 hour, stirring every 20 minutes, until tofu is firm and vegetables are caramelized. Remove from oven and serve.

Note: To make your own seasoning blend, combine any or all of the following: sea salt, freshly ground black pepper, dried basil, dried parsley, dried oregano, paprika, lemon peel and celery and mustard seeds.

SERVES 4

Pad Thai with Tofu

I FELL IN LOVE WITH PAD THAI at a small restaurant outside Boston and spent years trying to re-create it. This version features roasted tofu instead of the traditional eggs. The tofu can be prepared up to a day in advance or can be left out if time is limited.

STIR-FRY

½	pound fettuccine-style rice noodles
½	pound fresh firm tofu (not silken)
½	cup Bragg Liquid Aminos
½	cup water
2	tablespoons mirin
1	tablespoon grapeseed oil
3	garlic cloves, minced
½	cup thinly sliced snow peas
1½	cups mung bean sprouts, rinsed well
3	tablespoons chopped fresh cilantro
4	scallions, thinly sliced
	Juice of 1 lime
½	cup dry roasted peanuts

STIR-FRY SAUCE

1	teaspoon roasted red chili paste
1	tablespoon sucanat
1	tablespoon tamari
1	tablespoon lime juice
½	cup water

PREPARING NOODLES FOR STIR-FRY

Cook noodles according to directions on package. Drain and let sit in cold water. Drain just before using.

PREPARING TOFU FOR STIR-FRY

Cut tofu into ¼-inch slices and place in shallow tray. In separate bowl, combine liquid aminos, water and mirin. Pour over tofu and marinate 30 minutes.

Preheat oven to 375°F. Place marinated tofu on cookie sheet and roast 15 minutes. Turn pieces over and roast 15 minutes longer or until firm. Remove from oven and cut into uneven 1-inch pieces.

PREPARING SAUCE

In small bowl, whisk together all sauce ingredients until chili paste and sucanat are dissolved. Set aside.

FINISHING STIR-FRY

In large sauté pan or wok, sauté garlic in oil 1 minute. Add stir-fry sauce and cook until it starts to thicken. Add tofu and snow peas and stir another minute. Add noodles and sauté 2–3 minutes to heat through. Remove from heat and stir in bean sprouts, cilantro, scallions and lime juice. Top with peanuts and serve.

SERVES 4

Spicy Thai Tempeh with Cashews

MY HUSBAND LIKES NEARLY EVERYTHING that comes out of my kitchen, but tempeh is the one food he refused, hands down. I only wish I had my video camera when he tasted this dish and loved it. Since then, I've converted many more non-tempeh eaters into tempeh lovers. We serve this dish with Zesty Basmati Rice with Cinnamon and Cumin *(page 282)* and steamed bok choy or pac choy.

1	8-ounce package tempeh
1	tablespoon extra virgin olive oil
1	red onion, diced
1	roasted red bell pepper, diced
1	cup toasted cashews, chopped
1	tablespoon roasted red chili paste
2	tablespoons maple syrup
2	teaspoons tamari
⅓	cup water
4	scallions, finely chopped

Cut tempeh into large chunks and steam 8 minutes. Remove from heat and set aside until cool enough to handle.

In large cast-iron skillet or Dutch oven over medium heat, sauté onion in olive oil 10 minutes or until caramelized. Crumble chunks of tempeh directly into skillet. Add roasted red pepper and cashews and sauté 5 minutes.

In small bowl, whisk together chili paste, syrup, tamari and water. Pour over tempeh, and sauté another minute to combine flavors. Remove from heat, top with chopped scallions and serve.

SERVES 4

Sautéed Tempeh with Coconut Milk and Snow Peas

TEMPEH IS A WONDERFUL SOURCE of minerals, protein, vitamins and soy isoflavones. When steamed, it puffs up and is better able to absorb flavors from marinades and sauces. Serve this dish over basmati rice or forbidden rice.

---

2   8-ounce packages of tempeh

1   cup snow peas

2   tablespoons grapeseed oil

2   garlic cloves, minced

1   tablespoon grated fresh ginger

½   cup golden raisins

½   cup coconut milk

2   tablespoons tamari

2   tablespoons maple syrup

1   tablespoon mirin

Water as needed

5   scallions, chopped

½   cup chopped fresh cilantro

Cut tempeh into bite-size chunks and steam 8 minutes. Remove from heat and set aside.

Trim snow peas and place in bowl. Bring 2 cups water to boil, pour over peas. Leave for 2 minutes then drain. Rinse with cool water and set aside.

In large skillet over medium heat, sauté garlic and ginger in grapeseed oil until soft (about 2 minutes). Add tempeh, raisins, coconut milk, tamari, syrup and mirin and cook 5 minutes or until tempeh starts to brown, adding water as needed to deglaze pan. Add snow peas and cook 2 minutes longer. Remove from heat, top tempeh with scallions and cilantro and serve.

SERVES 6

Seitan Shepherd's Pie

THIS HEARTY CASSEROLE IS VERY SATISFYING, whether you're vegan, a meat-and-potatoes lover or somewhere in between.

POTATO TOPPING

5–6 small russet potatoes, quartered

¼ cup rice milk

¼ teaspoon sea salt

2 tablespoons extra virgin olive oil

Paprika

FILLING

16 ounces seitan

1 large portobello mushroom cap

1 tablespoon extra virgin olive oil

2 garlic cloves, minced

1 onion, chopped

½ teaspoon ground cumin

1 tablespoon dried basil

Water as needed

3 carrots, diced

½ cup corn, fresh or frozen

1 bunch kale or collards, chopped into bite-size pieces

¼ cup mirin

3 tablespoons tamari

1 cup vegetable stock mixed with 1 tablespoon kudzu

Sea salt and freshly ground black pepper

PREPARING POTATOES

Place potatoes in pot with enough water to cover. Bring to boil and cook until easily pierced with fork (about 20 minutes). Drain potatoes in a colander and return to pot. Add rice milk, salt and olive oil and mash until smooth and creamy. Set aside.

Preheat oven to 350°F.

PREPARING FILLING

Chop seitan and mushroom into large pieces, place together in food processor and process until coarse and crumbly.

In large pot or skillet over medium heat, sauté garlic and onion in olive oil until soft. Add seitan mushroom mixture, cumin and basil and cook 2–3 minutes. Add water as needed to prevent sticking. Add carrots, corn, kale, mirin, tamari and stock with kudzu. Stir to combine, cover and cook 5 minutes or until kale is tender and bright green. Season with salt and pepper to taste and pour into deep casserole.

FINISHING

Spread mashed potatoes over vegetable mixture and sprinkle with paprika. Bake uncovered 25–30 minutes until sauce starts to bubble. Remove from oven, cool slightly and serve.

GLUTEN-FREE OPTION
Substitute 16 ounces crumbled tempeh for seitan.

SERVES 6

Seitan Bourguignon

THIS RICH DISH COMBINES RED WINE, wild mushrooms and seitan in a distinctive, aromatic and filling main dish that requires hearty accompaniments that can hold their own, such as basmati or wild rice *(page 14)* and Sautéed Garlic Greens *(page 179)* or Ginger Sesame Greens *(page 180)*.

2	tablespoons extra virgin olive oil
2	garlic cloves, minced
6	shallots, thinly sliced
1	pound cremini mushrooms, thinly sliced
1	pound shiitake mushroom caps, thinly sliced
2	stalks celery, minced
1	tablespoon finely chopped fresh rosemary
1	tablespoon fresh thyme leaves
2	teaspoons finely chopped fresh sage
3	tablespoons tamari
2	cups dry red wine
2	pounds seitan, sliced into thin strips
1	bay leaf
½	cup vegetable stock
2	tablespoons arrowroot
Freshly ground black pepper	
¼	cup chopped fresh parsley

In large skillet over medium heat, sauté garlic and shallots in olive oil until soft. Add cremini and shiitake mushrooms, celery, rosemary, thyme, sage, tamari and wine. Bring to simmer, add seitan and bay leaf, cover and cook 15 minutes until mushrooms are tender.

In small bowl, whisk together vegetable stock and arrowroot until arrowroot dissolves. Slowly pour into skillet and continue whisking until sauce starts to thicken. Turn off heat and discard bay leaf. Season to taste with pepper, top with parsley and serve.

GLUTEN-FREE OPTION
Substitute tempeh for seitan.

SERVES 6

Wholegrain Pancakes

THIS GRAIN VERSION OF AN OLD FAVORITE, potato pancakes, is delicious served with maple syrup or applesauce and even a dash of cinnamon. Cooking grains in extra water will make them mushier, which helps them stick together. Experiment with different grains and amounts of water to find the texture you and your family like best. This is a great way to use up leftover grains.

---

1   cup uncooked or
    2½–3 cups cooked grain
    (brown rice, millet and
    quinoa all work well)

1   thumb-size piece kombu

2¼ cups water

1   tablespoon
    extra virgin olive oil

1   medium onion,
    finely chopped

½   cup grated raw carrot,
    sweet potato or winter
    squash

Sea salt

¼   cup brown rice flour

Maple syrup or applesauce
    as topping (optional)

Rinse grain and place in rice cooker or large pot with kombu and water. Bring to boil, then reduce heat and simmer until liquid is absorbed and grain is soft. Remove from heat, discard kombu and set aside. (If using refrigerated leftover grains, heat in skillet with ½ cup water and sauté 4–5 minutes.)

Preheat oven to 350°F.

In large skillet over medium heat, sauté onion and grated carrot, sweet potato or squash in olive oil for 6–8 minutes or until very soft. Add grain, season to taste with salt and fold together. Add flour 1 tablespoon at a time and mix until everything sticks together. You may not need all the flour. Remove from heat and set aside until cool enough to handle.

Using an ice cream scoop, form balls of grain mixture and place on parchment-lined cookie sheet. Flatten with fork to about ¼-inch thick. Bake 10 minutes, carefully flip pancakes and bake another 10 minutes. Serve with maple syrup or applesauce as desired.

SERVES 6

Zesty Basmati Rice with Cinnamon and Cumin

A SIMPLE YET DELICIOUS ACCOMPANIMENT to a variety of foods, such as sweet winter squash, sautéed Asian greens and warming Thai dishes.

---

1 cup brown basmati rice

2 cups water or vegetable stock

1 cinnamon stick

1 tablespoon grated fresh ginger

½ teaspoon ground cumin

¼ teaspoon sea salt

Zest of 1 orange

1 tablespoon toasted sesame oil

½ cup toasted cashew pieces

½ cup coarsely chopped fresh cilantro or parsley

Soak rice for 1 hour in bowl with enough water to cover. Drain and place in rice cooker or large pot with stock, cinnamon stick, ginger, cumin, salt and orange zest. Bring to boil, reduce heat and simmer covered until all liquid is absorbed (about 25 minutes). Remove from heat and discard cinnamon stick. Fluff with fork, toss with sesame oil, cashews and cilantro or parsley and serve.

SERVES 6

Sweet Brown Rice and Mung Beans with Indian Spices

HERBS, SPICES, LEGUMES AND VERY LITTLE EFFORT – that's all it takes to turn plain rice into something special. These Indian spices are warming to the body and especially comforting on a cold winter day.

¾ cup mung beans, soaked overnight in 4 cups water

¾ cup sweet brown rice

3 cups water

Pinch of sea salt

1 tablespoon grapeseed oil

1 large onion, diced

½ teaspoon ground cloves

½ teaspoon ground cinnamon

½ teaspoon ground cardamom

¼ teaspoon ground turmeric

Drain beans and rinse well.

Rinse rice and place in rice cooker or large pot. Add mung beans, water and salt. Bring to boil, reduce heat and simmer covered until water is absorbed and grains and beans are tender (about 45 minutes). Remove from heat and set aside to cool (fluffing too soon will yield mushy rice and beans).

In medium skillet over medium heat, sauté onion in oil until soft. Reduce heat to low and stir in all spices. Sauté another minute and remove pan from heat. Fluff rice and beans, gently fold in onion mixture and serve hot.

SERVES 6

Jasmine Rice with Sweet Peas

MANY RECIPES SUGGEST STEAMING JASMINE RICE in a double boiler or even wrapped in cheesecloth. I find that the heat in my rice cooker is indirect enough to turn out tender, fluffy jasmine rice every time. Be sure to follow the appropriate directions for the type of rice you are using (white or brown).

2 cups white jasmine rice or 1 cup brown jasmine rice

2 cups water

Pinch of sea salt

1½ cups peas, fresh or frozen

2 tablespoons lemon juice

1 tablespoon grated lemon peel

2 tablespoons chopped fresh parsley

Rinse and drain rice 3–4 times until water runs clear. Place in rice cooker with 2 cups water and salt and cook until liquid is absorbed, about 15 minutes for white rice and 25 minutes for brown rice.

Place peas in strainer. Bring 2 cups water to boil and pour over peas to blanch or thaw. Fold peas, lemon juice and lemon peel into cooked rice. Top with chopped parsley and serve.

SERVES 6

Millet with Cranberries and Pistachios

MILLET'S LIGHT FLAVOR MAKES IT A NICE ACCOMPANIMENT to winter squash, roasted nuts and dried fruit. It is high in protein and has no gluten. I like to pan-roast millet before cooking it to bring out its nutty flavor.

1½ cups millet

3 cups water

¾ cup dried cranberries

Pinch of sea salt

3 tablespoons extra virgin olive oil

4 dashes ume plum vinegar

¾ cup roasted pistachios, shelled

¼ cup chopped fresh parsley

Rinse and drain millet. Pan-roast in large skillet over medium heat for 3–4 minutes, until water evaporates and millet gives off a nutty aroma. Add 3 cups water, dried cranberries and salt, stir and bring to boil. Cover, reduce heat to low and cook 25 minutes or until all water is absorbed. Remove from heat and set aside for 5 minutes.

Fluff millet with fork, drizzle with olive oil and vinegar and gently fold to combine. Fold in pistachios and chopped parsley and serve.

SERVES 6

Polenta au Gratin

MADE FROM COARSELY GROUND CORN, polenta is a flavorful alternative to pasta. There are a variety of prepared polentas (both plain and seasoned) available in markets today that make this dish a breeze to throw together.

FILLING

1　tablespoon
　　extra virgin olive oil

2　garlic cloves, minced

1　large red onion,
　　thinly sliced

1　sprig fresh rosemary
　　leaves, minced

Water as needed

1　cup thinly sliced cremini
　　mushrooms

1　bunch Swiss chard,
　　chopped

Sea salt and freshly ground
　　black pepper

1½　cups prepared
　　pasta sauce

¼　cup grated soy or rice
　　mozzarella or parmesan

POLENTA

4　cups vegetable stock

½　teaspoon sea salt

1　cup polenta

Preheat oven to 350°F.

PREPARING CHARD FILLING

In large skillet over medium heat, sauté garlic, onion and rosemary in 1 tablespoon olive oil until soft, adding water 1 tablespoon at a time as needed to prevent sticking. Add mushrooms and chard, cover and cook 3–4 minutes or until chard is soft. Season to taste with salt and pepper, remove from heat and set aside.

PREPARING POLENTA

In medium Dutch oven or deep sauté pan over high heat, bring stock and salt to boil. Gradually stir in polenta, reduce heat and simmer stirring frequently to avoid sticking for 15 minutes. Remove from heat.

ASSEMBLING

Lightly oil 8 x 8-inch casserole and spread half the polenta evenly over the bottom. Cover with ¾ cup pasta sauce, the chard mixture, the remaining polenta, the remaining ¾ cup pasta sauce and grated soy or rice cheese. Cover with foil and bake for 15 minutes. Uncover and bake another 10 minutes. Remove from oven, let set 5 minutes and serve.

SERVES 6

Baked Stuffed Shells

MY OLDEST DAUGHTER IS A NUT FOR my Tofu Kale Lasagna *(page 213)*. This dish takes its key ingredients from the lasagna, but requires only half the time and effort and disappears every bit as quickly once it hits her plate.

---

8 ounces large pasta shells

3 tablespoons extra virgin olive oil

3 garlic cloves, minced

1 large onion, chopped

¼ cup mirin

2 teaspoons dried basil

2 teaspoons dried parsley

1½ pounds fresh firm tofu (not silken)

2 bunches kale or collard greens, chopped

Sea salt and freshly ground pepper

4 cups tomato sauce

1 cup grated soy or rice mozzarella

Preheat oven to 400°F.

Cook shells according to instructions on package, drain and set aside.

PREPARING FILLING

In large skillet or Dutch oven over medium heat, sauté garlic and onions in olive oil until soft (about 5 minutes). Stir in mirin, basil and parsley. Wrap tofu in paper towels and press to remove excess liquid. Crumble tofu into pot, mix to combine and cook 5 minutes.

Fold greens into tofu mixture and continue cooking until soft. Season to taste with salt and pepper, remove from heat and set aside until cool enough to handle.

ASSEMBLING

Stuff shells with filling and place in 9 x 12-inch lasagna pan. Cover stuffed shells with tomato sauce. Sprinkle top with soy or rice mozzarella, cover with foil and bake 20 minutes. Remove foil and bake uncovered 10 minutes. Remove from oven and let set 5 minutes before serving.

SERVES 4

Sinful Stuffed Dates

I USED TO MAKE THESE TREATS ON THE SLY. When the kids went to bed, I'd grab a date, slice it open and stuff it with some nuts, some chocolate chips…whatever I could get a hold of quickly. After much sneaking, I decided to admit my sins (OK, so I got caught) and turned my cheating into a legitimate – yet sinfully delicious – recipe.

Zest of 1 orange

½ cup chopped pecans

¼ teaspoon ground cinnamon

½ cup plus 2 tablespoons shredded dried unsweetened coconut

2 tablespoons maple syrup

1 tablespoon virgin coconut oil, melted

18 dates

Preheat oven to 350°F.

In small bowl, combine orange zest, chopped pecans, cinnamon, 2 tablespoons coconut, syrup and oil. Stir until evenly coated. Spread out on parchment-lined cookie sheet and roast 5–6 minutes until lightly browned. Remove from oven and set aside.

Carefully slice each date down one side and remove pit. If necessary, make small cuts in rounded ends of dates so they do not tear. Gently turn date inside out, placing sticky side down on work surface.

Press ¼ teaspoon roasted nut mixture into each date. Fold up edges and press seam and ends together to seal shut. Place remaining ½ cup coconut in small bowl, then press and roll sealed dates in coconut to coat. Arrange on tray and serve.

MAKES 18 dates

Coconut Cranberry Pecan Balls

THIS RECIPE WAS CREATED AT THE END OF A CLASS that did not include a dessert. The meal was a hit, but as soon as I served it, I felt desperate for something sweet. While everyone ate, I quickly pulled out my food processor and a couple of goodies from my cupboard, and this was the result.

¼ cup shredded dried unsweetened coconut

1½ cups toasted pecans

1 cup dried cranberries

½ cup almond butter

½ cup maple syrup

Place coconut in small bowl and set aside.

In food processor, combine remaining ingredients and process to form a stiff paste or meal. Form into tablespoon-size balls and roll in coconut to coat. Serve immediately or store in airtight container for up to 4 days.

MAKES 12–15 balls

Maple Spiced Almonds

I SERVE THESE AROMATIC NUTS AROUND THE HOLIDAYS and people devour them. They're also great sprinkled over a salad or granola or chopped and served over ice cream.

---

1 tablespoon walnut oil

3 tablespoons maple syrup

2 tablespoons pumpkin pie spice

3–4 dashes cayenne

3 cups whole almonds

Preheat oven to 350°F.

In large bowl, whisk together oil, syrup, pumpkin pie spice and cayenne. Add almonds, stir to coat and spread out in single layer on parchment-lined cookie sheet. Bake until nuts start to brown, 20–25 minutes. Remove from oven and cool completely. Break nuts apart and store in airtight container.

MAKES 3 cups

Sesame Almond Balls

THESE ALMOND BALLS ARE A PERFECT BITE-SIZE DESSERT. If you want something more to sink your teeth into, bake up some cinnamon-raisin mochi squares and stuff them with this mixture.

½ cup toasted sesame seeds

½ cup almond butter

¼ cup toasted sunflower seeds

¼ cup toasted almonds

4–5 dates, pitted

Place ¼ cup sesame seeds in small bowl and set aside.

In food processor, combine remaining ¼ cup sesame seeds with almond butter, sunflower seeds, almonds and dates. Process to form a stiff paste or meal. Form into tablespoon-size balls and roll in reserved sesame seeds to coat. Serve immediately or store in airtight container for up to 4 days.

MAKES 12–15 balls

Poached Winter Fruit Medley

THIS SIMPLE DESSERT WILL SATISFY your need for that little something sweet at the end of a meal, and you'll enjoy the added benefit of a home filled with the wonderful aroma of brewing spices. For an extra-special presentation, serve with vanilla bean ice cream and a sprig of mint.

1½ cups water

½ cup maple syrup

Zest of 1 orange

6 cloves

2 cinnamon sticks

½ teaspoon lemon extract

4 ripe but firm pears, peeled, cored and quartered

4 apples, peeled, cored and quartered

2 dried Calimyrna figs, quartered

¼ cup dried cranberries or cherries

Combine water, syrup, zest, cloves, cinnamon sticks and lemon extract in large pot over medium heat and bring to simmer. Place pears and apples in simmering syrup, reduce heat to medium-low and poach 10 minutes. Add figs and cranberries and cook another 10 minutes, or until fresh fruits are tender and syrup has reduced by half. Serve warm or chilled.

SERVES 4

Apple Tart

APPLES AND NEW ENGLAND ARE PRACTICALLY SYNONYMOUS.
I remember my parents bringing them home by the bushel and we would enjoy them straight through fall and winter. I was always partial to the most simple of recipes like this one that required little fuss and delivered lots of sweet satisfaction.

CRUST

1	cup millet flour
¾	cup almond flour
¼	teaspoon sea salt
¼	cup extra virgin coconut oil
¼	cup maple syrup

FILLING

4	apples
2	tablespoons lemon juice
2	tablespoons maple syrup
2	tablespoons sliced almonds

GLAZE

½	cup apricot jam or preserves
2	tablespoons water
1	teaspoon lemon juice
Zest of 1 lemon	

Preheat oven to 350°F.

PREPARING CRUST

Place millet flour, almond flour and salt in food processor and combine. Melt coconut oil over very low heat and whisk together with maple syrup. Add to food processor and pulse to combine and form dough. Transfer dough into 9-inch oiled tart pan. Press down to form crust. Pierce several times with fork and bake 15 minutes. Remove from oven and set aside.

ASSEMBLING TART

Peel apples, slice in half (from stem down) and remove stems and cores. Slice apples crosswise into ¼-inch slices. Keeping sliced halves together, fit apples into tart crust. When crust is full, tilt sliced apples to fan them. Combine lemon juice and maple syrup and brush over apples. Sprinkle with sliced almonds and bake 45 minutes to 1 hour or until apples are soft and lightly browned. Remove from oven and set aside to cool.

FINISHING WITH GLAZE

In small pan over low heat, thin apricot preserves in water. Remove from heat and stir in lemon juice. Pour through strainer into separate bowl. Stir in lemon zest, brush over tart and serve.

SERVES 8

Pear and Fig Tart in Pecan Crust

THIS NONTRADITIONAL TART is less sweet than many of my other desserts, makes an impressive presentation and has delicious rich flavor. Pair it with a scoop of vanilla bean ice cream and a glass of Port.

CRUST

2 cups pecans

1 cup brown rice flour

¼ cup virgin coconut oil, melted

¼ cup maple syrup

FIG FILLING

10 dried Calimyrna figs

1 cup water

2 cups pear or apple juice

1 tablespoon maple syrup

1 tablespoon orange zest

2 tablespoons tapioca flour

½ teaspoon vanilla extract

PEARS AND GLAZE

3 large D'Anjou pears

2 tablespoons lemon juice

1 cup pear or apple juice

1 tablespoon maple syrup

¼ teaspoon vanilla extract

2 teaspoons arrowroot

PREPARING CRUST

Preheat oven to 350°F. Place pecans in food processor and coarsely chop. Add brown rice flour and process briefly. Combine oil and syrup in small bowl, add to nut mixture and process until combined. Transfer to 11-inch tart pan and press to form crust. Pierce several times with fork and bake 15 minutes or until golden brown. Remove from oven and set on wire rack to cool.

PREPARING FILLING

Remove and discard tough ends of figs and cut figs into quarters. Place in pot with water and juice. Bring to boil, then reduce heat and simmer until figs are soft and 1½ cups of liquid remains (about 25 minutes). Remove from heat, add maple syrup and orange zest. Purée mixture with handheld blender until smooth. Gradually stir in tapioca flour and vanilla, pour into tart crust and spread evenly to cover bottom.

PREPARING PEARS

Peel, core and slice pears. Cut into equal-size thin, flat wedges and toss with lemon juice. Place in steamer basket and steam 3 minutes, or until just soft (oversteaming will make pears mushy). Remove steamer basket and cool pears. Arrange over fig filling in overlapping, fanlike pattern with ends pointing toward center of tart.

PREPARING GLAZE AND FINISHING

In small pan over no heat, combine pear or apple juice, maple syrup, vanilla and arrowroot. Place over medium heat and stir continuously until mixture thickens and becomes translucent. Spoon evenly over tart and refrigerate to set (about 1 hour). Serve at room temperature.

SERVES 8

Chocolate Pecan Pie

WHEN IT COMES TO THANKSGIVING, PECAN PIE IS A MUST. This version – made without the traditional eggs, brown sugar and butter – is free of guilt but full of rich flavor and will have you eating pecan pie more than once a year.

CRUST

1½	cups almonds
1	cup rolled oats
¼	cup cacao powder
¼	teaspoon sea salt
¼	cup walnut oil
¼	cup maple syrup

FILLING

2	tablespoons ground golden flax seeds
6	tablespoons water
1	cup apple juice
½	cup raisins
½	cup honey
½	cup cacao powder
Pinch of sea salt	
2	tablespoons cashew butter
1	teaspoon vanilla extract
2	cups lightly toasted pecans

Preheat oven to 350°F. Lightly oil 9-inch tart pan.

PREPARING CRUST

Place almonds, oats, cacao and salt in food processor and process to form a crumb-like mixture. Add oil and syrup and process to combine. Place mixture in tart pan and press to form crust. Pierce several times with fork and bake 12 minutes or until lightly browned. Remove from oven and cool on wire rack. Keep oven on.

PREPARING FILLING

Soak ground flax in bowl with 6 tablespoons water for 20 minutes. Meanwhile, in small pot, combine apple juice, raisins, honey, cacao powder and salt. Place over medium heat and simmer for 10 minutes (raisins will lose their form). Add cashew butter to soaked flax seed mixture and whisk into apple juice mixture. Continue whisking until texture is uniform or purée gently with handheld blender. Remove from heat, stir in vanilla and set aside.

ASSEMBLING

Arrange 1½ cups toasted pecans over cooked pie crust. Pour in filling and arrange remaining pecans on top. Cover loosely with foil and bake 50 minutes. Remove from oven and place on wire rack to set. Serve at room temperature.

SERVES 10–12

Chestnut Cream Pie

PREPARED CHESTNUTS ARE A SEASONAL SPECIALTY ITEM that you will find on sale as soon as the holidays are over. I stock up on them so I can easily enjoy making this pie all winter long. Store-bought crust makes this simple pie whip up in a snap. Not overly sweet or indulgent, the smooth texture and pungent cinnamon in this pie satisfy even my most stubborn cravings.

1   9-inch prepared pie crust

TOPPING

1   teaspoon virgin coconut oil, melted
1   teaspoon maple syrup
1   teaspoon ground cinnamon
1   cup coarsely chopped almonds

FILLING

2   cups prepared chestnuts
1   cup rice milk
2   teaspoons ground cinnamon
1½   teaspoons vanilla extract
Pinch of ground allspice
3   tablespoons maple syrup
2   tablespoons agar powder
½   cup apple juice

Preheat oven to 375°F.

Pierce pie crust 6–7 times and bake 20 minutes or until lightly browned. Remove from oven and cool on wire rack.

PREPARING TOPPING

In small bowl, combine oil, syrup and cinnamon. Add chopped almonds and toss to coat. Spread out nuts on parchment-lined cookie sheet and bake 10 minutes or until browned. Remove from oven and set aside.

PREPARING FILLING

In food processor, process chestnuts, rice milk, cinnamon, vanilla, allspice and maple syrup until smooth.

In small pot over medium heat, whisk together agar powder and apple juice until powder dissolves and mixture thickens. Remove from heat, add to food processor and process briefly to combine.

FINISHING

Pour mixture into pie crust and top with spiced nuts. Refrigerate 1 hour to set. Serve cold or at room temperature.

SERVES 8

Tiramisu

I'M NOT A COFFEE DRINKER, but I'm a nut for coffee-flavored treats like ice cream and tiramisu. To satisfy my taste for coffee ice cream, I combine almonds, ice, maple syrup and iced coffee in my Vitamix. To satisfy my taste for tiramisu, I developed this decadent recipe.

CAKES

1   cup ivory teff flour

½   cup almond meal

¼   cup tapioca flour

1   teaspoon baking powder

¼   teaspoon sea salt

½   cup maple syrup

¼   cup virgin coconut oil, melted, plus more to grease baking tins

2   tablespoons rice milk

2   tablespoons applesauce

2   teaspoons vanilla extract

TOFU CREAM

Prepare recipe as on page 155

SYRUP

¾   cup hot grain coffee substitute or coffee of choice

¼   cup maple syrup

1   tablespoon vanilla extract

1   teaspoon almond extract

Cacao powder for garnish

Preheat oven to 350°F.

PREPARING CAKES

Light oil two 8-inch round baking tins or springform pans. In large bowl, combine teff flour, almond meal, tapioca, baking powder and salt. In separate bowl, combine maple syrup, coconut oil, rice milk, applesauce and vanilla extract. Pour wet ingredients into dry and whisk until combined. Pour batter equally into prepared tins and bake 15 minutes or until cakes are lightly browned and a toothpick inserted into the center comes out clean. Remove from oven and place on wire rack to cool.

PREPARING SYRUP

Whisk together all syrup ingredients and set aside.

ASSEMBLING

Remove one cake from tin and place on cake plate. Drizzle half the syrup evenly over the cake and spread with half the cream. Remove second cake from tin, place on top of first and drizzle remaining syrup evenly over the top. Spread with remaining cream, top with a generous amount of sifted cacao powder and serve.

SERVES 8

There is no season such delights can bring as summer, autumn, winter and spring.

WILLIAM BROWNE

Snacks

By definition, snacks are light meals. But today, snack foods have become a multi billion-dollar industry of processed packaged foods, driven by our busy lifestyles and demand for everything to be quick and easy. All too often we sacrifice nutritional value for convenience. Reversing this trend can be as simple as slowing down, making conscious healthy choices and being prepared. Snacking isn't a bad thing when its purpose is to fuel metabolism and activity. So whether you're stocking your pantry with nuts and seeds, your refrigerator with crudités and dips, or your desk or backpack with raw chocolate, if you prepare for snacking you can easily make this mini meal clean and delicious. Sometimes fruit, vegetables, nuts or seeds will do the trick. Other times transforming leftovers into a spring roll or pizza is sure to entice! Whatever you choose – eat your snacks mindfully, enjoy every bite, and allow them to satisfy and nourish your need for that little something extra.

SNACKS

COOL AND REFRESHING

Vegetable Nori Rolls 304
Lettuce Wraps with Ginger Peanut Tofu 305
Super Smoothies 307
    Green Monster
    Carrot Cantaloupe Ginger
    Peanut Butter Cacao Banana
Rice Noodles and Peanut Sauce Rolled in Nori 308
Quick Homemade Pickles 309

SAVORY

Traditional Hummus 310
Muffaletto 311
Kale Chips 312
Crispy Roasted Chickpeas 314
Green Goddess Dip 315
Herbed White Bean Dip 316
Pita Chips 317
Leftover Soup 318
Baked Stuffed Sweet Potatoes 319
Toasted Sesame Nori Crisps 321
Tortilla Pizzas 322
Baked Stuffed Mochi 323

SWEETS

Maple Nut Granola 324
Brown Rice Pudding 326
Oatmeal Chocolate Chip (or Raisin) Cookies 327
Popcorn with Olive Oil, Sea Salt
    and Drizzled Dark Chocolate 329
Crispy Rice Squares 330
Raisin Nut Bars 331
Teff Peanut Butter Chocolate Chip Cookies 332
Teff Ginger Molasses Cookies 334

Vegetable Nori Rolls

IF YOU DINE AT JAPANESE RESTAURANTS, you've likely encountered vegetables and rice wrapped in nori. Of all the seaweeds, nori has the highest protein content and is the easiest to digest. These rolls make a great appetizer, snack or small meal.

---

2 cups sushi rice

3 cups water, plus more for rolls

Pinch of sea salt

2 tablespoons brown rice vinegar

10 sheets toasted nori

1 small cucumber, julienned

1 carrot, julienned

1 avocado, peeled, pitted and cut into strips

ACCOMPANIMENTS

Tamari

Pickled ginger

Wasabi paste

Combine rice, 3 cups water and salt in large pot and bring to boil. Cover, then reduce heat and simmer 20 minutes or until all water is absorbed. Remove from heat, add brown rice vinegar and fold to combine.

ASSEMBLING NORI ROLLS

Place a sheet of nori, shiny side down, on work surface or bamboo rolling mat, with short edge facing you. Press a layer of rice ¼-inch thick along the edge of the sheet closest to you. Place vegetables in a long thin strip across the middle of the rice. Carefully fold the end of nori over the rice and continue rolling away from you to form a log. Moisten the edge with water to seal, and let sit briefly until nori is soft enough to cut easily. Cut into ½-inch pieces and arrange on platter. Serve with tamari, pickled ginger and wasabi.

SERVES 6

VARIATION
For even greater health benefits, substitute short grain brown rice for the sushi rice and increase your water to 4 cups.

Lettuce Wraps with Ginger Peanut Tofu

I CAN FIND A REASON TO ADD PEANUT BUTTER to just about any recipe, but this one is far from a stretch. Rich and salty peanut butter is the perfect complement to crisp and refreshing lettuce. Make the tofu in advance so when you want a snack, all you have to do is wash a piece of lettuce, add the tofu and go. That's what I call "fast food!"

---

15 ounces, fresh firm tofu
⅓ cup chopped chives
⅓ cup julienned carrots
8 whole leaves bib or Boston lettuce

PEANUT SAUCE

½ cup vegetable stock
¼ cup crunchy peanut butter
2 cloves garlic, minced
1 tablespoon grated ginger root
1 tablespoon lime juice
1 tablespoon maple syrup

Preheat oven to 350°F.

Cut tofu into ½-inch cubes, place in 8 x 8-inch baking dish and set aside.

In small mixing bowl, whisk together sauce ingredients. (If peanut butter is firm, break it up with a knife and slowly blend it in with the other ingredients.) Pour sauce over tofu and place in oven. Bake 15 minutes, toss to redistribute sauce and bake an additional 15 minutes. Remove from heat and set aside to cool and allow sauce to thicken (about 30 minutes).

Add chives and carrot to cooled tofu and toss to combine. Place one lettuce leaf on cutting board with stem end closest to you. Place a scoop of tofu mixture into the middle of the leaf. Fold in sides and then roll lettuce away from you to fully enclose mixture. Use smaller leaves like cups. Repeat until all lettuce and filling is used. Serve at room temperature.

MAKES 8 lettuce cups

Super Smoothies

SMOOTHIES ARE MY PROOF that children are more likely to eat (or at least try) foods they prepare themselves. If I make the smoothies, my children are suspicious. But if they make them, they disappear before I even get a taste. To avoid excess sugar, we have one rule in our house – every smoothie has to have at least one vegetable in it. For finicky eaters, smoothies can be a great place to hide super-foods. You'd be surprised how well frozen blueberries cover up powdered greens or kelp!

GREEN MONSTER

6   kale leaves

2   bananas, peeled

1   apple, peeled and cored

1   cup apple juice

1–1½ cups ice

CARROT CANTALOUPE GINGER

1½ cups chopped cantaloupe

1   peach, peeled and pitted

2   teaspoons grated fresh ginger

1   tablespoon lime juice

1   cup carrot juice

1–1½ cups ice

PEANUT BUTTER CACAO BANANA

2   bananas, peeled

½   cup peanut butter

¼   cup cacao beans (raw chocolate beans)

¼   cup sliced almonds

1   cup rice milk

1–1½ cups ice

Using a blender with a powerful motor, place all ingredients and 1 cup of ice in blender and turn on the lowest speed. Gradually increase blender speed to high and blend until smooth. Add more ice as needed, blend to achieve desired consistency and serve.

Each recipe SERVES 2

VARIATIONS

Experiment with these super-nutritional add-ins to create your own unique smoothie combination: coconut water, avocado, chia seeds, powdered greens, powdered kelp, rice protein powder, acai berries, goji berries, cacao (beans, nibs or powder), nuts and seeds or nut and seed butters.

Rice Noodles and Peanut Sauce Rolled in Nori

NORI IS A STAPLE IN MY HOME. My kids love it plain (as does the dog), and we've tried just about everything we can think of as a filling. This combination delivers a surprising and satisfying trio: spicy peanut sauce, cool and refreshing noodles, and the tang of pickled ginger. They disappear so quickly when I make them that I hide extra sauce and noodles in the refrigerator just so that there's something left for me once the kids are done.

Rice noodles or bean thread noodles – 1 cup cooked per serving

Nori sheets – one per person

Pickled ginger

PEANUT SAUCE

¼	cup peanut butter
2	tablespoons coconut milk
1	teaspoon red chili paste
2	tablespoons maple syrup
2	tablespoons lime juice
1	teaspoon tamari
3	tablespoons toasted sesame oil or 2 tablespoons hot sesame oil

Water

Prepare noodles according to directions on package. Rinse with cool water, drain and set aside.

PREPARING SAUCE

Whisk together all sauce ingredients. Thin with water 1 tablespoon at a time to achieve desired consistency.

ASSEMBLING

Place a sheet of nori, shiny side down, on work surface or bamboo sushi rolling mat with the short edge facing you. Arrange a serving of noodles over the closest one-third of the sheet. Top with peanut sauce and pickled ginger. Carefully fold closest end of nori over noodles and continue rolling away from you to form a log. Seal by dampening edge with water. Let sit briefly until the nori is soft enough to cut easily. Cut into ½-inch pieces, arrange on platter and serve with peanut sauce.

SINGLE SERVING: 1 sheet nori yields 5–6 bite-size pieces

Quick Homemade Pickles

MACROBIOTICS TEACHES US that pickles aid digestion. This approach to pickling is quick and easy and works great with cucumbers, daikon, radishes, cabbage, carrots and more. The possibilities are endless.

3   cups thinly sliced
     vegetables of choice

¼   cup water

¼   cup brown rice vinegar

3   tablespoons sucanat

½   teaspoon sea salt

Place sliced vegetables in glass bowl and set aside.

In medium pot over high heat, combine remaining ingredients. Bring to boil, reduce heat and simmer until sucanat dissolves. Remove from heat and cool 2–3 minutes. Pour over vegetables, cover and refrigerate. If liquid does not cover vegetables completely, stir every 30 minutes and marinate until vegetables break down and liquid covers all (about 2 hours). Store pickles refrigerated in pickling liquid in glass container.

MAKES 2½ cups

Traditional Hummus

THE ORIGINAL VEGAN SNACK FOOD! Hummus was the first dish
I figured out on my own, and years later I still make it by the tubful.
Whether stuffed in pita pockets with vegetables and sprouts, or served
as an appetizer or midday snack with carrot sticks or rice crackers,
hummus is easy to make, healthy and enjoyed by all. For variety, try
adding roasted garlic or roasted red peppers.

---

1 garlic clove, peeled

2 cups cooked chickpeas

3 tablespoons
extra virgin olive oil

2 tablespoons tahini

½ teaspoon ground cumin

2 tablespoons lemon juice

¼ teaspoon sea salt

Water

With food processor running, drop in garlic clove and process until
minced. Turn off processor, scrape down sides and add chickpeas,
olive oil, tahini, cumin, lemon juice and salt. Restart processor and
slowly add water, making hummus slightly thinner than desired, as it
will thicken when refrigerated. Season to taste with extra cumin, lemon
juice and/or salt as desired. Chill to combine flavors before serving.

MAKES 1½ cups

Muffaletto

THIS CONDIMENT WHIPS UP IN SECONDS and has many wonderful uses. Try it in a wrap with hummus and arugula, serve it as an appetizer with Pita Chips *(page 317)* or toasted baguette rounds, or thin it with a bit of wine and some chopped tomatoes and use it as a pasta sauce.

---

1 cup black and green olives, pitted

1 cup roasted red pepper

2 garlic cloves, peeled

¼ cup chopped fresh parsley

1 tablespoon red wine vinegar

Freshly ground black pepper

Extra virgin olive oil

Combine olives, roasted pepper, garlic, parsley and vinegar in food processor and pulse to chop ingredients. (Be sure not to purée – chunks are good!) Season to taste with pepper and drizzle with olive oil. Cover and refrigerate 3 hours. Before serving, stir and bring to room temperature.

MAKES 1¼ cups

Kale Chips

I PROMISE, THESE CHIPS TASTE JUST LIKE POTATO CHIPS, if not better! This is the perfect recipe for introducing non-kale eaters to the wonders of kale, and my children are the proof. Not only do they devour them almost instantly fresh out of the oven, but they request them so much I can barely make them fast enough.

---

1   large bunch kale (about 4 cups firmly packed)

1   tablespoon extra virgin olive oil

¼   teaspoon sea salt

Freshly ground black pepper

Preheat oven to 300°F and line two rimmed baking sheets with parchment paper.

Remove stems of kale by holding stem with one hand and with other hand pinch stem at base of leaves and slowly pull stem toward top of the leaf. Discard stems. Wash and dry leaves thoroughly and place in large mixing bowl. Drizzle with olive oil, sprinkle with salt and massage into leaves. Add pepper to taste and spread out kale in single layer on prepared baking sheets. Place in oven and bake for 10–15 minutes or until kale is dry and crispy and just barely brown on the edges. Remove from heat, transfer to bowl and serve.

SERVES 2

VARIATIONS
Once you master the classic recipe, experiment with a variety of herb and spice combinations, such as cumin and cayenne, onion powder and dill, and even curry or herbs de Provence.

Crispy Roasted Chickpeas

I STRONGLY ENCOURAGE YOU to double, triple or even quadruple this recipe, because once they come out of the oven they're nearly impossible to resist.

3   cups cooked chickpeas

2–3 tablespoons
       extra virgin olive oil

Sea salt

Seasoning of choice
       (see variations at right)

Preheat oven to 400°F.

Rinse chickpeas and drain well. Pat dry with a towel and spread evenly over parchment-lined baking sheet. Drizzle with olive oil and rub chickpeas with fingers to make sure they are coated. Sprinkle with a generous amount of sea salt and seasoning(s) of choice, and roast for 30 minutes or until golden and crisp on the inside but not burnt on the outside.

MAKES 3 cups

VARIATIONS
Experiment with a variety of different spices such as garlic powder, cumin, chili powder, cayenne, Chinese five spice, nutmeg, wasabi powder or your own unique spice blend.

Green Goddess Dip

WHEN I PUT DINNER ON THE TABLE, my children quickly fill up on the least nutritious part of the meal and then complain they're too full to eat their vegetables. This dip is my solution. I serve it as an appetizer with crudités so that my children feel like they're getting a treat, and I succeed in adding more vegetables to their diet. Everybody wins!

---

12 ounces extra firm silken tofu

3 scallions, chopped

3 tablespoons firmly packed fresh parsley or cilantro

3 tablespoons extra virgin olive oil

2 tablespoons maple mustard

1 tablespoon mellow white miso

1 tablespoon apple cider vinegar

2 teaspoons maple syrup

Juice of 1 lemon

Wrap tofu in paper towels and press gently to remove excess water. Place in food processor or blender and process until smooth. Add remaining ingredients and process to combine. Cover and refrigerate to thicken and allow flavors to blend. Store in airtight container in refrigerator for up to 3 days.

MAKES 2 cups

VARIATIONS
This dip can be thinned with water and used as a salad dressing, or made with 1½ cups great northern or navy beans instead of tofu.

Herbed White Bean Dip

THIS DIP CAN BE MADE IN ADVANCE and stored in an airtight container in the refrigerator, but the flavors will be best at room temperature or slightly heated. Serve with Garlic Crostini *(page 240)*, Pita Chips *(page 317)*, crudités or in a sandwich with baby field greens and sliced tomato.

---

2 tablespoons
  extra virgin olive oil

2 garlic cloves, minced

2 shallots or 1 small sweet
  onion, diced

2 tablespoons mirin

1 tablespoon minced
  fresh rosemary

1 tablespoon fresh thyme
  or lemon thyme leaves

¼ teaspoon sea salt

2 cups cooked white beans
  (navy, great northern or
  cannellini)

4–5 dashes hot pepper sauce
  or cayenne

Zest of 1 lemon

In small skillet over medium heat, sauté garlic and shallots in olive oil until soft (about 3 minutes). Add mirin, rosemary, thyme and salt and reduce heat to medium-low. Cook for 5 minutes, then remove from heat.

In large bowl, combine beans with sautéed shallot mixture and purée with handheld blender. Season to taste with hot pepper sauce, top with lemon zest and serve at room temperature.

MAKES 1½ cups

Pita Chips

THESE CHIPS ARE DELICIOUS ON THEIR OWN and also make a perfect accompaniment to soups, bean dips, Muffaletto *(page 311)* or Olive Tapenade *(page 239)*. Season them any way you want for a variety of flavors.

6–8 small pita pockets

OPTION 1

Extra virgin olive oil

All-purpose seasoning blend
*Prepare recipe as on
page 275*

OPTION 2

Toasted sesame oil

Gomasio

Preheat oven to 350°F.

Split each pita into 2 rounds and place, rough side up, on cookie sheet. Pour oil into small bowl and brush onto each pita. Sprinkle lightly with seasoning, cut into triangular wedges and bake 6–8 minutes or until lightly browned. Baking time will vary according to the thickness of pitas. Remove from oven, cool and serve. Store in airtight container.

GLUTEN-FREE OPTION
Substitute rice or corn tortillas for pita.

SERVES 4

VARIATIONS
Try seasoning chips with olive oil, ground mustard and garlic powder. Melted virgin coconut oil with either pumpkin pie spice, curry, nutmeg or cinnamon are other favorite combinations.

Leftover Soup

THIS IS THE GREENEST WAY I KNOW to satisfy the need for a quick and delicious snack as well as to reduce the amount of waste coming out of your kitchen. There's really nobody in my family who gets excited about reheating leftover veggies, but I definitely get excited about putting together a meal in just minutes and this soup is my solution.

---

2   teaspoons extra virgin olive oil, plus extra for drizzling

1   clove garlic, minced

¼   cup chopped onion

¾   cup chopped carrots and celery

1½ cups leftover sautéed or steamed leafy greens or broccoli

1   cup leftover cooked grains, beans or both

3   cups vegetable stock, plus more as desired

1   teaspoon ume plum vinegar

Freshly ground black pepper

Chopped fresh parsley to garnish

In Dutch oven over medium heat, sauté garlic and onion in olive oil until soft, about 2–3 minutes. Add carrots and celery and continue sautéing until vegetables are just soft. Add leftover vegetables, grains and/or beans and stock. Simmer until all ingredients are heated through. Add extra stock to thin to desired consistency. Remove from heat, stir in vinegar and season to taste with pepper. Top with a drizzle of olive oil and a sprinkle of parsley and serve.

SERVES 4

VARIATIONS
Turn roasted root vegetables into a cream soup by adding stock and puréeing. Season any soup with fresh herbs and spices that go with your leftovers – try curry, turmeric, ginger, oregano or even nutmeg.

Baked Stuffed Sweet Potatoes

SWEET POTATOES ARE SO NATURALLY SWEET, delicious and satisfying that I rarely feel the need to top them at all. But when I do, a simple switch from chopped nuts and dates to caramelized onions and greens can take this dish from breakfast to lunch to snack time and even dinner with little fuss.

---

2 medium sweet potatoes

TOPPING SUGGESTIONS

NORI, SESAME SEEDS AND SEA SALT

½ sheet toasted nori

2 tablespoons toasted sesame seeds

Coarse sea salt

CARAMELIZED ONIONS AND GREENS

1 teaspoons extra virgin olive oil

1 small onion (any variety), chopped

1 cup firmly packed chopped greens (kale, collards, broccoli...)

2 dashes ume plum vinegar

MAPLE, ALMONDS AND CINNAMON

1 tablespoon maple syrup

¼ cup toasted sliced almonds

Cinnamon

Preheat oven or toaster over to 350°F.

Wash sweet potatoes and pierce several times with a fork. Place in glass baking dish, cover with foil and bake until soft (50–60 minutes). Prepare topping of choice based on desired quantity and taste. Remove potatoes from oven, slice open lengthwise, squeeze in the ends to open and fill with prepared topping. Serve warm.

PREPARING NORI TOPPING
Using mortar and pestle, grind together all ingredients. Sprinkle over baked sweet potatoes and serve.

PREPARING GREENS TOPPING
In skillet over medium heat, sauté onion in olive oil until soft (about 3 minutes). Add greens and continue sautéing until bright and just soft. Add ume plum vinegar, toss and serve over baked sweet potatoes.

PREPARING ALMOND TOPPING
In mixing bowl, combine maple syrup, almonds and cinnamon to taste. Spoon over baked sweet potatoes and serve.

VARIATIONS
Experiment with different toppings such as diced avocado with red onion and cilantro; roasted Brussels sprouts and shiitake mushrooms; or black beans and sweet corn with scallion and crumbled corn chips.

MAKES 2 stuffed sweet potatoes

Toasted Sesame Nori Crisps

MANY YEARS AGO I DISCOVERED SESAME NORI CRISPS at my local health food store. They came in a tiny deli-style container, and I devoured them in less than a minute. Even my kids couldn't get enough. Now I make them in huge batches, as they are always a welcome gift for family and friends. Serve nori crisps with any meal, save them for a nutritionally packed and satisfying snack or use them as a garnish for fish, grains or salads.

3   sheets toasted nori
½   cup extra virgin olive oil
½   cup brown rice syrup
Cayenne
1½ cups sesame seeds
Spice of choice
      (nutmeg, cinnamon,
      pumpkin pie spice…)
Sea salt

Preheat oven to 350°F.

Stack nori sheets, cut into 2-inch strips, stack again and cut in half. Cover cookie sheet with parchment paper, and lay individual strips of nori side by side on paper. In small bowl, whisk together oil, syrup, and a pinch of cayenne.

Using a pastry brush, generously coat the top of each piece of nori with syrup mixture. Oil and syrup tend to separate, so continue to mix as you work. When all nori pieces are coated, sprinkle with sesame seeds, spice of choice and salt. Toast in oven 5–7 minutes (keep a close eye as they burn easily). When seeds are light brown, remove from oven and set aside to cool until nori is firm enough to handle.

Flip nori pieces, brush with syrup mixture and sprinkle with sesame seeds, seasoning and salt. Return to oven for another 5–7 minutes. Remove from oven and cool completely. Repeat until all ingredients are used. Store in airtight container.

MAKES 30 crisps

Tortilla Pizzas

TORTILLAS MAKE THE PERFECT super-thin and crispy pizza crust and they cook up in no time. Simply top with your favorite toppings, broil and within minutes you have a light and delicious pizza. My kids like to make their own which always yields new and unexpected topping combinations, and is also a whole lot of fun.

SAVORY

2 brown rice tortillas (or variety of choice)

¼ cup pesto

¼ cup tomato sauce

½ cup firmly packed basil leaves

1 cup firmly packed fresh spinach

2 medium tomatoes, sliced thinly

2 thin slices red onion

2 tablespoons pine nuts

SWEET

2 brown rice tortillas (or variety of choice)

¼ cup apple butter

2 apples or pears, cored and thinly sliced

1 tablespoon maple syrup

1 tablespoon lemon juice

¼ cup sliced almonds

3–4 dashes ground nutmeg

Set oven to broil and place rack on second setting from the top (pizzas directly under broiler will burn). Place baking sheet or pizza stone on rack to preheat.

SAVORY OPTION

Remove baking sheet or pizza stone from oven and place tortillas on whichever you are using. Spread pesto and tomato sauce on tortillas leaving ¼-inch clean around outside edge. Top with basil leaves, spinach, tomatoes, onion and pine nuts. Broil 3–5 minutes or until tomatoes are soft and edges of tortillas are lightly browned and crispy. Remove from oven and serve.

SWEET OPTION

Remove baking sheet or pizza stone from oven and place tortillas on whichever you are using. Spread apple butter on tortillas leaving ¼-inch clean around outside edge. Top with apple or pear slices placed in a fanned pattern. In separate bowl, combine maple syrup and lemon juice and brush on apple slices. Sprinkle sliced almonds evenly over the top and season with ground nutmeg. Broil 3–5 minutes or until fruit is just soft. Remove from oven and serve.

SERVES 2 tortilla pizzas

Baked Stuffed Mochi

LIMITLESS OPTIONS… that's what I like about mochi. This pressed brown rice puffs up in the oven and makes a great pocket for stuffing with your favorite sweet or savory fillings. While I use cinnamon raisin mochi or garlic mochi for almost everything, there is a chocolate mochi that is not quite as commonly sold, but makes for some over-the-top decadent snacking (especially when filled with peanut butter)!

1   12½ ounce package mochi

OPTIONAL
SWEET FILLINGS

Apple butter

Peanut butter and jelly
    or banana

Almond butter and
    sliced peach or pear

Cashew butter and berries

Chopped almonds and dates

Chopped almonds and
    chocolate chips

OPTIONAL
SAVORY FILLINGS

Pesto and sliced tomato

Hummus and grated carrot

Muffaletto

Olive Tapenade

Salsa and avocado

Roasted squash

Pizza sauce

Preheat oven to 350°F.

Cut mochi into 1½-inch pieces and place on parchment-lined baking sheet. Bake for 10–12 minutes or until mochi puffs up and lightly browns. Remove from oven and set aside for 1 minute or until cool enough to touch. Cut open and stuff with filling of choice.

SERVES 4

Maple Nut Granola

THE KEY TO MAKING DELICIOUS GRANOLA is to bake it at a low temperature for a long time. Of course, a little bit of shredded coconut and a lot of cinnamon and maple syrup help, too. My husband devours this granola every morning and at the end of each week leaves the nearly empty Mason jar on the counter to remind me to make more.

4	cups rolled oats
2	cups crispy brown rice cereal
1½	cups unsweetened coconut flakes
1	cup sliced almonds
1	cup chopped walnuts
2	tablespoons ground cinnamon
¼	teaspoon ground cloves
½	cup virgin coconut oil, melted
½	cup maple syrup
1	teaspoon almond extract

Preheat oven to 250°F.

In large bowl, mix together all dry ingredients. In separate bowl, whisk together oil, syrup and almond extract. Pour wet mixture over dry and stir to coat. Transfer mixture to two 9 x 12-inch glass casseroles and spread out evenly. Bake 60 minutes or until golden. Turn off oven, but do not remove granola until completely cooled and set. Remove from oven and use spatula to release granola and break into chunks. Store in airtight container.

MAKES 12 cups

VARIATIONS
Experiment with adding different nuts and seeds to find your own special blend. To make this recipe oil-free, substitute an equal amount of cooked pumpkin or applesauce for the coconut oil.

Brown Rice Pudding

MY MOTHER HAS BEEN MAKING THIS RECIPE for as long as I can remember. In my home, we eat it for breakfast, lunch, dinner or dessert. It's also become quite popular at my children's school. We like it warm with a bit of cold rice milk poured over the top.

2½ cups cooked brown rice

12 ounces extra firm silken tofu

1 cup rice milk, plus more for serving

½ cup maple syrup

½ teaspoon nutmeg

2 teaspoons vanilla

1 tablespoon kudzu or arrowroot, dissolved in 2 tablespoons rice milk

½ cup raisins

¼ cup semi-sweet or dark chocolate chips

Ground cinnamon

Preheat oven to 350°F.

In food processor, combine cooked rice with tofu and rice milk. Add maple syrup, nutmeg and vanilla and process to combine. Add dissolved kudzu and pulse to combine. Lightly oil 9 x 12-inch casserole and pour in mixture. Sprinkle top with raisins and chocolate chips and press down with a wooden spoon to incorporate into pudding. Sprinkle cinnamon evenly over top and bake 50 minutes or until top is bubbling and browned. Remove from oven and cool slightly. Serve warm on its own or with a little rice milk poured over it as desired.

SERVES 8

Oatmeal Chocolate Chip (or Raisin) Cookies

I USUALLY FOLLOW MY OWN ADVICE when it comes to not keeping things in the house that I don't want to eat, and then one day it backfired on me. I simply had to have a cookie and it *had* to have chocolate in it. Within 20 minutes I was saved (and the rest of the family thanked me). If you prefer raisins, substitute them for the chocolate chips, or better yet, use both.

2	cups rolled oats
1	cup brown rice flour
¾	cup shredded unsweetened coconut
1	tablespoon ground cinnamon
¼	teaspoon sea salt
¾	cup maple syrup
½	cup canola oil
1	teaspoon vanilla extract
1	cup chopped toasted walnuts
½	cup semisweet or dark chocolate chips or raisins

Preheat oven to 350°F.

In large bowl, combine oats, flour, shredded coconut, cinnamon and salt. In separate bowl, whisk together syrup, oil and vanilla. Pour wet ingredients into dry and stir until evenly combined. Fold in walnuts and chocolate chips or raisins. Press dough into 1½-inch balls, place onto parchment-lined cookie sheet and bake 15 minutes or until lightly browned. Remove from oven – and do your best not to eat them all in one sitting!

MAKES 2 dozen

Popcorn with Olive Oil, Sea Salt and Drizzled Dark Chocolate

POPCORN GETS A BUM RAP as a result of the non-nutritional toppings that so often dress it. Add to that the toxicity of microwave popcorn, and many steer clear of this light and nutritious snack with good reason. In fact, popcorn is low in calories and touts health benefits such as fiber and zinc. Add air popping and nutritional toppings and you have a snack that you can feel good about.

½ cup popcorn kernels

¼ cup dark chocolate chips

2 tablespoons plus 1 teaspoon extra virgin olive oil

Sea salt

Ground cinnamon

Pop popcorn in air popper and set aside. Place chocolate chips in small pan over low heat and stir continuously until melted. Remove from heat and stir in one teaspoon olive oil. Drizzle remaining 2 tablespoons olive oil over popcorn and toss with sea salt and a dash of cinnamon. Drizzle with melted chocolate and serve.

SERVES 4 (about 3 cups per person)

VARIATIONS
Experiment with melted virgin coconut oil in place of olive oil and different herbs, spices and spice blends such as garlic powder, brewers yeast, cacao powder, pumpkin pie spice, fajita seasoning, curry powder and more.

Crispy Rice Squares

MOMS HAVE BEEN MAKING crispy rice treats forever. I feel good about this healthy version, and have never met a child (or adult) who doesn't love these. If you are allergic to nuts, use sunflower butter instead of cashew butter.

½ cup brown rice syrup or coconut nectar

½ cup maple syrup

½ cup cashew butter

¼ cup semi-sweet or dark chocolate chips

3 cups crispy brown rice cereal

½ cup toasted sesame seeds

In medium Dutch oven over medium-low heat, combine syrups and cashew butter until smooth. Add chocolate chips and stir until melted. Fold in rice cereal and sesame seeds and stir to coat everything. Press stiff batter into 8 x 8-inch casserole and refrigerate until firm (at least 20 minutes). Cut into squares and serve or store in airtight container.

GLUTEN-FREE OPTION
To ensure that this recipe is gluten-free, use rice cereal that is not sweetened with barley malt.

MAKES 1–1½ dozen 1-inch squares

Raisin Nut Bars

THESE YUMMY BARS CAME INTO BEING when we realized that our daughter was sensitive to wheat, corn, soy and dairy – all of my usual baking staples. They're delicious even if you have no food allergies!

1½ cups raisins
1 cup brown rice flour
1 cup rolled oats
1 cup toasted walnuts, chopped
½ teaspoon sea salt
¼ cup virgin coconut oil
¼ cup maple syrup
Apple juice as needed

Preheat oven to 350°F.

Place raisins in bowl and cover with boiling water. Let sit 10 minutes or until soft. Drain and press out excess water. Chop softened raisins and set aside.

In large bowl, combine flour, oats, walnuts and salt. In small pan over very low heat, dissolve coconut oil. Add syrup and whisk to combine. Pour wet ingredients over dry ingredients, add raisins and mix until blended. Dough should be just moist enough to stick together. Add apple juice one tablespoon at a time to achieve this consistency.

Oil 6 x 9-inch glass casserole and press in batter so it sticks together and is consistently thick throughout. Pre-cut into squares and bake 25 minutes. Remove from heat and let cool completely before removing from pan. Store in airtight container.

MAKES 16 squares

Teff Peanut Butter Chocolate Chip Cookies

IT SIMPLY DOESN'T MATTER HOW CLOSELY I follow my own dietary guidelines. When all is said and done, I still love cookies, and so do my children. Rather than deny ourselves, we came up with this decadent recipe that keeps the wheat out of our diets, but the cookies in!

1½ cups teff flour
(preferably ivory)

¼ teaspoon sea salt

1 teaspoon baking soda

1 cup chunky
100% peanut butter

1 cup maple syrup

½ cup semisweet or
dark chocolate chips

Preheat oven to 350°F.

Combine flour, salt and baking soda in one bowl and peanut butter and syrup in another. Pour wet ingredients over dry and blend until just combined. Fold in chocolate chips.

Line cookie sheet with parchment paper. Drop batter by heaping teaspoons onto cookie sheet. Leave cookies free-form or press down dough with tines of fork in crisscross pattern. Bake 13 minutes or until just lightly browned. (The key to these cookies is not to overbake them.) Remove from oven and place on wire rack to cool.

MAKES 20 cookies

Teff Ginger Molasses Cookies

TEFF IS SUCH A SMALL GRAIN that it is impossible to hull before grinding into flour, making its nutritional value nearly identical to that of the whole grain. These cookies are a high-protein, non-gluten, nutritious treat. Nobody will ever believe that they are made without wheat, eggs, milk, butter or brown sugar.

2   cups brown teff flour
1   teaspoon baking soda
¼   teaspoon sea salt
1   teaspoon
      ground cinnamon
¼   teaspoon ground cloves
½   teaspoon
      powdered mustard
½   cup almond butter
½   cup molasses
2   teaspoons tamari
1   tablespoon
      grated fresh ginger
½   cup maple syrup

Preheat oven to 350°F.

Combine all dry ingredients in large bowl and all wet ingredients in another. Pour wet ingredients over dry and blend until just combined.

Line cookie sheet with parchment paper. Drop batter by heaping teaspoons onto cookie sheet and bake 12 minutes. Remove from oven and place on wire rack to cool.

MAKES 24 cookies

ometimes the best place to start is at the very end. This index is a resource and a tool to help you turn Clean Food into delicious and nourishing meals. Select one new item each time you go to the grocery store or farmers market, and by the end of one year you will have significantly improved your diet with variety and nutritional value. Pick whatever catches your attention, look it up in this index and select the recipe that appeals to you. One item, one recipe and one choice at a time — these are the ingredients to make your kitchen the heart of a healthy home.

INDEX

ADUKI BEANS, 16–17, 27
Marinated Aduki Beans, 76
Millet, Aduki Beans and Corn
  with Lemon Dressing, 203
Savory "Unbaked" Beans, 272
Three Bean Chili, 249
Tuscan Bean Soup, 251
Winter Squash and
  Aduki Bean Soup, 252

AGAR, 27
Blueberry Kanten
  with Cashew Cream, 86
Chestnut Cream Pie, 298
Fresh Fruit Tart
  with Almond Crust, 147
Lemon Berry Cream Pie, 152
Mixed Berry Couscous Cake, 87
Mixed Berry Tart, 154
Nuts Over Strawberry
  Rhubarb Pie, 146
Silky Sweet Potato Pie, 198
Strawberry Rhubarb Compote
  with Cashew Cream, 150

AGAVE NECTAR, 20, 27

AIOLI
(See Grapeseed Oil Mayonnaise)

ALMONDS,
ALMOND FLOUR 18–19, 23, 27
Apple Tart, 294
Baked Stuffed Sweet Potatoes, 319
Butternut Squash Casserole, 266
Chestnut Cream Pie, 298
Chocolate Pecan Pie, 297
Fresh Fruit Tart
  with Almond Crust, 147
Ginger Pear Crisp, 225
Lemon Almond Cookie Tart
  with Strawberry Topping, 91
Maple Nut Granola, 324
Maple Spiced Almonds, 291
Nuts Over Strawberry
  Rhubarb Pie, 146
Peanut Butter Cacao Banana
  Smoothie, 307
Quinoa with Arame,
  Toasted Nuts and Seeds, 72

Quinoa with Almonds
  and Currants, 218
Sesame Almond Balls, 292
Teff Ginger Molasses Cookies, 334
Tortilla Pizzas, 322
Wild Rice Pilaf, 85
Winter Squash and
  Chestnut Casserole, 267

AMARANTH, 13, 27

APPLE BUTTER
Maple Apple Vinaigrette, 236
Tortilla Pizzas, 322
Savory "Unbaked" Beans, 272

APPLE CIDER
Apple Chutney, 164
Butternut Squash Casserole, 266
Cranberry Applesauce, 241
Spiced Kukicha Iced Tea, 160
Winter Squash and
  Chestnut Casserole, 267

APPLE CIDER VINEGAR, 27

APPLES, 20, 23
Apple Chutney, 164
Apple Crisp, 224
Apple Squash Soup, 166
Apple Tart, 294
Chestnut Stuffing, 269
Cranberry Applesauce, 241
Cranberry Chutney, 163
Green Monster Smoothie, 307
Lentil Apple Walnut Loaf, 271
Maple Apple Vinaigrette, 236
Poached Winter Fruit Medley, 293
Tortilla Pizzas, 322

APRICOTS,
APRICOT JUICE, 23
Fruity Balsamic Vinaigrette, 97
Quinoa and Black Bean Salad
  with Apricot Lime Vinaigrette, 141
Sautéed Fennel and Asian Greens
  with Ginger and Apricot, 59
Spring Greens
  with Apricot Vinaigrette, 49
Sprouted Quinoa
  with Strawberries and Lime, 143

ARAME, 16, 27
(See also Sea Vegetables)

ARROWROOT, 27
Fresh Berries with Tofu Cream, 155
Fresh Fruit Tart
  with Almond Crust, 147
Lemon Berry Cream Pie, 152
Mixed Berry Tart, 154
Pear and Fig Tart
  in Pecan Crust, 296
Silky Sweet Potato Pie, 198
Strawberry Rhubarb Compote
  with Cashew Cream, 150

ARTICHOKES, 16
Artichokes, Fennel and Olives
  over Penne, 66
Lemony Artichoke Dip, 40
Seared Artichokes
  with Red Pepper Aioli, 61

ARUGULA
Artichokes, Fennel and Olives
  over Penne, 66
White Bean Salad with
  Roasted Tomatoes and Arugula, 134
Winter Green Salad with
  Sugared Walnuts, Crispy Pears
  and Pomegranate, 256

ASIAN GREENS
Asian Coleslaw, 112
Bok Choy and Chickpeas
  with Cashews, 63
Bok Choy and Mung Bean
  Sprout Sauté with
  Peanuts and Scallions, 255
Ginger Sesame Greens, 180
Mango Sesame Tatsoi, 60
Sautéed Fennel and Asian Greens
  with Ginger and Apricot, 59
Sautéed Garlic Greens, 179
Seaweed and Cabbage Sauté, 70

ASPARAGUS, 16, 23, 27
Asparagus with Mustard Vinaigrette
  and Toasted Pecans, 62
Chopped Salad with
  Shallot Poppy Seed Dressing, 52
Cream of Asparagus Soup, 46
Roasted Squash with
  Fennel and Asparagus, 195

AVOCADOS, 16, 23, 27
Black Bean Patties with
  Pineapple Guacamole, 133
Heirloom Tomato Salad, 109
Jícama Strawberry Guacamole, 98
Mango Salsa, 101
Mexican Layer Dip, 242
Raw Kale Salad
  with Great Northern Beans
  and Kalamata Olives, 185
Sprouted Quinoa
  with Strawberries and Lime, 143
Traditional Guacamole, 100
Vegetable Nori Rolls, 304
Watercress, Daikon and
  Avocado Salad with
  Mustard Seed Dressing, 51

BALSAMIC VINEGAR, 27
Baby Greens with
  Grilled Balsamic Pears, 114
Basic Balsamic Vinaigrette, 43
Pomegranate Vinaigrette, 237

BANANAS
Banana Coconut
  Chocolate Chip Cookies, 88
Chocolate Pudding
  with Fresh Berries, 153
Green Monster Smoothie, 307
Peanut Butter Cacao Banana
  Smoothie, 307

BARLEY, 13–14, 27
Barley with Lemon and Herbs, 84
Goodness Soup, 243
Multigrain Pilaf with
  Toasted Sunflower Seeds, 216
Stovetop Barley
  with Sweet Vegetables, 219
Wild Rice, Barley
  and Arame Salad, 201

BARLEY MALT, 20, 28

BASIL
Grilled Vegetables with Pasta, 121
Heirloom Tomato Salad, 109
Pesto Pasta Salad, 144
Summer Rolls
  with Lemon Basil Pesto, 127
Tortilla Pizzas, 322

BASMATI RICE, 13–14, 28
Wild Rice Pilaf, 85
Zesty Basmati Rice
  with Cinnamon and Cumin, 282

BEETS, 15, 21
Golden Beet and
  Snap Pea Salad, 120
Julienned Beet, Broccoli Stem
  and Carrot Salad, 176
Swiss Chard with Roasted
  Golden Beets and Sweet Peas, 67

BERRIES, 20–21, 23
Blueberry Kanten
  with Cashew Cream, 86
Chocolate Pudding
  with Fresh Berries, 153
Fresh Berries with Tofu Cream, 155
Fresh Fruit Tart
  with Almond Crust, 147
Lemon Berry Cream Pie, 152
Mixed Berry Couscous Cake, 87
Mixed Berry Tart, 154
Nuts Over Strawberry
  Rhubarb Pie, 146
Sprouted Quinoa
  with Strawberries and Lime, 143
Strawberry Custard with
  Fresh Berries and Lemon Peel, 148
Strawberry Rhubarb Compote
  with Cashew Cream, 150

BLACK BEANS, 16–17, 28
Black Bean, Corn
  and Tomato Salsa, 102
Black Bean Patties
  with Pineapple Guacamole, 133
Black Bean Salad, 132
Millet Black Bean Patties
  with Corn, 83
Multibean Salad
  with Fresh Herbs, 73
Quinoa and Black Bean Salad
  with Apricot Lime Vinaigrette, 141
Savory Black Bean Soup, 173
Savory "Unbaked" Beans, 272
Sweet Potato and Black Bean
  Burritos with Cashew Cheese, 206
Thai Black Beans with
  Mangoes and Cilantro, 270
Three Bean Chili, 249

BLACK-EYED PEAS, 17
Collard Greens and
  Black-Eyed Peas, 258

BLUEBERRIES, 20, 23
Blueberry Kanten
  with Cashew Cream, 86
Honeydew Cucumber Soup, 107
Lemon Berry Cream Pie, 152

BOK CHOY, 15, 27
Asian Coleslaw, 112
Bok Choy and Chickpeas
  with Cashews, 63
Bok Choy and Mung Bean
  Sprout Sauté with
  Peanuts and Scallions, 255
Cucumber Noodles with
  Bok Choy and Peanut Sauce, 119
Sautéed Fennel and Asian Greens
  with Ginger and Apricot, 59
Warm Greens with Citrus Dressing
  and Pomegranate, 175

BRAGG LIQUID
AMINOS, 25, 28

BREAD
Chestnut Stuffing, 269
Garlic Crostini, 240
Pita Chips, 317

BROCCOLI, 15, 23
Baked Stuffed Sweet Potatoes, 319
Creamy Shiitake and
  Chickpea Soup, 172
Julienned Beet, Broccoli Stem
  and Carrot Salad, 176
Pesto Pasta Salad, 144
Quick Boiled Broccoli and Stems
  with Toasted Sesame Seeds, 178
Stir-Fried Broccoli with Arame, 199
Sweet and Sour Stir-Fry, 68
Tree of Life Stir-Fry, 264

BROWN RICE, 13–14, 28
Brown Rice Pudding, 326
Brown Rice with Ginger
  and Umeboshi Plums, 80
Crispy Rice Squares, 330

Kabocha Squash
  Stuffed with Brown Rice
  and Chickpea Pilaf, 220
Stovetop Barley
  with Sweet Vegetables, 219
Wholegrain Pancakes, 281

BROWN RICE FLOUR
Chocolate Lover's Tart, 227
Nuts Over Strawberry
  Rhubarb Pie, 146
Peach, Fresh Fig and Bourbon
  Crisp with Pecan Topping, 149
Pear and Fig Tart
  in Pecan Crust, 296
Raisin Nut Bars, 331

BROWN RICE SYRUP, 20, 28
Crispy Rice Squares, 330
Seitan Walnut Stuffed
  Collard Greens, 211
Toasted Sesame Nori Crisps, 321
Winter Squash and
  Chestnut Casserole, 267

BROWN RICE VINEGAR, 28

BRUSSELS SPROUTS, 15
Roasted Brussels Sprouts
  with Fennel and
  Shiitake Mushrooms, 260
Roasted Root Vegetables
  with Truffle Oil, 187
Sesame Brussels Sprout Sauté, 192
Stovetop Barley
  with Sweet Vegetables, 219

BURDOCK, 15, 28
Super-Strengthening Stew, 248

BURRITOS
Sweet Potato and Black Bean
  Burritos with Cashew Cheese, 206

CABBAGE, 15, 23
Mochi Dumplings, 79
Seaweed and Cabbage Sauté, 70
Traditional Coleslaw, 111
Winter Vegetable Soup, 254

CACAO
(See Chocolate)

CANNELLINI BEANS, 17, 28

CANOLA OIL, 23, 28

CANTALOUPE, 23
(See also Melons)

CARROTS, 15, 23
Arame Sauté, 129
Autumn Harvest Soup, 167
Carrot Cantaloupe Ginger
  Smoothie, 307
Carrot Fruit Soup, 108
Carrot Ginger Soup, 171
Carrot Raisin Salad, 56
Crispy Sesame Carrots, 57
Fingerling Potato Salad
  with Fresh Herbs, 122
Goodness Soup, 243
Julienned Beet, Broccoli Stem
  and Carrot Salad, 176
Marinated Aduki Beans, 76
Pesto Pasta Salad, 144
Root Veggie Fries, 190
Seaweed and Cabbage Sauté, 70
Stovetop Barley
  with Sweet Vegetables, 219
Super-Strengthening Stew, 248
Sweet and Sour Stir-Fry, 68
Tree of Life Stir-Fry, 264
Vegetable Nori Rolls, 304
Winter Vegetable Soup, 254

CASHEWS,
CASHEW BUTTER, 19
Blueberry Kanten
  with Cashew Cream, 86
Bok Choy and Chickpeas
  with Cashews, 63
Chocolate Lover's Tart, 227
Crispy Rice Squares, 330
Curry Tempeh
  with Raisins and Cashews, 139
Fresh Berries with Tofu Cream, 155
Marinated Tofu with Ginger
  Cashew Dipping Sauce, 209
Savory Stuffed Pumpkins, 196
Spicy Thai Tempeh
  with Cashews, 277
Strawberry Rhubarb Compote
  with Cashew Cream, 150
Sweet Potato and Black Bean
  Burritos with Cashew Cheese, 206

Wild Rice, Barley
  and Arame Salad, 201
Zesty Basmati Rice
  with Cinnamon and Cumin, 282

CAULIFLOWER, 15, 23
Tree of Life Stir-Fry, 264

CELERIAC (Celery Root), 15
Sweet and Savory
  Root Vegetable Stew, 246

CHESTNUTS
Chestnut Cream Pie, 298
Chestnut Stuffing, 269
Winter Squash and
  Chestnut Casserole, 267

CHIA SEEDS, 19, 28

CHICKPEA FLOUR
Silky Sweet Potato Pie, 198

CHICKPEAS, 16–17, 28
Bok Choy and Chickpeas
  with Cashews, 63
Chickpea and Cherry Tomato Salad
  with Cilantro Dressing, 131
Creamy Shiitake and
  Chickpea Soup, 172
Crispy Chickpea Fritters, 78
Crispy Roasted Chickpeas, 314
Cucumber, Mango
  and Chickpea Salad, 130
Julienned Beet, Broccoli Stem
  and Carrot Salad, 176
Kabocha Squash
  Stuffed with Brown Rice
  and Chickpea Pilaf, 220
Mediterranean Pasta
  with Greens, 223
Multibean Salad
  with Fresh Herbs, 73
Traditional Hummus, 310
Tuscan Bean Soup, 251

CHILI PEPPERS
Mexican Layer Dip, 242
Refried Pinto Beans with Chiles, 204
Spicy Coconut Pumpkin Soup, 253

CHOCOLATE, 21
Banana Coconut
  Chocolate Chip Cookies, 88
Chocolate Coconut Granola Bites, 90
Chocolate Lover's Tart, 227
Chocolate Pecan Pie, 297
Chocolate Pudding
  with Fresh Berries, 153
Crispy Rice Squares, 330
Oatmeal Chocolate Chip
  (or Raisin) Cookies, 327
Peanut Butter Cacao Banana
  Smoothie, 307
Popcorn with Olive Oil, Sea Salt
  and Drizzled Dark Chocolate, 329
Teff Peanut Butter
  Chocolate Chip Cookies, 332

CHUTNEY (See also Sauces)
Apple Chutney, 164
Cranberry Chutney, 163

CILANTRO
Black Bean, Corn
  and Tomato Salsa, 102
Black Bean Patties
  with Pineapple Guacamole, 133
Black Bean Salad, 132
Chickpea and Cherry Tomato Salad
  with Cilantro Dressing, 131
French Lentil Salad with
  Lemon, Radish and Cilantro, 74
Garlic Scape and Walnut Pesto, 44
Green Goddess Dip, 315
Lettuce Soup with Cilantro
  and Hot Sesame Oil, 45
Mango Salsa, 101
Pad Thai Summer Rolls
  with Tamarind Dipping Sauce, 128
Pad Thai with Tofu, 276
Tangy Tomato
  and Tomatillo Salad, 110
Thai Black Beans with
  Mangoes and Cilantro, 270
Traditional Guacamole, 100
Zesty Basmati Rice
  with Cinnamon and Cumin, 282

CINNAMON, 28
Baked Stuffed Sweet Potatoes, 319
Chestnut Cream Pie, 298
Poached Winter Fruit Medley, 293

Sinful Stuffed Dates, 289
Spiced Kukicha Iced Tea, 160
Sweet Brown Rice and Mung Beans
  with Indian Spices, 283
Zesty Basmati Rice
  with Cinnamon and Cumin, 282

COCONUT
Banana Coconut
  Chocolate Chip Cookies, 88
Chocolate Coconut Granola Bites, 90
Coconut Cranberry Pecan Balls, 290
Maple Nut Granola, 324
Oatmeal Chocolate Chip
  (or Raisin) Cookies, 327
Sinful Stuffed Dates, 289

COCONUT MILK, 28
Apple Squash Soup, 166
Marinated Tofu with Ginger
  Cashew Dipping Sauce, 209
Rice Noodles and Peanut Sauce
  Rolled in Nori, 308
Sautéed Tempeh with
  Coconut Milk and Snow Peas, 278
Spicy Coconut Pumpkin Soup, 253

COCONUT OIL (VIRGIN),
  19–20, 28

COLESLAW
Asian Coleslaw, 112
Traditional Coleslaw, 111

COLLARD GREENS, 15, 23, 29
Autumn Harvest Soup, 167
Baked Stuffed Shells, 287
Baked Stuffed Sweet Potatoes, 319
Collard Greens and
  Black-Eyed Peas, 258
Ginger Sesame Greens, 180
Sautéed Garlic Greens, 179
Seitan Shepherd's Pie, 279
Seitan Walnut Stuffed
  Collard Greens, 211
Shiitake Mushrooms
  and Bitter Greens in Filo, 259
Tuscan Bean Soup, 251
Warm Greens with Citrus Dressing
  and Pomegranate, 175

COOKIES
Banana Coconut
  Chocolate Chip Cookies, 88
Lemon Almond Cookie Tart
  with Strawberry Topping, 91
Oatmeal Chocolate Chip
  (or Raisin) Cookies, 327
Teff Ginger Molasses Cookies, 334
Teff Peanut Butter
  Chocolate Chip Cookies, 332

CORN, 16, 23
Black Bean, Corn
  and Tomato Salsa, 102
Black Bean Salad, 132
Corn Chowder, 170
Green Beans and Sweet Corn
  with Summer Vinaigrette, 117
Grilled Polenta
  with Mushroom Ragoût, 145
Millet, Aduki Beans and Corn
  with Lemon Dressing, 203
Millet Black Bean Patties
  with Corn, 83
Quinoa with Sweet Corn, 215
Seitan Shepherd's Pie, 279
Skillet Cornbread, 214
Sweet Potato, Corn and
  Kale Chowder, 168
Three Sisters Deep-Dish Pie, 191
Winter Vegetable Soup, 254

CORNMEAL
Black Bean Patties
  with Pineapple Guacamole, 133
Root Veggie Fries, 190
Skillet Cornbread, 214
Sweet Potato and
  Parsnip Pancakes, 263

COUSCOUS, 13
Mixed Berry Couscous Cake, 87

CRANBERRIES, 21
Chocolate Coconut Granola Bites, 90
Coconut Cranberry Pecan Balls, 290
Cranberry Applesauce, 241
Cranberry Chutney, 163
Millet with Cranberries
  and Pistachios, 285
Poached Winter Fruit Medley, 293
Seitan Walnut Stuffed
  Collard Greens, 211

Sweet Dumpling Squash
  with Orange-Scented Quinoa
  Stuffing, 222
Wild Rice Pilaf, 85

CREMINI MUSHROOMS
(See Mushrooms)

CUCUMBERS, 16
Cucumber, Mango
  and Chickpea Salad, 130
Cucumber Noodles with
  Bok Choy and Peanut Sauce, 119
Gazpacho, 105
Heirloom Tomato Salad, 109
Honeydew Cucumber Soup, 107
Quick Homemade Pickles, 309
Sprouted Quinoa Tabbouleh, 140
Vegetable Nori Rolls, 304

CURRANTS
Inca Red Quinoa with Currants, 81
Kale with Pine Nuts
  and Currants, 182
Quinoa with Almonds
  and Currants, 218
Wheatberry Salad, 142

CURRY
Curry Tempeh
  with Raisins and Cashews, 139

DAIKON, 15, 29
Arame with
  Caramelized Shiitakes, 200
Quick Homemade Pickles, 309
Roasted Root Vegetables
  with Truffle Oil, 187
Super-Strengthening Stew, 248
Watercress, Daikon and
  Avocado Salad with
  Mustard Seed Dressing, 51

DANDELION GREENS, 15, 29
Ginger Sesame Greens, 180
Sautéed Garlic Greens, 179
Shiitake Mushrooms
  and Bitter Greens in Filo, 259
Winter Green Salad with
  Sugared Walnuts, Crispy Pears
  and Pomegranate, 256

DATES
Sesame Almond Balls, 292
Sinful Stuffed Dates, 289

DELICATA SQUASH, 15
(See also Squash)

DESSERTS
Apple Crisp, 224
Apple Tart, 294
Banana Coconut
  Chocolate Chip Cookies, 88
Blueberry Kanten
  with Cashew Cream, 86
Brown Rice Pudding, 326
Chestnut Cream Pie, 298
Chocolate Coconut Granola Bites, 90
Chocolate Lover's Tart, 227
Chocolate Pecan Pie, 297
Chocolate Pudding
  with Fresh Berries, 153
Coconut Cranberry Pecan Balls, 290
Crispy Rice Squares, 330
Fresh Berries with Tofu Cream, 155
Fresh Fruit Tart
  with Almond Crust, 147
Ginger Pear Crisp, 225
Glazed Oranges
  with Pomegranate Seeds, 231
Green Tea Poached Pears
  with Pomegranate Glaze and
  Pistachios, 229
Lemon Almond Cookie Tart
  with Strawberry Topping, 91
Lemon Berry Cream Pie, 152
Maple Poached Pears, 228
Maple Spiced Almonds, 291
Mixed Berry Couscous Cake, 87
Mixed Berry Tart, 154
Nuts over Strawberry
  Rhubarb Pie, 146
Oatmeal Chocolate Chip
  (or Raisin) Cookies, 327
Peach, Fresh Fig and Bourbon
  Crisp with Pecan Topping, 149
Pear and Fig Tart
  in Pecan Crust, 296
Poached Winter Fruit Medley, 293
Popcorn with Olive Oil, Sea Salt
  and Drizzled Dark Chocolate, 329
Raisin Nut Bars, 331
Sesame Almond Balls, 292
Sinful Stuffed Dates, 289

Strawberry Custard with
  Fresh Berries and Lemon Peel, 148
Strawberry Rhubarb Compote
  with Cashew Cream, 150
Teff Ginger Molasses Cookies, 334
Teff Peanut Butter
  Chocolate Chip Cookies, 332
Tiramisu, 299
Toasted Sesame Nori Crisps, 321
Tofu Pumpkin Pie
  with Gingersnap Crust, 230
Tortilla Pizzas, 322

DIPS AND DRESSINGS
(See also Sauces)
Apricot Lime Vinaigrette, 141
Apricot Vinaigrette, 49
Basic Balsamic Vinaigrette, 43
Caesar Salad Dressing, 53
Cilantro Dressing, 131
Citrus Dressing, 175
Creamy Miso Dressing, 41
Fruity Balsamic Vinaigrette, 97
Ginger Sesame Vinaigrette, 43
Green Goddess Dip, 315
Herbed Aioli, 103
Herbed White Bean Dip, 316
Jícama Strawberry Guacamole, 98
Lemon Basil Pesto, 127
Lemon Dill Dressing, 124
Lemony Artichoke Dip, 40
Lentil Walnut Pâté, 165
Maple Apple Vinaigrette, 236
Maple Mustard Vinaigrette, 43
Mexican Layer Dip, 242
Muffaletto, 311
Mustard Seed Dressing, 51
Mustard Vinaigrette, 62
Olive Tapenade, 239
Pesto Pasta Salad, 144
Pineapple Guacamole, 133
Pomegranate Vinaigrette, 237
Red Pepper Aioli, 61
Shallot Poppy Seed Dressing, 52
Summer Vinaigrette, 117
Sun-dried Tomato Aioli, 65
Traditional Guacamole, 100

DUMPLINGS
Mochi Dumplings, 79

DUMPLING SQUASH, 15
(See also Squash)

EDAMAME, 29

EGGPLANT, 23
Grilled Vegetables with Pasta, 121

EGG REPLACER, 29
Skillet Cornbread, 214

ENDIVE, 16
Chopped Salad with
   Shallot Poppy Seed Dressing, 52
Marinated Bitter Greens, 174

ESCAROLE, 16
Super-Strengthening Stew, 248
White Beans and Escarole, 205

FARRO, 13

FENNEL, 15, 29
Apple Chutney, 164
Artichokes, Fennel and Olives
   over Penne, 66
Fennel and Orange Salad, 50
Quinoa with Arame,
   Toasted Nuts and Seeds, 72
Roasted Brussels Sprouts
   with Fennel and
   Shiitake Mushrooms, 260
Roasted Root Vegetables
   with Truffle Oil, 187
Roasted Squash with
   Fennel and Asparagus, 195
Sautéed Fennel and Asian Greens
   with Ginger and Apricot, 59
Seared Fennel with Meyer Lemon, 58
Stovetop Barley
   with Sweet Vegetables, 219
Sweet and Savory
   Root Vegetable Stew, 246
Traditional Coleslaw, 111

FERMENTED BLACK BEANS, 29
Thai Black Beans with
   Mangoes and Cilantro, 270

FIGS
Peach, Fresh Fig and Bourbon
   Crisp with Pecan Topping, 149
Pear and Fig Tart
   in Pecan Crust, 296
Poached Winter Fruit Medley, 293

FILO DOUGH
Shiitake Mushrooms
   and Bitter Greens in Filo, 259

FLAX SEEDS, 19, 29
Black Bean Patties
   with Pineapple Guacamole, 133
Chocolate Pecan Pie, 297
Lentil Apple Walnut Loaf, 271
Sweet Potato and
   Parsnip Pancakes, 263

GALANGAL, 29
Spicy Coconut Pumpkin Soup, 253

GARBANZO BEANS
(See Chickpeas)

GARLIC, GARLIC SCAPES, 15, 29
Garlic Crostini, 240
Garlic Scape and Walnut Pesto, 44
Roasted Tofu with Green Beans, 275
Sautéed Garlic Greens, 179
Simply Delicious
   Spaghetti Squash, 265
White Beans and Escarole, 205
Zucchini with
   Garlic and Oregano, 125

GINGER, 15, 30
Carrot Cantaloupe Ginger
   Smoothie, 307
Carrot Ginger Soup, 171
Gingered Arame with Snow Peas, 71
Ginger Pear Crisp, 225
Ginger Pear Sauce, 161
Ginger Sesame Greens, 180
Ginger Sesame Vinaigrette, 43
Lettuce Wraps with
   Ginger Peanut Tofu, 305
Marinated Tofu with Ginger
   Cashew Dipping Sauce, 209
Orange Ginger Tofu, 274
Rutabaga Purée
   with Orange and Ginger, 194

Sautéed Fennel and Asian Greens
   with Ginger and Apricot, 59
Sautéed Yams
   with Ginger and Lime, 189
Teff Ginger Molasses Cookies, 334

GOMASIO, 30

GRANOLA
Chocolate Coconut Granola Bites, 90
Maple Nut Granola, 324

**GRAPESEED OIL
MAYONNAISE, 25**
Herbed Aioli, 103
Lemony Artichoke Dip, 40
Roasted Portobello Sandwich
   with Sun-dried Tomato Aioli, 65
Seared Artichokes
   with Red Pepper Aioli, 61
Tempeh Salad, 77
Tofu Salad, 135
Traditional Coleslaw, 111

GREAT NORTHERN BEANS
Raw Kale Salad
   with Great Northern Beans
   and Kalamata Olives, 185

GREEN BEANS, 16
Fingerling Potatoes and Green Beans
   with Lemon Dill Dressing, 124
Green Beans and Sweet Corn
   with Summer Vinaigrette, 117
Multibean Salad
   with Fresh Herbs, 73
Roasted Tofu with Green Beans, 275
Three Sisters Deep-Dish Pie, 191

GREEN TEA
Green Tea Poached Pears
   with Pomegranate Glaze and
   Pistachios, 229

GUACAMOLE
Jícama Strawberry Guacamole, 98
Pineapple Guacamole, 133
Traditional Guacamole, 100

HIJIKI, 30

HONEY, 20, 30

HONEYDEW
(See Melon)

HUMMUS
Traditional Hummus, 310

JASMINE RICE, 13–14
Jasmine Rice with Sweet Peas, 284

JÍCAMA, 30
Arame Sauté, 129
Black Bean Patties
    with Pineapple Guacamole, 133
Jícama Strawberry Guacamole, 98
Mango Salsa, 101
Quinoa and Black Bean Salad
    with Apricot Lime Vinaigrette, 141
Sprouted Quinoa
    with Strawberries and Lime, 143

JOB'S TEARS, 13, 30

KABOCHA SQUASH, 15
(See also Squash)

KAFFIR LIMES, 30
(See also Limes)

KALE, 15, 23, 30
Autumn Harvest Soup, 167
Baked Stuffed Shells, 287
Baked Stuffed Sweet Potatoes, 319
Kale Chips, 312
Ginger Sesame Greens, 180
Green Monster Smoothie, 307
Kale with Caramelized Shallots, 181
Kale with Pine Nuts
    and Currants, 182
Mediterranean Pasta
    with Greens, 223
Raw Kale Salad
    with Great Northern Beans
    and Kalamata Olives, 185
Roasted Kabocha Squash
    with Kale, 268
Sautéed Garlic Greens, 179
Seitan Shepherd's Pie, 279
Sweet Potato, Corn and
    Kale Chowder, 168

Tofu Kale Lasagna, 213
Tuscan Bean Soup, 251
Warm Greens with Citrus
    Dressing and Pomegranate, 175

KELP, 16, 30
(See also Sea Vegetables)

KIDNEY BEANS, 16–17, 30
Multibean Salad
    with Fresh Herbs, 73

KOMBU, 13, 14, 16, 31

KUDZU (Kuzu), 31
Brown Rice Pudding, 326
Tree of Life Stir-Fry, 264

KUKICHA TWIG TEA
(See Teas)

LASAGNA
Tofu Kale Lasagna, 213

LEEKS, 15, 31
Roasted Kabocha Squash and
    Creminis with Fresh Herbs, 197
Roasted Tofu with Green Beans, 275
Winter Vegetable Soup, 254

LEMON BALM
Summer Rolls
    with Lemon Basil Pesto, 127

LEMONGRASS, 31
Spicy Coconut Pumpkin Soup, 253

LEMONS
Baked Stuffed Sweet Potatoes, 319
Barley with Lemon and Herbs, 84
Fingerling Potatoes and Green Beans
    with Lemon Dill Dressing, 124
French Lentil Salad with
    Lemon, Radish and Cilantro, 74
Fresh Herb Salad
    with Lemon and Olive Oil, 115
Fruity Balsamic Vinaigrette, 97
Grilled Cipollini Onions, 116
Grilled Vidalia Onions
    with Wild Mushrooms
    and Lemon Zest, 54

Lemon Almond Cookie Tart
    with Strawberry Topping, 91
Lemon Berry Cream Pie, 152
Lemony Artichoke Dip, 40
Millet, Aduki Beans and Corn
    with Lemon Dressing, 203
Seared Fennel with Meyer Lemon, 58
Sprouted Quinoa Tabbouleh, 140
Strawberry Custard with
    FreshBerries and Lemon Peel, 148

LENTILS, 17, 31
French Lentil Salad with
    Lemon, Radish and Cilantro, 74
Goodness Soup, 243
Lentil Apple Walnut Loaf, 271
Lentil Soup, 244
Lentil Walnut Pâté, 165

LETTUCE, 15, 23
Baby Greens with
    Grilled Balsamic Pears, 114
Caesar Salad, 53
Fresh Herb Salad
    with Lemon and Olive Oil, 115
Lettuce Wraps with
    Ginger Peanut Tofu, 305
Lettuce Soup with Cilantro
    and Hot Sesame Oil, 45
Marinated Bitter Greens, 174
Pad Thai Summer Rolls
    with Tamarind Dipping Sauce, 128
Spring Greens
    with Apricot Vinaigrette, 49
Winter Green Salad with
    Sugared Walnuts, Crispy Pears
    and Pomegranate, 256

LIMES
Quinoa and Black Bean Salad
    with Apricot Lime Vinaigrette, 141
Sautéed Yams
    with Ginger and Lime, 189
Spicy Coconut Pumpkin Soup, 253
Sprouted Quinoa
    with Strawberries and Lime, 143

MANGOES, 23
Carrot Fruit Soup, 108
Cucumber, Mango
    and Chickpea Salad, 130
Mango Salsa, 101

Mango Sesame Tatsoi, 60
Quinoa and Black Bean Salad
  with Apricot Lime Vinaigrette, 141
Thai Black Beans with
  Mangoes and Cilantro, 270

MAPLE SYRUP, 20, 31
Baked Maple Mustard Tempeh, 210
Baked Stuffed Sweet Potatoes, 319
Coconut Cranberry Pecan Balls, 290
Maple Apple Vinaigrette, 236
Maple Mustard Vinaigrette, 43
Maple Nut Granola, 324
Maple Poached Pears, 228
Maple Spiced Almonds, 291
Poached Winter Fruit Medley, 293
Sinful Stuffed Dates, 289
Tiramisu, 299

MELON, 23
Carrot Cantaloupe Ginger
  Smoothie, 307
Carrot Fruit Soup, 108
Honeydew Cucumber Soup, 107

MILLET,
MILLET FLOUR, 13–14, 31
Apple Tart, 294
Millet, Aduki Beans and Corn
  with Lemon Dressing, 203
Millet Black Bean Patties
  with Corn, 83
Millet with Cranberries
  and Pistachios, 285
Multigrain Pilaf with
  Toasted Sunflower Seeds, 216
Pan-Roasted Millet
  with Pumpkin Seeds, 217
Wholegrain Pancakes, 281

MISO, 18, 25, 31
Caesar Salad, 53
Carrot Ginger Soup, 171
Creamy Miso Dressing, 41
Marinated Tofu with Ginger
  Cashew Dipping Sauce, 209
My Favorite Miso Soup, 47
Tree of Life Stir-Fry, 264

MOCHI, 31
Baked Stuffed Mochi, 323
Mochi Dumplings, 79
Seitan Walnut Stuffed
  Collard Greens, 211

MOLASSES, 20
Lentil Soup, 244
Savory "Unbaked" Beans, 272
Teff Ginger Molasses Cookies, 334

MUFFALETTO, 311

MUNG BEANS,
MUNG BEAN SPROUTS, 17, 31
Bok Choy and Mung Bean
  Sprout Sauté with
  Peanuts and Scallions, 255
Pad Thai Summer Rolls
  with Tamarind Dipping Sauce, 128
Pad Thai with Tofu, 276
Sweet Brown Rice and Mung Beans
  with Indian Spices, 283

MUSHROOMS, 16, 23
(See also Shitake Mushrooms)
Chestnut Stuffing, 269
Goodness Soup, 243
Grilled Polenta
  with Mushroom Ragoût, 145
Grilled Vegetables with Pasta, 121
Grilled Vidalia Onions
  with Wild Mushrooms
  and Lemon Zest, 54
Polenta au Gratin, 286
Roasted Kabocha Squash and
  Creminis with Fresh Herbs, 197
Roasted Portobello Sandwich
  with Sun-dried Tomato Aioli, 65
Roasted Tofu with Green Beans, 275
Savory Stuffed Pumpkins, 196
Seitan Bourguignon, 280
Seitan Shepherd's Pie, 279
Seitan Walnut Stuffed
  Collard Greens, 211
Sweet Dumpling Squash
  with Orange-Scented Quinoa
  Stuffing, 222
Tofu Kale Lasagna, 213
Wild Rice Pilaf, 85

MUSTARD
Asparagus with Mustard Vinaigrette
  and Toasted Pecans, 62
Baby Spinach Salad
  with Mustard Vinaigrette, 48
Baked Maple Mustard Tempeh, 210
Maple Mustard Vinaigrette, 43
Watercress, Daikon and
  Avocado Salad with
  Mustard Seed Dressing, 51

MUSTARD GREENS, 15, 32
Ginger Sesame Greens, 180
Sautéed Garlic Greens, 179
Shiitake Mushrooms
  and Bitter Greens in Filo, 259
Tamari-Braised Mustard Greens, 183

NAPA CABBAGE, 15
Asian Coleslaw, 112
Sautéed Fennel and Asian Greens
  with Ginger and Apricot, 59
Seaweed and Cabbage Sauté, 70

NAVY BEANS, 17

NORI, 16, 32
(See also Sea Vegetables)

OATS, 13–14, 32
Apple Crisp, 224
Banana Coconut
  Chocolate Chip Cookies, 88
Carrot Ginger Soup, 171
Chocolate Coconut Granola Bites, 90
Chocolate Pecan Pie, 297
Fresh Fruit Tart
  with Almond Crust, 147
Ginger Pear Crisp, 225
Maple Nut Granola, 324
Oatmeal Chocolate Chip
  (or Raisin) Cookies, 327
Raisin Nut Bars, 331

OLIVE OIL, 19–20, 25, 32
Popcorn with Olive Oil, Sea Salt
  and Drizzled Dark Chocolate, 329

OLIVES
Artichokes, Fennel and Olives
 over Penne, 66
Caesar Salad, 53
Mexican Layer Dip, 242
Muffaletto, 311
Olive Tapenade, 239
Pesto Pasta Salad, 144
Raw Kale Salad
 with Great Northern Beans
 and Kalamata Olives, 185

ONIONS, 15, 23
(*See also* Scallions)
Arame Sauté, 129
Baked Stuffed Sweet Potatoes, 319
Grilled Cipollini Onions, 116
Grilled Vegetables with Pasta, 121
Grilled Vidalia Onions
 with Wild Mushrooms
 and Lemon Zest, 54
Quinoa with Arame,
 Toasted Nuts and Seeds, 72
Three Bean Chili, 249

**ORANGES,
ORANGE JUICE, 23**
Carrot Ginger Soup, 171
Carrot Raisin Salad, 56
Fennel and Orange Salad, 50
Glazed Oranges
 with Pomegranate Seeds, 231
Orange Ginger Tofu, 274
Rutabaga Purée
 with Orange and Ginger, 194
Spiced Kukicha Iced Tea, 160
Sweet Dumpling Squash
 with Orange-Scented Quinoa
 Stuffing, 222
Warm Greens with Citrus Dressing
 and Pomegranate, 175

OREGANO
Zucchini with
 Garlic and Oregano, 125

PARSLEY, 15, 21, 25, 32
Sprouted Quinoa Tabbouleh, 140

PARSNIPS, 15, 32
Curried Parsnips, 186
Not Mashed Potatoes, 261
Root Veggie Fries, 190
Sweet and Savory
 Root Vegetable Stew, 246
Sweet Potato and Parsnip
 Pancakes, 263

PASTA/NOODLES
Artichokes, Fennel and Olives
 over Penne, 66
Baked Stuffed Shells, 287
Grilled Vegetables with Pasta, 121
Mediterranean Pasta
 with Greens, 223
Pad Thai Summer Rolls
 with Tamarind Dipping Sauce, 128
Pad Thai with Tofu, 276
Pesto Pasta Salad, 144
Rice Noodles and Peanut Sauce
 Rolled in Nori, 308
Sweet and Sour Stir-Fry, 68
Tofu Kale Lasagna, 213

PÂTÉ
(*See also* Dips and Dressings)
Lentil Walnut Pâté, 165

PEACHES, 23
Carrot Cantaloupe Ginger
 Smoothie, 307
Carrot Fruit Soup, 108
Fresh Fruit Tart
 with Almond Crust, 147
Peach, Fresh Fig and Bourbon Crisp
 with Pecan Topping, 149
Wheatberry Salad, 142

PEANUTS, 19, 21, 23
Bok Choy and Mung Bean
 Sprout Sauté with
 Peanuts and Scallions, 255
Cucumber Noodles with
 Bok Choy and Peanut Sauce, 119
Lettuce Wraps with
 Ginger Peanut Tofu, 305
Pad Thai Summer Rolls
 with Tamarind Dipping Sauce, 128

Pad Thai with Tofu, 276
Peanut Butter Cacao Banana
 Smoothie, 307
Rice Noodles and Peanut Sauce
 Rolled in Nori, 308
Teff Peanut Butter
 Chocolate Chip Cookies, 332

PEARS
Baby Greens with
 Grilled Balsamic Pears, 114
Ginger Pear Crisp, 225
Ginger Pear Sauce, 161
Green Tea Poached Pears
 with Pomegranate Glaze and
 Pistachios, 229
Maple Poached Pears, 228
Pear and Fig Tart
 in Pecan Crust, 296
Poached Winter Fruit Medley, 293
Tortilla Pizzas, 322
Winter Green Salad with
 Sugared Walnuts, Crispy Pears,
 and Pomegranate, 256

PEAS/SNAP PEAS, 16, 23
Golden Beet and
 Snap Pea Salad, 120
Jasmine Rice with Sweet Peas, 284
Swiss Chard with Roasted
 Golden Beets and Sweet Peas, 67

PECANS, 19
Asparagus with Mustard Vinaigrette
 and Toasted Pecans, 62
Chocolate Lover's Tart, 227
Chocolate Pecan Pie, 297
Coconut Cranberry Pecan Balls, 290
Kabocha Squash
 Stuffed with Brown Rice
 and Chickpea Pilaf, 220
Maple Nut Granola, 324
Nuts Over Strawberry
 Rhubarb Pie, 146
Peach, Fresh Fig and Bourbon Crisp
 with Pecan Topping, 149
Pear and Fig Tart
 in Pecan Crust, 296
Silky Sweet Potato Pie, 198
Sinful Stuffed Dates, 289

PEPPERS, 21
French Lentil Salad with
  Lemon, Radish and Cilantro, 74
Gazpacho, 105
Grilled Vegetables with Pasta, 121
Muffaletto, 311
Seared Artichokes
  with Red Pepper Aioli, 61
Three Bean Chili, 249

PESTO
Garlic Scape and Walnut Pesto, 44
Pesto Pasta Salad, 144
Summer Rolls
  with Lemon Basil Pesto, 127
Tortilla Pizzas, 322

PICKLED GINGER, 32
Brown Rice with Ginger
  and Umeboshi Plums, 80
Rice Noodles and Peanut Sauce
  Rolled in Nori, 308

PICKLES
Quick Homemade Pickles, 309

PIES (See Desserts)

PINEAPPLE, 23
Black Bean Patties
  with Pineapple Guacamole, 133
Pineapple Tempeh Kebabs, 137
Sweet and Sour Stir-Fry, 68

PINE NUTS, 18
Kabocha Squash
  Stuffed with Brown Rice
  and Chickpea Pilaf, 220
Kale with Pine Nuts
  and Currants, 182
Pesto Pasta Salad, 144
Raw Kale Salad
  with Great Northern Beans
  and Kalamata Olives, 185
Summer Rolls
  with Lemon Basil Pesto, 127
Sweet Dumpling Squash
  with Orange-Scented Quinoa
  Stuffing, 222

PINTO BEANS, 17, 32
Refried Pinto Beans with Chiles, 204
Three Bean Chili, 249

PISTACHIO NUTS, 19, 32
Green Tea Poached Pears
  with Pomegranate Glaze and
  Pistachios, 229
Millet with Cranberries
  and Pistachios, 285

PITA CHIPS, 317

PIZZA
Tortilla Pizza, 322

POLENTA
Grilled Polenta
  with Mushroom Ragoût, 145
Polenta au Gratin, 286

POMEGRANATE, 32
Glazed Oranges
  with Pomegranate Seeds, 231
Green Tea Poached Pears
  with Pomegranate Glaze and
  Pistachios, 229
Pomegranate Vinaigrette, 237
Spiced Kukicha Iced Tea, 160
Warm Greens with Citrus Dressing
  and Pomegranate, 175
Winter Green Salad with
  Sugared Walnuts, Crispy Pears
  and Pomegranate, 256

POPCORN
Popcorn with Olive Oil, Sea Salt
  and Drizzled Dark Chocolate, 329

POPPY SEEDS
Chopped Salad with
  Shallot Poppy Seed Dressing, 52

PORTOBELLO MUSHROOMS, 16
(See also Mushrooms)

POTATOES, 23
Fingerling Potatoes and Green Beans
  with Lemon Dill Dressing, 124
Fingerling Potato Salad
  with Fresh Herbs, 122
Not Mashed Potatoes, 261
Seitan Shepherd's Pie, 279
Winter Vegetable Soup, 254

PUMPKIN, 15
(See also Squash)

PUMPKIN SEEDS, 18–19, 33
Baby Spinach Salad
  with Mustard Vinaigrette, 48
Chopped Salad with
  Shallot Poppy Seed Dressing, 52
Pan-Roasted Millet
  with Pumpkin Seeds, 217
Quinoa with Arame,
  Toasted Nuts and Seeds, 72
Watercress, Daikon and
  Avocado Salad with
  Mustard Seed Dressing, 51

QUINOA, 13–14, 33
Inca Red Quinoa with Currants, 81
Quinoa and Black Bean Salad
  with Apricot Lime Vinaigrette, 141
Quinoa with Arame,
  Toasted Nuts and Seeds, 72
Quinoa with Almonds
  and Currants, 218
Quinoa with Sweet Corn, 215
Sprouted Quinoa Tabbouleh, 140
Sprouted Quinoa
  with Strawberries and Lime, 143
Sweet Dumpling Squash
  with Orange-Scented Quinoa
  Stuffing, 222
Wholegrain Pancakes, 281

RADICCHIO
Chopped Salad with
  Shallot Poppy Seed Dressing, 52
Marinated Bitter Greens, 174

RADISHES
French Lentil Salad with
  Lemon, Radish and Cilantro, 74

RAISINS
Apple Chutney, 164
Carrot Raisin Salad, 56
Cranberry Chutney, 163
Creamy Shiitake and
  Chickpea Soup, 172
Curry Tempeh
  with Raisins and Cashews, 139
Maple Nut Granola, 324
Oatmeal Chocolate Chip
  (or Raisin) Cookies, 327
Raisin Nut Bars, 331

RHUBARB, 21
Nuts Over Strawberry
   Rhubarb Pie, 146
Strawberry Rhubarb Compote
   with Cashew Cream, 150

ROLLS
Lettuce Wraps with
   Ginger Peanut Tofu, 305
Pad Thai Summer Rolls
   with Tamarind Dipping Sauce, 128
Rice Noodles and Peanut Sauce
   Rolled in Nori, 308
Summer Rolls
   with Lemon Basil Pesto, 127
Vegetable Nori Rolls, 304

ROMAINE LETTUCE, 15
(See also Lettuce)
Caesar Salad, 53
Fresh Herb Salad
   with Lemon and Olive Oil, 115
Lettuce Soup with Cilantro
   and Hot Sesame Oil, 45
Marinated Bitter Greens, 174
Winter Green Salad with
   Sugared Walnuts, Crispy Pears
   and Pomegranate, 256

RUTABAGAS, 15, 33
Roasted Root Vegetables
   with Truffle Oil, 187
Root Veggie Fries, 190
Rutabaga Purée
   with Orange and Ginger, 194
Stovetop Barley
   with Sweet Vegetables, 219
Super-Strengthening Stew, 248
Sweet and Savory
   Root Vegetable Stew, 246

SALADS
Baby Greens with
   Grilled Balsamic Pears, 114
Baby Spinach Salad
   with Mustard Vinaigrette, 48
Black Bean Salad, 132
Caesar Salad, 53
Carrot Raisin Salad, 56
Chickpea and Cherry Tomato Salad
   with Cilantro Dressing, 131

Chopped Salad with
   Shallot Poppy Seed Dressing, 52
Cucumber, Mango and
   Chickpea Salad, 130
Fennel and Orange Salad, 50
Fingerling Potato Salad
   with Fresh Herbs, 122
French Lentil Salad with
   Lemon, Radish and Cilantro, 74
Fresh Herb Salad
   with Lemon and Olive Oil, 115
Golden Beet and
   Snap Pea Salad, 120
Heirloom Tomato Salad, 109
Julienned Beet, Broccoli Stem
   and Carrot Salad, 176
Marinated Bitter Greens, 174
Multibean Salad with
   Fresh Herbs, 73
Pesto Pasta Salad, 144
Quinoa and Black Bean Salad
   with Apricot Lime Vinaigrette, 141
Raw Kale Salad
   with Great Northern Beans
   and Kalamata Olives, 185
Spring Greens
   with Apricot Vinaigrette, 49
Sprouted Quinoa Tabbouleh, 140
Sprouted Quinoa
   with Strawberries and Lime, 143
Tangy Tomato and
   Tomatillo Salad, 110
Tempeh Salad, 77
Tofu Salad, 135
Watercress, Daikon and
   Avocado Salad with
   Mustard Seed Dressing, 51
Wheatberry Salad, 142
White Bean Salad with
   Roasted Tomatoes and Arugula, 134
Wild Rice, Barley
   and Arame Salad, 201
Winter Green Salad with
   Sugared Walnuts, Crispy Pears
   and Pomegranate, 256

SALSA
Black Bean, Corn
   and Tomato Salsa, 102
Mango Salsa, 101

SAUCES
(See also Chutney; Dips and Dressings)
Cranberry Applesauce, 241
Ginger Peanut Sauce, 305
Ginger Pear Sauce, 161
Marinated Tofu with Ginger
   Cashew Dipping Sauce, 209
Tamarind Dipping Sauce, 128

SCALLIONS, 15
Bok Choy and Mung Bean
   Sprout Sauté with
   Peanuts and Scallions, 255
Mexican Layer Dip, 242
Wild Rice, Barley
   and Arame Salad, 201

SEA SALT, 25, 33
Popcorn with Olive Oil, Sea Salt
   and Drizzled Dark Chocolate, 329

SEA VEGETABLES, 16, 27, 30, 31, 33
Arame and Sunflower Seeds, 69
Arame Sauté, 129
Arame with
   Caramelized Shiitakes, 200
Baked Stuffed Sweet Potatoes, 319
Gingered Arame with Snow Peas, 71
My Favorite Miso Soup, 47
Quinoa with Arame,
   Toasted Nuts and Seeds, 72
Rice Noodles and Peanut Sauce
   Rolled in Nori, 308
Seaweed and Cabbage Sauté, 70
Stir-Fried Broccoli with Arame, 199
Tempeh Salad, 77
Toasted Sesame Nori Crisps, 321
Tree of Life Stir-Fry, 264
Vegetable Nori Rolls, 304
Wild Rice, Barley
   and Arame Salad, 201

SEITAN, 33
Seitan Bourguignon, 280
Seitan Shepherd's Pie, 279
Seitan Walnut Stuffed
   Collard Greens, 211

SESAME SEEDS, SESAME OIL,
   18–19, 20, 25, 33
Asian Coleslaw, 112
Baked Stuffed Sweet Potatoes, 319

Crispy Rice Squares, 330
Crispy Sesame Carrots, 57
Ginger Sesame Greens, 180
Ginger Sesame Vinaigrette, 43
Lettuce Soup with Cilantro
    and Hot Sesame Oil, 45
Mango Sesame Tatsoi, 60
Quick Boiled Broccoli and Stems
    with Toasted Sesame Seeds, 178
Sesame Almond Balls, 292
Sesame Brussels Sprout Sauté, 192
Sweet and Sour Stir-Fry, 68
Toasted Sesame Nori Crisps, 321
Wild Rice, Barley
    and Arame Salad, 201

SHALLOTS, 15
Arame with
    Caramelized Shiitakes, 200
Chopped Salad with
    Shallot Poppy Seed Dressing, 52
Kale with Caramelized Shallots, 181
Roasted Kabocha Squash
    with Kale, 268
Roasted Squash with
    Fennel and Asparagus, 195
Seitan Bourguignon, 280
Sweet and Savory
    Root Vegetable Stew, 246
Sweet Dumpling Squash
    with Orange-Scented Quinoa
    Stuffing, 222

SHIITAKE MUSHROOMS, 16, 33
Arame with
    Caramelized Shiitakes, 200
Autumn Harvest Soup, 167
Bok Choy and Mung Bean
    Sprout Sauté with
    Peanuts and Scallions, 255
Creamy Shiitake and
    Chickpea Soup, 172
Lettuce Soup with Cilantro
    and Hot Sesame Oil, 45
Mochi Dumplings, 79
Roasted Brussels Sprouts
    with Fennel and
    Shiitake Mushrooms, 260
Seitan Bourguignon, 280
Shiitake Mushrooms
    and Bitter Greens in Filo, 259
Stir-Fried Broccoli with Arame, 199

SHOYU, 18, 33

SMOOTHIES
Carrot Cantaloupe Ginger, 307
Green Monster, 307
Peanut Butter Cacao Banana, 307

SNOW PEAS
Asian Coleslaw, 112
Brown Rice with Ginger
    and Umeboshi Plums, 80
Gingered Arame with Snow Peas, 71
Pad Thai Summer Rolls
    with Tamarind Dipping Sauce, 128
Pad Thai with Tofu, 276
Sautéed Tempeh with
    Coconut Milk and Snow Peas, 278
Sweet and Sour Stir-Fry, 68

SOBA/UDON NOODLES, 35
Sweet and Sour Stir-Fry, 68

SOUPS AND STEWS
Apple Squash Soup, 166
Autumn Harvest Soup, 167
Carrot Fruit Soup, 108
Carrot Ginger Soup, 171
Corn Chowder, 170
Cream of Asparagus Soup, 46
Creamy Shiitake and
    Chickpea Soup, 172
Gazpacho, 105
Golden Split Pea Soup, 245
Goodness Soup, 243
Honeydew Cucumber Soup, 107
Leftover Soup, 318
Lentil Soup, 244
Lettuce Soup with Cilantro
    and Hot Sesame Oil, 45
My Favorite Miso Soup, 47
Savory Black Bean Soup, 173
Spicy Coconut Pumpkin Soup, 253
Super-Strengthening Stew, 248
Sweet and Savory
    Root Vegetable Stew, 246
Sweet Potato, Corn and
    Kale Chowder, 168
Three Bean Chili, 249
Tuscan Bean Soup, 251
Winter Squash and
    Aduki Bean Soup, 252
Winter Vegetable Soup, 254

SOUR CREAM
Mexican Layer Dip, 242
Tofu Sour Cream, 104

SPINACH, 21, 23
Baby Spinach Salad
    with Mustard Vinaigrette, 48
Tortilla Pizzas, 322

SPLIT PEAS, 17
Golden Split Pea Soup, 245

SQUASH, 15, 34, 35
Apple Squash Soup, 166
Butternut Squash Casserole, 266
Grilled Vegetables with Pasta, 121
Kabocha Squash
    Stuffed with Brown Rice
    and Chickpea Pilaf, 220
Roasted Kabocha Squash and
    Creminis with Fresh Herbs, 197
Roasted Kabocha Squash
    with Kale, 268
Roasted Squash with
    Fennel and Asparagus, 195
Savory Stuffed Pumpkins, 196
Simply Delicious
    Spaghetti Squash, 265
Spicy Coconut Pumpkin Soup, 253
Sweet Dumpling Squash
    with Orange-Scented Quinoa
    Stuffing, 222
Three Sisters Deep-Dish Pie, 191
Tofu Pumpkin Pie
    with Gingersnap Crust, 230
Winter Squash and
    Aduki Bean Soup, 252
Winter Squash and
    Chestnut Casserole, 267

STEVIA, 20

STRAWBERRIES, 21, 23
Baby Spinach Salad
    with Mustard Vinaigrette, 48
Jícama Strawberry Guacamole, 98
Lemon Almond Cookie Tart
    with Strawberry Topping, 91
Nuts Over Strawberry
    Rhubarb Pie, 146
Sprouted Quinoa
    with Strawberries and Lime, 143

Strawberry Custard with
Fresh Berries and Lemon Peel, 148
Strawberry Rhubarb Compote
with Cashew Cream, 150

SUMMER SQUASH, 15, 34
(See also Zucchini)

SUN-DRIED TOMATOES
Grilled Polenta
with Mushroom Ragoût, 145
Roasted Portobello Sandwich
with Sun-dried Tomato Aioli, 65
Tofu Kale Lasagna, 213

SUNFLOWER SEEDS, 19, 23, 34
Arame and Sunflower Seeds, 69
Maple Nut Granola, 324
Multigrain Pilaf with
Toasted Sunflower Seeds, 216
Quinoa with Arame,
Toasted Nuts and Seeds, 72
Sesame Almond Balls, 292
Wheatberry Salad, 142

SUSHI RICE, 13–14, 34
Vegetable Nori Rolls, 304

SWEET BROWN RICE, 13–14, 34
Multigrain Pilaf with
Toasted Sunflower Seeds, 216
Savory Stuffed Pumpkins, 196
Sweet Brown Rice and Mung Beans
with Indian Spices, 283

SWEET POTATOES, 15, 23
Baked Stuffed Sweet Potatoes, 319
Silky Sweet Potato Pie, 198
Spiced Sweet Potato Fries, 188
Sweet and Savory
Root Vegetable Stew, 246
Sweet Potato and Black Bean
Burritos with Cashew Cheese, 206
Sweet Potato and
Parsnip Pancakes, 263
Sweet Potato, Corn and
Kale Chowder, 168

SWISS CHARD, 21
Polenta au Gratin, 286
Swiss Chard with Roasted Golden
Beets and Sweet Peas, 67

TAHINI, 34
Creamy Miso Dressing, 41
Ginger Sesame Vinaigrette, 43
Savory "Unbaked" Beans, 272
Traditional Hummus, 310

TAMARI, 18, 25, 34
Tamari-Braised Mustard Greens, 183

TAMARIND, 34
Pad Thai Summer Rolls
with Tamarind Dipping Sauce, 128

TARTS (See Desserts)

TATSOI
Mango Sesame Tatsoi, 60
Sautéed Fennel and Asian Greens
with Ginger and Apricot, 59

TEAS
Green Tea Poached Pears
with Pomegranate Glaze and
Pistachios, 229
Herbal Iced Tea, 96
Spiced Kukicha Iced Tea, 160

TEFF (Ivory and Dark), 13–14, 34
Mixed Berry Tart, 154
Peach, Fresh Fig and Bourbon Crisp
with Pecan Topping, 149
Teff Ginger Molasses Cookies, 334
Teff Peanut Butter
Chocolate Chip Cookies, 332
Tiramisu, 299

TEMPEH, 18, 34
Baked Maple Mustard Tempeh, 210
Curry Tempeh
with Raisins and Cashews, 139
Pineapple Tempeh Kebabs, 137
Sautéed Tempeh with
Coconut Milk and Snow Peas, 278
Savory Stuffed Pumpkins, 196
Spicy Thai Tempeh
with Cashews, 277
Tempeh Quesadillas, 136
Tempeh Salad, 77

TOFU, 18, 34
Baked Stuffed Shells, 287
Brown Rice Pudding, 326
Caesar Salad, 53
Chocolate Lover's Tart, 227
Chocolate Pudding
with Fresh Berries, 153
Fresh Berries with Tofu Cream, 155
Green Goddess Dip, 315
Lemon Berry Cream Pie, 152
Lettuce Wraps with
Ginger Peanut Tofu, 305
Marinated Tofu with Ginger
Cashew Dipping Sauce, 209
Mexican Layer Dip, 242
My Favorite Miso Soup, 47
Orange Ginger Tofu, 274
Pad Thai with Tofu, 276
Roasted Tofu with Green Beans, 275
Scrambled Tofu, 208
Strawberry Custard with
Fresh Berries and Lemon Peel, 148
Tiramisu, 299
Tofu Kale Lasagna, 213
Tofu Pumpkin Pie
with Gingersnap Crust, 230
Tofu Salad, 135
Tofu Sour Cream, 104

TOMATILLOS, 35
Black Bean Salad, 132
Sprouted Quinoa
with Strawberries and Lime, 143
Tangy Tomato and
Tomatillo Salad, 110

TOMATOES
(See also Sun-Dried Tomatoes)
Artichokes, Fennel and Olives
over Penne, 66
Baked Stuffed Shells, 287
Black Bean, Corn
and Tomato Salsa, 102
Chickpea and Cherry Tomato Salad
with Cilantro Dressing, 131
Chopped Salad with
Shallot Poppy Seed Dressing, 52
Gazpacho, 105
Green Beans and Sweet Corn
with Summer Vinaigrette, 117
Grilled Polenta
with Mushroom Ragoût, 145

Grilled Vegetables with Pasta, 121
Heirloom Tomato Salad, 109
Mediterranean Pasta
  with Greens, 223
Mexican Layer Dip, 242
Pesto Pasta Salad, 144
Polenta au Gratin, 286
Sprouted Quinoa Tabbouleh, 140
Tangy Tomato
  and Tomatillo Salad, 110
Three Bean Chili, 249
Tofu Kale Lasagna, 213
Tortilla Pizzas, 322
Tuscan Bean Soup, 251
White Bean Salad with
  Roasted Tomatoes and Arugula, 134

TURNIPS, 15
Sweet and Savory
  Root Vegetable Stew, 246

UDON/SOBA NOODLES, 35
Sweet and Sour Stir-Fry, 68

UMEBOSHI PLUMS, 35
Brown Rice with Ginger
  and Umeboshi Plums, 80

VEGETABLE STOCK, 25

WAKAME, 16, 35
(See also Sea Vegetables)

WALNUTS, 18–19, 35
Baby Greens with
  Grilled Balsamic Pears, 114
Garlic Scape and Walnut Pesto, 44
Lentil Apple Walnut Loaf, 271
Lentil Walnut Pâté, 165
Nuts Over Strawberry
  Rhubarb Pie, 146
Oatmeal Chocolate Chip
  (or Raisin) Cookies, 327
Raisin Nut Bars, 331
Seitan Walnut Stuffed
  Collard Greens, 211
Winter Green Salad with
  Sugared Walnuts, Crispy Pears
  and Pomegranate, 256

WATERCRESS, 15, 35
Chopped Salad with
  Shallot Poppy Seed Dressing, 52
Marinated Bitter Greens, 174
Warm Greens with Citrus Dressing
  and Pomegranate, 175
Watercress, Daikon and
  Avocado Salad with
  Mustard Seed Dressing, 51
Winter Green Salad with
  Sugared Walnuts, Crispy Pears
  and Pomegranate, 256

WATERMELON RADISHES, 15, 35
Jícama Strawberry Guacamole, 98
Sprouted Quinoa
  with Strawberries and Lime, 143
Tangy Tomato and
  Tomatillo Salad, 110
Traditional Coleslaw, 111

WHEATBERRIES, 13–14, 35
Savory Stuffed Pumpkins, 196
Wheatberry Salad, 142

WHITE BEANS, 17
Autumn Harvest Soup, 167
Goodness Soup, 243
Herbed White Bean Dip, 316
Lemony Artichoke Dip, 40
Tuscan Bean Soup, 251
White Bean Salad with
  Roasted Tomatoes and Arugula, 134
White Beans and Escarole, 205

WILD RICE, 13–14, 35
Wild Rice, Barley
  and Arame Salad, 201
Wild Rice Pilaf, 85

WINTER SQUASH, 15, 35
(See also Squash)

WRAPS
(See Rolls)

YAMS, 15
Sautéed Yams
  with Ginger and Lime, 189
Super-Strengthening Stew, 248

ZUCCHINI
Grilled Vegetables with Pasta, 121
Zucchini with
  Garlic and Oregano, 125

As you cook your way to a clean and healthy life, you're bound to discover variations, substitutions and food combinations that you particularly like. You may also want to keep track of important information such as the hours of the farmers market, the sign-up date for your CSA, or online resources for your favorite producers, products or tools. Menus from your favorite meals, restaurants you don't want to forget, meals shared with family and friends…all provide inspiration and nourishment and can be noted here. Use the pages that follow to personalize your CLEAN FOOD so that it can even better support you and your journey to eat clean and live well.

SPRING

SUMMER

....
....
....
....
....
....
....
....
....
....
....
....
....
....
....
....
....
....

FALL

WINTER

....

....

....

....

....

....

....

....

....

....

....

....

....

....

....

....

....

SNACKS

Be nourished by the
fruits and beauty
of nature and make
every day a celebration
of the rhythms of the
seasons. *Terry*